The Yankee Plague

Civil War America

Peter S. Carmichael, Caroline E. Janney,
and Aaron Sheehan-Dean, editors

This landmark series interprets broadly the history and culture of
the Civil War era through the long nineteenth century and beyond.
Drawing on diverse approaches and methods, the series publishes
historical works that explore all aspects of the war, biographies of
leading commanders, and tactical and campaign studies, along with
select editions of primary sources. Together, these books shed new
light on an era that remains central to our understanding of American
and world history.

The Yankee Plague

Escaped Union Prisoners and the Collapse of the Confederacy

Lorien Foote

The University of North Carolina Press *Chapel Hill*

The University of North Carolina Press has been a member
of the Green Press Initiative since 2003.

Jacket illustrations: Front, from *Four Years in Secessia* by Junius Henri Browne
(Hartford: O. D. Case and Company, 1865). Back, from *The Secret Service, the Field,
the Dungeon, and the Escape* by Albert D. Richardson (Hartford: American Publishing
Company, 1865).

Library of Congress Cataloging-in-Publication Data
Names: Foote, Lorien, 1969– author.
Title: The Yankee plague : escaped Union prisoners and the collapse
   of the Confederacy / Lorien Foote.
Other titles: Civil War America (Series)
Description: Chapel Hill : University of North Carolina Press, [2016] |
   Series: Civil War America | Includes bibliographical references and index.
Identifiers: LCCN 2016000575 | ISBN 9781469630557 (cloth : alk. paper) |
   ISBN 9781469630564 (ebook)
Subjects: LCSH: Escaped prisoners of war—United States—History—19th century. |
   United States—History—Civil War, 1861–1865—Prisoners and prisons. | Prisoners
   of war—United States—History—19th century. | United States. Army—Officers—
   History—19th century. | North Carolina—History—Civil War, 1861–1865. |
   South Carolina—History—Civil War, 1861–1865.
Classification: LCC E611 .F66 2016 | DDC 973.7/71—dc23 LC record available at
   http://lccn.loc.gov/2016000575

Portions of chapters 1, 3, and 6 were published in "They Cover the Land Like the
Locusts of Egypt: Fugitive Federal Prisoners of War and the Collapse of the
Confederacy," *Journal of the Civil War Era* 6, no. 1 (March 2016): 30–55. Portions of
chapters 1, 2, 4, and the epilogue were published in "The Fugitives," *Civil War Monitor*
(Winter 2014): 55–63, 76–77. Portions of chapters 1, 3, and 6 were published in "A Futile
Attempt at Imprisonment," *Civil War Times* (April 2015): 38–43. Used with permission.

To the One Who Rescued Me

Contents

Illustrations and Maps

Illustrations

Maps

Acknowledgments

This book is proof that I am surrounded by supportive people who have contributed their time, expertise, and hospitality to its production. My research was possible because generous friends and family opened their homes to me for weeks at a time: Greg and Sarah Jane Eastman, Holly and Kevin Fletcher, Shirley Sennhauser, and Dedra and Eric Overholt. The words written here seem inadequate to express my gratitude. Greg Eastman is my research rock—he has opened his home to me for three successive books and has already promised I can come back for the next one!

The insights I gained into my sources were possible because a range of people contributed time and knowledge to helping me build a working database of escaped prisoners. I trusted Erin Hope, the best undergraduate student I have ever encountered, to meticulously enter data from manuscript sources into Excel. A Faculty Research Grant from Sponsored Programs at the University of Central Arkansas paid her bills. Robin Roe deserves credit for verifying and mapping locations and names in the database. Ken Merrick, Doug Bell, and David Villar performed similar work. David Holcomb, of the Carl Vinson Institute of Government at the University of Georgia, set up a collaborative version of the database and created initial maps of its data set. Stephen Berry, historian and writer extraordinaire, and codirector of the Center for Virtual History at the University of Georgia, worked with me on grant-writing to support potential Digital Humanities components, and has enthusiastically encouraged this project from its inception. Laura Mandell, director of the Initiative for Digital Humanities, Media, and Culture at Texas A&M University, and Kathy Weimer, head of the Kelley Center for Government Information, Data and Geospatial Services at Rice University, contributed time and expertise to grant-writing.

I was also privileged to enjoy the support of numerous institutions during the research phase of this book. I am grateful for receiving a 2011 Andrew W. Mellon Foundation Fellowship at the Huntington Research Library in San Marino, California, where I spent an entire summer reading about escaped prisoners. The University Research Council at the

University of Central Arkansas awarded me a Faculty Research Grant that supported a fall 2011 tour of archives in South Carolina and North Carolina. Texas A&M University provided me with generous start-up research funds, allowing trips to North Carolina and Washington, D.C., and the advantage of joining its outstanding History Department, jump-starting progress on my writing. The staff and librarians of the archives I visited were uniformly helpful and professional: the National Archives, the Library of Congress (particularly Michelle A. Krowl), the Charleston Library Society, the Huntington Library, the North Carolina State Archives (particularly Chris Meekins), the David M. Rubenstein Library at Duke University (particularly Elizabeth Dunn), the South Carolina Department of Archives and History (particularly Patrick McCawley), the South Carolina Historical Society, the South Caroliniana Library at the University of South Carolina, the Southern Historical Collection (particularly Laura Clark Brown) and the North Carolina Collection (particularly Jason Tomberlin) in the Wilson Library at the University of North Carolina–Chapel Hill, and the Special Collections, University of Tennessee–Knoxville (particularly Elizabeth Graham Wilson).

The writing and production phase of this book would not have been possible without the contribution of many people. Aaron Sheehan-Dean, who knows more about the scholarship being produced on the Civil War than anyone I know, believed in this book before I wrote it and has given me the benefit of his expertise and friendship along the entire way. Mark Simpson-Vos, one of the great editors working in the business, has fulfilled all the guarantees he made to me about what it would be like to move this book through the University of North Carolina Press. I am grateful to numerous scholars and historians who read portions of the manuscript: Patrick McCawley, Walter Edgar, Andrew Fialka, and the members of the History Department Colloquium at Texas A&M University, particularly Rebecca Schloss and April Hatfield for their detailed comments. Thank you to Terry Johnston of *Civil War Monitor* and Dana Shoaf of *Civil War Times* for soliciting articles that gave me the opportunity to practice writing readable history. I am deeply appreciative of Bill Blair and the three anonymous reviewers for the *Journal of the Civil War Era*, whose feedback at earlier stages of the writing made this a better book than it would have been. Several historians for whom I have the utmost respect read the entire manuscript and offered invaluable suggestions. My sincere thanks to Chip Dawson, Brian Linn, Adam Seipp, Earl J. Hess, Stephen Berry, and Aaron Sheehan-Dean. Members of my family, including my thirteen-year-old nephew, read the whole manuscript to make sure that non-historians would enjoy it. I love you, Bob and Sharon Foote, and Heather, Mark, and Eric Bauman. Working with the staff at this press has been both professional and pleasant. I extend my sincere gratitude to Lucas Church, Jay Mazzocchi, Mikala Guyton, and Ellen Lohman.

During the summer that I wrote the second half of the manuscript, I adopted a thirteen-week-old Shih Tzu puppy. Considering the fact that readers of the manuscript version had few to no comments for revisions on that portion of the work, it obviously helped my writing to take a break every hour to pet and play with him. So thank you, Buzz.

I cannot end these acknowledgments without thanking J. Madison Drake, Charles Porter Mattocks, Willard Worcester Glazier, and John V. Hadley, who told their own stories so superbly. I am proud to have the opportunity to reintroduce these heroes to a modern audience.

Abbreviations in the Text

AG	Adjutant General
CLS	Charleston Library Society
GO	General Orders
HL	The Huntington Library
LC	Library of Congress
NA	National Archives
NCSA	North Carolina State Archives
OR	*The War of the Rebellion: A Compilation of the Official Records of the Union and Confederate Armies*
PMG	Provost Marshal General
PMM	Pritzker Military Museum
RBPMG	Record Book of the Provost Marshal General
RG	Record Group
RL	David M. Rubenstein Library
SCDAH	South Carolina Department of Archives and History
SCHS	South Carolina Historical Society
SCL	South Caroliniana Library
SCTN	Special Collections, University of Tennessee–Knoxville
SHC	Southern Historical Collection
SO	Special Orders

The Yankee Plague

Introduction

The Plague

The Yankees spread across the South Carolina and North Carolina countryside like a plague of biblical proportions, according to one observer. They dug sweet potatoes out of farmers' fields, broke into barns, and burrowed into haylofts. Their bodies were infested with millions of lice and they carried these vermin to every place they stopped for the night. Every day one of the pestilential Yankees accosted an unsuspecting white or black southerner going about his or her daily business. In Caldwell County, North Carolina, the Reverend Isaac Oxford discovered a Yankee napping underneath his fodder. The Federal awoke and attacked Oxford, who finally subdued the man after a brutal fistfight. Oxford later captured three others that he encountered while squirrel hunting. In the same county, near Lenoir, the wife of the local doctor used her watchdog to subdue a Yankee trying to slip past the fence on her property. Slaves who lived near the road between Columbia and Spartanburg in South Carolina awoke to find a Yankee who had entered their cabins looming over their beds. He wanted food and a guide.[1]

"They seem to be everywhere," a local South Carolina newspaper lamented. "They actually cover the land like the locusts of Egypt."[2] The Yankees swarming the interior of the Carolinas were not armed soldiers marching with Major General William Tecumseh Sherman on his campaign. They were unarmed and ravenous escaped prisoners of war on a desperate quest to escape the Confederacy and return to Union lines. And there were more than 2,800 of them on the loose in the winter of 1864 and 1865.[3]

Confederate officials unwittingly unleashed the Yankee plague when they relocated prisoners of war from Georgia to South Carolina in September 1864 and placed them in open fields rather than enclosed stockades. Nine hundred Federal prisoners escaped: 400 enlisted men from Florence and 500 officers from Charleston, Columbia, and points in between. These Yankees spread out in one of three directions in their quest to find the safety of Union military lines. Some chose an arduous journey through the piedmont region of South Carolina, across the Blue Ridge Mountains of North Carolina, to reach Knoxville, Tennessee.

Others headed for the Atlantic coast and the Federal forces occupying Hilton Head Island, South Carolina. Some, hoping to find William Tecumseh Sherman's army, moved toward Augusta, Georgia.

A second major outbreak occurred in February 1865 when Confederate officials transferred their Yankee prisoners from South Carolina to North Carolina. This time over 1,900 Federals escaped during a process that merged the collapse of the Confederate prison system with the collapse of Confederate military defense of the Carolinas. Federal armies invading North Carolina from multiple directions trapped the Rebels in a vise that left them with no place to contain their prisoners. Prison authorities realized that there was no longer any location within the Confederacy that was safe from the operation of Union armies.[4]

Local residents in the Carolinas mobilized to hunt the escaped prisoners. They formed pickets on the roads and patrolled on horseback the paths and byways through the woods. Anyone who spotted a fugitive sent for help, and neighbors rallied to the hunt with lanterns and bloodhounds. But at the same time, white and black southerners organized to assist the Yankees. When the townspeople of Jalapa, South Carolina, formed a picket on the road to intercept some escapees, slaves in the area formed a counter-picket on the road below in order to alert the Yankees and guide them around the trap their masters had set. White and black families provided essential provisions and cooperated in guiding fugitives to hiding places and to routes that would lead them to greater safety. Black guides took a Yankee captain to the home of a county sheriff who arranged for his journey into Tennessee. Children were put on war footing. A father sent his twelve-year-old daughter alone at night over a mountain to warn some escaped prisoners that Home Guard units had learned of their hiding place.[5]

Historians of the American Civil War have missed this important and compelling story. Scholars who study Confederate prisons tend to write community histories that stand in isolation from other narratives of the war or to focus on questions of blame for the horrifying conditions within such prisons. This book integrates the story of prisoners of war and the collapse of the Confederate prison system with the story of how the Confederate States of America ended. It uncovers for the first time the scale of escapes from prisons in the Carolinas between September 1864 and March 1865. The numbers amounted to the size of a fully staffed army brigade. Because each escapee encountered at least one, and usually dozens, of the Confederacy's inhabitants, tension-filled interactions and their consequences multiplied into the tens of thousands. This created the widespread impression of "plague"-like conditions. Yet the value of the story presented here is not in its head count of Yankee prisoners loose in a vast countryside, but in its unique viewpoint of the war's final months.[6]

This book explores the timing and the process of defeat as the journey of fugitive Federals converged with a series of collapses in the Carolinas. Thousands of escaped Yankee prisoners moved through a landscape where slavery was breaking down, where the government no longer provided local security, where home fronts merged with battle fronts, where movement broke through and altered imagined sovereign borders, and where military defense against invasion crumbled. These intertwined collapses after September 1864 triggered a "general crisis" in the Carolinas, or a spectrum of political, social, economic, and military failures that culminated in the disintegration of a society during war. Most historians assume that Sherman's famous invasion of the two states ended the Confederacy there. They overlook the critical breakdowns that occurred *before* he arrived. Sherman helped to complete the process, but the Confederate government ceased to function in South Carolina and in significant portions of North Carolina in the weeks before Union armies invaded the interior.[7]

Because this story takes place in a relatively understudied region of the Confederacy and brings together unfamiliar sources, it changes what we thought we knew about the end of the Civil War. It reveals the full extent of the Confederacy's political collapse at the local level preceding the final Union offensives of 1865. It provides the most nuanced look we have at what happened to individuals living in the South when the state failed. Neither the military nor the state stopped the escaped prisoners who swept across the land, and citizens were forced to protect themselves while the Confederacy died around them. This book brings together portions of states—South Carolina, North Carolina, Tennessee, and Virginia—that historians have generally studied separately. In doing so, it uncovers why the Confederacy did not adequately defend the region and how the sweeping movements of thousands of people contributed to interrelated breakdowns there. Because we see this story through the eyes of escaped prisoners, rather than the more standard fare of soldiers marching with an invading army, we gain an intimate view of the slaves and deserters upon whom the fugitives depended. We witness the complexities of slavery's destruction and watch the war zone spread into communities, neighborhoods, and homes. And for the first time, we grasp the connection between the story of the Civil War's prisoners and the story of its campaigns and battles.

We are reminded that the end of the Civil War was not an event but rather a process that took place at different times and in different ways in different places within the Confederacy. The process extended back into the first year of the war and proceeded forward into the months that historians label "Reconstruction." This book picks up the story at a particular moment in time and presents a tale that is intensely personal. Amid the grand upheavals that ended the war, individuals struggled to survive, learned to see the world in new ways, and clung to what they knew before the conflict started.

Although this book is set in the Confederacy and tells of its collapse, the Yankees who fled as the Confederacy crumbled are the central characters. We will follow the full adventures of four Yankee escape parties, along with incidents in the journeys of more than fifty others, to understand the different ways that fugitive Federals interpreted the epic events happening around them and in part because of them. Through J. Madison Drake, a New Jersey journalist and fireman with a brave soul and a penchant for self-promotion, we will enter the homes of women participating in irregular warfare and follow disaffected southern men crossing the borders of the Confederacy. As we walk hundreds of miles with Charles Porter Mattocks, an aristocrat from Maine whose shy demeanor masked an iron will, we will meet the old men and young boys tracking escaped Yankees through their communities and taking over the functions of the state. As we encounter slaves with John V. Hadley, an Indiana lawyer traveling with his wisecracking best friend, we will witness how they seized opportunities to subvert their masters. With Willard Worcester Glazier, a New York cavalry officer who possessed a terrible sense of direction, we will listen outside the window of southern homes and wander across lands emptied of people.

One Federal who experienced the chaotic movements that led to the mass escapes of February 1865 observed that the Confederacy was trembling down to its core. Prisoners of war and those who guarded them were in a prime position to feel those death throes. This book narrates their story, and in doing so, lifts a shroud that has covered the passing away of the Confederate States of America.

1

Escape

The story of fugitive Federals and the collapse of the Confederacy begins in September 1864, when the Confederacy was staggering under myriad external and internal threats to its existence. On the military front, Confederate armies were giving up ground and casualties in every region. In the spring of that year, Lieutenant General Ulysses S. Grant, the newly appointed commander of all Union armies, ordered coordinated offenses in order to apply pressure at all points and take advantage of superior manpower. He was the first general to implement such a strategy during the war. In response, Confederate generals Robert E. Lee in Virginia and Joseph E. Johnston in Georgia adopted defensive maneuvers and entrenched positions that inflicted appalling casualties on Union armies and that seemed to stymie their breakthroughs on both fronts. Impatient and war-weary northerners feared the war had become a stalemate, even though Union armies were on the doorsteps of Richmond and Atlanta, and in August President Abraham Lincoln worried he would not be reelected.

Confederate armies expended maximum blood and treasure to stall Union offensives, yet the enemy continued its heavy punches. In the meantime, the Union's blockade of the Confederacy contributed to shortages and an inflation rate that reached 9,000 percent in 1864. The blockade was not the only source of economic troubles. The Confederate government printed fiat money without making such currency legal tender. Speculators roamed the country in the guise of Confederate officials, bought produce from hard-pressed farmers, and hoarded the goods to sell at astronomic prices. The drain of manpower from farms to battlefield, the slowdown of work on the part of slaves, the refusal of some planters to grow food for the armies rather than cotton for the blockade-runners, and the incursions of Union armies in various locations caused a downslide in agricultural production. Confederate states implemented welfare programs to provide relief for thousands of soldiers' wives who could not feed their families.

With these pressing military and economic problems, the Confederacy faced additional political and social turmoil during 1864. President

Jefferson Davis battled constant and increasing opposition in the Confederate Congress and from state governors over taxation, conscription policies, and the disposition of Confederate troops. State legislatures passed bills that contradicted national laws in order to keep men out of Confederate armies fighting in Virginia and Georgia. In the Appalachian Mountain regions of Virginia, Tennessee, the Carolinas, and Georgia, thousands of deserters from the Confederate army and disgruntled elements who defied Confederate authority stole provisions from loyal Confederate citizens, attacked state and Confederate units sent to capture them, engaged in guerrilla warfare with Confederates, and contributed to the descent into chaos and anarchy in some counties. Slaves in regions adjacent to Union armies ran away in droves, defied their masters, and constantly watched for opportunities to subvert the Confederacy's most important economic and social institution.[1]

Within this context of multiplying and enlarging threats, Union military offensives injected an unexpected element: Federal prisoners of war. According to a cartel established between the Union and the Confederacy in July 1862, prisoners captured in battle were immediately released on parole, which was a signed promise not to fight again until both governments agreed upon an exchange of prisoners. But neither side adhered to the terms of the cartel. The system soon broke down under the weight of mistrust and mutual recriminations. The Confederacy refused to treat African American soldiers who fought for Union armies as prisoners of war and President Lincoln insisted that they do so. By 1864 general exchanges of prisoners stopped. During the massive Union offensives in Virginia and Georgia between May and August, tens of thousands of Federal prisoners accumulated behind the lines in the Confederacy. They were a galling problem that sapped the Confederate infrastructure of manpower and provisions under the necessity of guarding and (barely) feeding them. Grant and U.S. Secretary of War Edwin Stanton were not really interested in exchanging prisoners of war. The Union had an advantage, since it held more prisoners than the Confederacy did. Grant wanted Rebels in northern prison camps rather than in Rebel armies, even if that meant thousands of Union soldiers died of hunger, exposure, and disease in Confederate camps. In the long run, Grant believed, such a policy would end the war faster and ultimately save more lives than it cost.[2]

The Confederate government shifted thousands of Yankees from Richmond to Georgia when Grant's offensives filled beyond their capacity the notorious Libby and Belle Isle prisons located in the Confederate capital. Enlisted men, more than 30,000 of them, shipped off to Camp Sumter in Andersonville, and 1,500 Federal officers transferred to Camp Oglethorpe in Macon. The blame for the death and suffering that transpired in these two camps during the summer of 1864 remains contentious to this day. The prisoners believed—most of those who survived never wavered in this belief—that the Confederate government deliberately starved, robbed, and tortured them. Defenders of the Lost Cause, then and now, blamed Lincoln for not exchanging prisoners and Union armies and navies for ravaging southern resources. With Rebel armies going hungry, they claimed, there was nothing to spare for Yankee prisoners. Modern scholarship on Civil War prisons points to the gross incompetence of Confederate authorities who mismanaged every aspect of the prison system, from selecting sites for camps to distributing available stocks of food.[3]

Confederate mismanagement was on stark display when the movement of Union armies in September 1864 once again necessitated the shifting of Federal prisoners. This time, though, authorities in Richmond unleashed a chain reaction that had vast repercussions in the daily lives of Confederate citizens who lived in the Carolinas. On September 2, 1864, Major General William Tecumseh Sherman captured Atlanta. Samuel Cooper, the Confederate adjutant and inspector general, decided to remove most Federal prisoners from Georgia to keep the Union army from liberating the captives. When he ordered the evacuation of Andersonville and Macon prisons on September 5, there were not adequate shelters prepared anywhere else in the region to house the hungry and ill-clad Yankees. Nor was there an effective command-and-control structure over the Confederate prison system. There was no commissary general of prisoners in September 1864 but rather divided responsibility between Brigadier General John Winder and Brigadier General William Gardner, neither of whom was entirely clear about his lines of responsibility and authority. Winder was in charge of the evacuation, and he decided to send the prisoners to Savannah and Charleston.[4]

No one bothered to notify Confederate departmental military commanders about the transfer of thousands of prisoners to Savannah. Major General Lafayette McLaws was flummoxed when 1,500 Federal prisoners arrived in the city on September 8. "There must be some strange misconception as to the force in this district," he protested. "I have now not a single man in reserve to support any point that may be threatened by the enemy. I have no place stockaded or palisaded or fenced in where the prisoners can be kept. No place where there is running water." McLaws placed an officer in charge of the emergency, who immediately impressed slaves wherever they could be found on the city's streets. They worked through the night lengthening a three-sided fence that partially enclosed an open area behind the local jail. They left one end open in order to extend the sides as more prisoners arrived. Crews continued to work until September 17, when the stockade reached the capacity to contain 10,000 prisoners.[5]

Cooper and Gardner did notify Major General Samuel Jones, commander of the Department of South Carolina, Georgia, and Florida, that prisoners were on the way from Andersonville to Charleston. They had not, however, consulted him about how the transfer of thousands of prisoners might thwart his defense of a city besieged by ongoing and active Union military operations. On September 8, Jones frankly threatened Secretary of War James A. Seddon that if Union forces advanced he would withdraw all guards from the prisoners and send them out of the city under the care of the railroad companies. "I am compelled to send prisoners of war where I can, not where I will," an annoyed Seddon responded.[6]

Jones scrambled to find guards. He contacted Brigadier General James Chesnut Jr., commander of the Confederate Reserves in South Carolina, who had earlier informed Richmond that his entire force was not sufficient to guard the prisoners from Georgia. Chesnut tried to cooperate. He telegraphed Jones on the ninth that he would "call out citizens temporarily." But on the tenth he reported he could not get "a single man from the militia" to help and that he had to obey orders from Richmond sending the reserves to escort the prisoners *to* Charleston. "I must respectfully at present decline to take charge of prisoners," he wrote.[7]

When more than 1,400 Union officers and nearly 6,000 enlisted men accumulated in Charleston on September 12, Jones again protested furiously to Seddon that he did not have sufficient troops to guard the prisoners and defend the city. A few days later, medical officials reported a yellow fever epidemic. Without notifying prison authorities or consulting anyone in Richmond about locations, Jones removed the Federal prisoners from Charleston. Between September 12 and 18, he sent batches of the enlisted men to Florence and put them in an open field with only a force of 125 South Carolina Reserves to guard them. The prisoners, veterans of a summer in Andersonville prison, immediately mutinied in a

desperate attempt to flee the area before Major F. F. Warley could construct a stockade. More than 400 of them broke loose from the guards,
plundered the citizens in the vicinity of the camp for food and clothing,
and attempted to destroy the railroad. Others headed for the woods in a
quest to escape. Two of these were Simon Dufur and George Hull of the
First Vermont Cavalry. The night was pitch dark, and Dufur and Hull
could not see each other, so they had to talk to keep in contact. The woods
were full of fugitives and they heard voices in every direction around
them. In the mass confusion, Dufur lost his companion, but soon joined
a Wisconsin soldier named Orange Ayers and five men from Michigan.
The party raided the outbuilding of a large farmhouse and headed into
some nearby swamps.[8]

When Warley telegraphed to Charleston that his force was completely
overpowered and the railroad might be destroyed, Jones immediately
deployed the Waccamaw Light Artillery, a cavalry unit, and every infan-
tryman he could spare from Charleston to Florence. Over the next several
days, these forces and local citizens patrolled the area and rounded up
nearly all of the fugitives. Warley placed an appeal to citizens in the
Darlington *Southerner* and asked them to look out for escaped prisoners and detain them. The cavalry caught Dufur six days after his escape
thirty-three miles from Florence. Citizens brought hundreds of others
back, some of whom had crossed the line into North Carolina. Only
twenty-three of the September mutineers arrived safely inside Union
lines. Sixteen of these made an arduous quest to Knoxville, Tennessee,
reporting there at various times between November and February.[9]

Despite the temporary influx of troops from Charleston, Confederate officers in Florence resorted to mobilizing the local population in
order to restore order and assert authority over the prisoners. The hastily built stockade, although not complete, was ready to receive the prisoners being guarded in the open field on September 30, and an additional
6,000 were on the way from Charleston. Citizens from the countryside
surrounding Florence assembled on that morning, each carrying whatever arms he possessed, and came to the prison site to help put the Yankees inside the new stockade. Prison officials were able to restore order
and contain the prisoners only with the help of the local population. Prisoners continued to arrive at the compound without prior notice until
the end of November.[10]

Jones's precipitous creation of a site at Florence only partially handled
the prisoner of war crisis in Charleston. Jones had sent off the enlisted

This portrait of J. Madison Drake appeared in *Fast and Loose in Dixie* (1880).

men, but he still had more than 1,500 Federal officers on his hands. He sent them to Columbia on October 5 and 6 with similar disastrous results. An unknown number of Yankees escaped in Charleston as they were marched down King Street to the train station. Slaves, free blacks, white Unionists, and a number of Irish and German immigrants hid these escaped prisoners, sometimes for weeks at a time, while they waited for opportunities to escape the city. The citizens who aided the fugitives used the streets of Charleston as pathways to transfer the Yankees from place to place when Confederate troops searched neighborhoods. Captain William H. Telford, Fiftieth Pennsylvania, traveled through six locations in the city, including a shoemaker's shop on King Street, a store on Cummings Street, a bachelor's house on Calhoun Street, and a family residence near the Negro Hospital. Eventually the fugitives ended up on one of the city wharves, where slave pilots moved them out by boat under the cover of darkness to Union lines on Hilton Head. Twenty-six of these fugitive Federals made it safely to the island by January 1865.[11]

More than 100 Federal officers escaped from the train on the way to Columbia, jumping off at one or the other of its two stops to fill up with water, first at Branchville, then at Kingsville. Among the latter were Lieutenant J. Madison Drake, and Captains Jared E. Lewis, Harry H. Todd, and Albert Grant, who were in the boxcar immediately in front of the caboose. Later, none of them could remember or explain how they survived the landing uninjured. As soon as they stopped rolling, they ran into a dark woods by the side of the railroad tracks, and then into a huge cypress swamp. The plan, forged during hours of studying an old atlas

More than 100 Federal officers escaped from the train carrying prisoners between Charleston and Columbia. Depicted here is the leap of J. Madison Drake and his comrades near Kingsville. Sketch from *Fast and Loose in Dixie* (1880).

they found in the Marine Hospital where they were kept in Charleston, was to march northwest to the Union lines near Knoxville, Tennessee.[12]

During his exploits as a fugitive inside the Confederacy, J. Madison Drake proved to be the heroic leader of men that his earlier war career foretold. A journalist and foreman of a fire company in Trenton, New Jersey, Drake enlisted immediately after the fall of Fort Sumter in a three-month regiment along with thirty-two other members of the American Hose Company. He recruited dozens more men for Company C of the Third New Jersey, but declined his election to captain and instead served as the color-bearer. Drake later joined the Ninth New Jersey as a sergeant and was first lieutenant of Company K when he was captured on May 16, 1864, at the Battle of Drury's Bluff. His courage at the battle earned him a Congressional Bronze Medal for Gallantry. Witnesses to his actions on October 6 attested to Drake's cool and collected behavior on the day his group initiated their preplanned escape. While the others talked to the guards who rode in the car with them, and shared pieces of cake the prisoners had bought at a railroad stop along the journey, Drake lay on the floor and with steady hands silently removed the percussion caps from all seven of the rifles the guards held in their hands.[13]

The Federals who did not escape from the train arrived in Columbia in two shifts on October 5 and 6, just one day after Jefferson Davis gave a speech in the city exhorting southerners to give their all for the cause of Confederate independence. The war-swollen capital city was bustling. An influx of refugees from other parts of the state, war workers, and soldiers had doubled the prewar population of 8,000. In the fairgrounds, medical laboratories for the Confederate army pumped out chloroform and 500 gallons of alcohol a day. Citizens who turned in their scabs for army use obtained free smallpox vaccines. A dozen branches of the Confederate government operated in the business district. Two hundred female Treasury Department employees worked six hours a day signing 3,200 Confederate bills per day per worker. The "Bee Store" created hubbubs when blockade runners filled its stock with imported luxuries. The Central Association for the Relief of South Carolina soldiers boxed and shipped over $1.1 million of donated supplies to soldiers on the front during the year. Weekly public concerts and luxurious private dinners entertained the city's elites, while its outnumbered police force battled a criminal underworld and the plethora of unlicensed grog shops.[14]

When the Yankees emerged from the trains, they walked past the Wayside Home at the depot, where women served 300 meals a day to Confederate soldiers who passed through Columbia. The guards marched the Federals to a rise of ground near the banks of the Saluda River about two miles west of the city. They turned them out into a scrubby pine field with no structures or fence and provided the 1,400 prisoners with eight axes to build shelters. Just a quarter of a mile from the field, the manager of the Saluda Mills, which employed and housed 400 women making cloth for the Confederate army, watched in horror as the Yankees spilled into the open space. He dashed off a letter to Confederate authorities in Charleston begging them to remove the prisoners to a more remote location. He worried that the prisoners would steal the factory's stock of cows, pigs, and chickens, or that some vengeful Federal would set fire to the factory. Even worse was the threat that the Yankees would seek out intimate contact with the female workers. "The associations growing out of the close proximity of these soldiers, must prove of the most dangerous & deadly character, in view of the possible influence it may have on the health of my operatives," he wrote. "Particularly in those diseases, affecting the personal habits of those concerned."[15]

Bureaucratic chaos ensued. Before Confederate officials in Richmond had a handle on what Jones had done, the War Department replaced him with Lieutenant General William J. Hardee. Adjutant and Inspector General Cooper sent an emissary to Columbia to investigate the situation. He reported on October 26 that the guards for this open field—nicknamed "Camp Sorghum" for the molasses that was the staple of the prisoners' diet—consisted of only 350 raw South Carolina Reserves who themselves needed constant watching and that the prisoners had not been issued any meat since their arrival. Cooper referred this report to Gardner and asked if the prisoners were under his control; Gardner testily responded that Jones had moved the prisoners without his knowledge, that the officer in charge of the prisoners at Columbia now reported to Hardee rather than to him, and that the War Department had ignored his repeated complaints. Cooper's underlings commented, "It is impossible to rectify evils where no responsible party can be reached." When shown this correspondence, Secretary of War Seddon claimed that he was never informed of the embarrassing situation at Columbia. Utter political incompetence and a broken command structure are two signs of a nation undergoing a "general crisis," and both were on stark display in the prison transfer debacle.[16]

Meanwhile, South Carolina governor Milledge L. Bonham vehemently protested the presence of the Federal prisoners at Columbia and the transfer of enlisted men to Florence. On October 12, Gardner responded that he knew nothing of the prisoners at Florence, who were sent there without his knowledge. Bonham was further incensed to learn that Gardner planned to build a permanent prison facility at Columbia and that an engineer had already chosen a site. On October 29, Bonham wrote President Davis, who interfered on the governor's behalf. This forced Gardner to negotiate with Bonham about a potential new location and to send additional inspectors from Richmond to settle disputes among Confederate and state officials over the suitability of proposed sites. Seddon halted construction of the new prison on November 21.

Nearly a month of fruitless wrangling left the 1,400 prisoners of war without adequate shelter or guard. Winder, who was appointed commissary general of prisoners on November 21, reported the result when he traveled to South Carolina in early December to resolve the problem. By December 6, a total of 373 officers had escaped from Columbia. Winder moved the remaining prisoners onto the grounds of Columbia's Lunatic Asylum on December 12. The 500 escapees from Charleston, the trains, and Camp Sorghum in October, November, and the first part of December amounted to 33 percent of the Federal officers imprisoned in South

Carolina. By the end of February, as we will see, nearly half of the total would successfully abscond.[17]

Escaping Camp Sorghum was the easy part of a difficult journey for Union officers who were healthy enough to try. The absence of a fence or stockade helped, of course. The main reason for the mass flight from Sorghum, however, was the utter incompetence, and often downright disloyalty, of the prison guards. When General Hardee received word in mid-October that Camp Sorghum was in "a dangerous condition," he reinforced the four companies of South Carolina Reserves, composed of seventeen-year-olds and men over the age of fifty, with three companies of the Thirty-Second Georgia and an artillery detachment. The supplemental forces hindered rather than helped security at the camp. One escaped prisoner reported that the private soldiers of the Thirty-Second Georgia "are loyal, and do all they dare for us." Another Federal put the matter succinctly: "The guards is careless and express sentiments in our favor." It seemed that only the diligent supervision of their officers stopped the guards from allowing more prisoners to get away.[18]

Most Federals escaped by simply walking out. Major Charles Porter Mattocks, Lieutenant Charles O. Hunt, and Captain Julius B. Litchfield did so on November 3. Because prisoners were in an open field, the prison commandant, Lieutenant Colonel Robert Means, allowed prisoners to give their parole not to escape in order to pass into the woods to bring back wood for fires and for building makeshift shelters. Because honor was essential to Federal officers, men who signed such paroles would not escape. But the guards rarely bothered to check whether men passing out to the woods had a parole or not. Mattocks and his companions grabbed their moment to escape when they saw the large number of men passing in and out of the field on parole. Lacking such a document themselves, they simply tucked a map and compass in their clothes, picked up a few small sticks to carry, and passed right through the line of sentinels. One hour later, they were on the banks of the Saluda River, hiding until darkness provided the cover they needed to swim the river without being seen by the guards on a nearby bridge.[19]

Mattocks, who was captured at the Battle of the Wilderness, was the leader of the party. Morally upright, literate, elitist, and shy around the ladies, he ruled soldiers with an iron hand. The twenty-four-year-old graduate of Bowdoin College was the stepson of a successful Maine lumber merchant. Commissioned as a first lieutenant in the Seventeenth Maine in 1862, he disciplined his company with the zeal born of his con-

Charles Porter Mattocks. Courtesy of the Baldwin Historical Society.

viction that gentlemen of his social class were the natural leaders of society. He cared nothing for the opinion of enlisted men. A soldier in the Seventeenth Maine wrote that Mattocks had "yards and yards of superfluous red tape about him." In September 1863, he had charge of a steamer transporting hundreds of conscripts to their various regiments on the front. When a drunken group of roughs instigated a boxing match below-decks, Mattocks entered the ring and gave both opponents "a good choking." His superiors noted with approval these kinds of exploits and assigned him to take command of the First U.S. Sharp Shooters, a unit censured by inspectors for its lack of discipline and poor performance in drills. Within a month, Mattocks brought the regiment's officers to heel through courts-martial and examination boards. He spent several hours daily studying military textbooks and expected other officers to do the same. Mattocks enjoyed command. "It is one of the easiest things in the world," he wrote his mother, "if a man only is *lavish* of the immense power which is by the military code granted to a Regimental commander."[20]

Mattocks remained a stickler for military order and discipline even while he was a prisoner of war. When the Federal officers confined in Macon, Georgia, learned that they were being transferred to Charleston, some of them plotted to overpower the guards, capture the train, run it to Pocotaligo, South Carolina, and escape en masse to the Union lines at Hilton Head, an island twenty miles northeast of Savannah. Mattocks declined a request to participate. He thought the plot would not succeed, but he was also concerned that it violated the laws of war. Every prisoner

had the duty, whether alone or in groups, to try to escape, but the Pocotaligo Plot involved killing, and Mattocks believed that an officer who
delivered up his sword and accepted quarter from the enemy made a
promise to desist from bloodshed until he returned to his own lines.
Mattocks also cited the laws of war as Francis Lieber encapsulated them
in General Orders 100, the code that governed the conduct of Union
armies in the field. Article 77 proclaimed that prisoners of war who con-
spired to effect a general escape of prisoners were liable to the death
penalty. Mattocks was brave enough to risk death on a chance to escape,
as his subsequent flight from Camp Sorghum demonstrated, but he was
not willing to kill for it.[21]

When the chance came on a bitterly cold and rainy November 3,
Mattocks took it, and his pluck and innate optimism got his companions through their first night. After darkness descended, the three Maine
officers placed the blankets they brought with them on an eight-foot-
long plank, plunged into the Saluda River, took hold of the plank, and
kicked toward the opposite shore. The chill of the air and the river
soaked deep into their bones, their blood felt thin, and the progress was
slow. Hunt looked back to measure the distance they had made.

"Don't look back," Mattocks said. "Look ahead and kick out."

After a long struggle, Litchfield exclaimed, "My God, Mattocks! We
never can get across."

"Yes, we can. Look ahead and kick out."

After what seemed an age, the Yankees reached the shore. Too exhausted to scramble up the foliage-entangled bank, they sucked in air
while they clung to the bushes. Eventually they dragged themselves to
dry land, wrung out their clothes, drained their knee-high boots, crossed
a field, and ventured into the woods. As happened to Dufur and the men
who escaped from Florence in September, once they entered the woods
they could not see each other in the dark. To avoid separation, they
formed a single-file line and held on to the shirt of the man in front. At
9:00 P.M. they struck a road that led north from Columbia. As the New
Jersey fireman J. Madison Drake and his party had done a month earlier, Mattocks, Hunt, and Litchfield planned to find their way to Union
lines at Knoxville. They had a small map with the principal towns and
roads of South Carolina, North Carolina, and Tennessee on it, and they
determined to take a northwest course through Newberry, Laurens, and
Greenville Counties in South Carolina to Asheville, North Carolina,
where they hoped to follow the French Broad River to Knoxville.[22]

The choice of which direction to flee after walking past Camp Sorghum's deadline was an example of picking poisons. Every option held different dangers and different advantages, and the stress of the decision weighed heavily on the fugitives. The day after Mattocks escaped, Lieutenant John V. Hadley and Lieutenant Homer Chisman, both of the Seventh Indiana, mingled in with one of the wood parties that gathered at the deadline to throw collected wood into the camp. Once in the woods, they linked their fortunes with two other fugitives, Lieutenant Simeon Baker, Sixth Missouri, and Lieutenant Thomas G. Good, First Maryland Cavalry. Escape parties typically had just such a mixture of prisoners who were strangers to each other and prisoners who were with friends they had known before the misfortunes of battle placed them in enemy hands. Mattocks and Hunt knew each other during their college days at Bowdoin, but did not socialize until fortune brought them together in the Confederate prisons at Macon and Charleston, where they became messmates and intimate friends.

Hadley and Chisman were unusually close. Before their separation and individual captures at the Battle of the Wilderness, they were the only two midwesterners on the staff of Brigadier General James C. Rice. They bunked together for nearly two years and built castles in the air about a future partnership in business. Equally sick of army life and equally in love, they planned to resign from the army in the fall of 1864, get married, and make their fortune as army sutlers. Their wives would live together while they were on the road. Needless to say, it was not part of the plan to find each other among the crowd of prisoners of war at the officers' prison in Macon in June. Upon their reunion in a Rebel prison, they paired up to spur each other to survival and escape. By then, soldiering and killing had hardened Hadley's naturally sentimental and romantic nature, but nothing had squelched Chisman's vivacious and witty personality. Hadley loved to tell the story of Chisman's reaction to a beautiful young Rebel in a crowd who jeered the Yankee officers as they marched from the train station to the prison camp. She waved the bonnie blue flag right in the lieutenant's face. He presented her with his rear end, pointed to the hole in his pants located there, and said, "Miss, if you've got time, I wish you would tack that rag on here."[23]

Brothers that they were to each other, they quarreled on their first night out of Sorghum. Chisman wanted the party to head toward Knoxville. The route encompassed over 260 miles and the hazardous physical challenge of crossing the Appalachian Mountains in winter, but

Chisman relied on the reports he heard that there were Union men in those mountains. He was confident that once they crossed the Blue Ridge into North Carolina, they would secure the help of loyal whites. Hadley, Good, and Baker wanted to strike toward the railroad between Chattanooga and Atlanta. It was a shorter distance to travel and they assumed few Rebel forces were positioned along that route. Although Chisman was outnumbered three to one, through the force of his personality, the others agreed to put off the decision until the next evening.[24]

The disagreement reminded the Federal officers that any successful military undertaking, as their escape was to them, required organization and unit discipline. They immediately adopted a set of field regulations that governed their journey, similar to those other fugitives were simultaneously adopting from their hiding places in the woods outside the prison camp. Every twenty-four hours, starting at 9:00 P.M. that night, they rotated command of the expedition. The commander made all decisions on behalf of the party. They traveled at night on the roads and never spoke above a whisper. They marched in single file at intervals of three paces, with the leader scanning in front of him, the second man observing the right side of the line, the third looking left, and the fourth responsible for the rear. A "hiss" was the signal to leave the road and hide. With the discipline in place, the party moved out in a westward direction, hoping that the next twenty-four hours would enable them to come to the unanimous vote necessary to determine the ultimate objective of their journey.[25]

Fireman Drake, elitist Mattocks, and wisecracking Chisman believed the best poison was the long route whose antidote was the Unionism of the Appalachian mountain folk. Nearly half of the officers who successfully escaped from Columbia eventually reported to Union authorities in Knoxville.[26] But other fugitives from the South Carolina prison-transfer debacle picked a different poison. They traded the shortest geographic distance for an increased likelihood of encountering Confederate forces. They traveled toward the Union lines at Hilton Head, the coastal island northeast of Savannah and ninety miles south of Charleston. Dangerous swamps and portions of the small Confederate army defending Charleston, particularly the companies posted at stations along the Charleston & Savannah Railroad, were between them and their objective. All but fifteen of the 100 Federals who jumped off the train on October 5 and 6 were recaptured, and fourteen of the successful men traveled to Knoxville. Unfortunate escape parties who headed toward the

Willard Worcester Glazier, taken from the frontispiece of *The Capture, the Prison Pen, and the Escape* (1865).

coast often stumbled into patrols. Bloodhounds belonging to a Confederate cavalry regiment cornered naval paymaster Luther Billings and his three companions twelve miles from the unit's camp at Adams Run Station just three days after the Yankees escaped. Recaptured prisoners were taken to Camp Sorghum, and there they gave advice about routes to those who made later attempts.[27]

This advice created new routes of escape from Columbia to Hilton Head. From late October through December, escapees from Sorghum followed either the Edisto or Congaree River that flowed southeast into the Atlantic and journeyed through the districts around them. These rivers served as highways to the coast and to the Union gunboats that patrolled there. Major Joseph Steele and two companions escaped from Camp Sorghum on November 19 and stole a canoe on the Congaree River fourteen miles below Columbia. They paddled down the Congaree to the Santee River, then to South Island near Georgetown, where they signaled a Union gunboat on November 29. Sixty-four fugitives who escaped from Columbia between October and December successfully reported to Union lines in Hilton Head, as did thirty-six fugitives from other parts of the state. Military authorities there also processed eighty-seven Federals who escaped from makeshift Confederate prisons in Savannah during November and December.[28]

Some fugitives headed west in order to link up with Sherman's rapidly moving army in Georgia. This was the choice of Lieutenant Willard Glazier, of New York's Harris Light Cavalry, and Lieutenant Moses W. Lemon, Fourteenth New York Heavy Artillery. Glazier waited long weeks in Camp Sorghum to find his moment to escape. In early November he was so weak with illness that he could not walk without the aid of a friend. During that time, officers who escaped in October but were recaptured brought the good news that slaves provided them with plenty of corn bread and bacon, and that it was worth an escape attempt just to get a few square meals. On November 26, Glazier and Lemon walked across the camp's deadline as if they had a parole to get wood. A sentinel actually halted them, but Glazier boldly bluffed him. "Do you stop paroled prisoners here?" he asked with the air of unquestioned authority that Civil War officers knew how to employ. "No, sir," the youth replied. And thus two more Yankees emerged from Sorghum. The New Yorkers struck toward Augusta, Georgia. They incorrectly assumed, as did Confederate military commanders in the region, that Sherman would occupy that position. It was the riskiest route, since the fugitives would have to pass through any Confederate forces deployed to meet Sherman's advance. But Glazier was impatient, and it was the direction that he thought would bring him soonest to the Federal camps. He and his companion headed west down the road toward Lexington, South Carolina.[29]

Fugitives from Columbia fanned out along three corridors for movement in South Carolina during October and November, a few weeks behind those already on the move from their escape points at Florence, Charleston, or the railroad tracks. They traveled on a northwest route through Newberry into the upcountry piedmont region that encompassed Greenville, Anderson, Pickens, and Spartanburg districts, and then passed across the border into North Carolina. They journeyed southeast, following the rivers that flowed into the Atlantic. They struck westward on the roads that led to Augusta, passing through Lexington, Edgefield, and Barnwell districts on their way. The Yankees were on the move, more than 500 strong. And it was only the beginning. Nearly 2,000 more would follow as the winter and spring progressed.

They were a different kind of invading army, one that was weak and unarmed. They never fought a conventional battle. But they heralded the collapse of the Confederate States of America.

2

The World in Black and White

The Collapse of Slavery

At twilight on the first night of their escape, Willard Glazier and Moses Lemon moved out of their hiding place in the woods near Columbia and struck west. The Yankees had in mind only one plan for success in their quest to get out of South Carolina: seek help from blacks and avoid all white men. The New Yorkers counted on getting food and directions from slaves as they moved toward Augusta. But they immediately encountered a potentially fatal flaw in their plan. As the fugitives walked on the road to Lexington, they heard voices behind them and realized to their horror that they could not tell if the voices belonged to black men or white men. "Their manner of conversation is precisely alike in many portions of the South," Glazier commented when he later published an account of his adventure. Northern soldiers expected southern blacks to speak in the typecast vernacular absolutely distinct from white speech that novelists and minstrel shows used to portray black speech. Glazier and Lemon saw the world in black and white, and they assumed that in the dark they would be able to hear in black and white.

Glazier boldly faced the situation and determined to discover the race of the men behind him. "A pleasant evening, gentlemen," he said. "Indeed it is," came the response. This answer offered no clue, so Glazier and Lemon immediately quickened their pace in anticipation of having to run for their lives. This suspicious behavior alerted the astute black men behind them to their identity as escaped Yankees. The slaves revealed themselves and readily agreed to guide the fugitives along the next stage of their journey. But once the guides left them, Glazier and Lemon struggled to navigate through a South that did not look or sound like they expected. Two weeks later, in Georgia, they saw a collection of houses that fit their stereotype of slave cabins. Glazier knocked on the door and someone inside yelled out, "Whose thar?" Frustrated that yet again he could not guess someone's race, Glazier yelled out, "Are you black or white in there?" Faced with an offended white occupant, Glazier pretended to be an injured Rebel soldier who needed food, and he obtained some small provisions through this deception.[1]

Other escape parties had similar problems in their quest to find friendly slaves in South Carolina. Captain Daniel Langworthy and four other New York officers walked out of Camp Sorghum on October 11. After several exhausting days on the march, the fugitives risked a small fire where they were hiding in a patch of woods. A woman approached with three young girls. Her plain cotton apparel, hanging loosely from her shoulders, looked like a night dress to the Yankees, and they all assumed she was black. Rather than run or hide, they greeted her, "Hello, Auntie." But instead she was a white woman who knew they were escaped prisoners, since they were not the first to trespass on her land that week. She listened to their frantic descriptions of the wives and daughters who waited to hear that they were safe, and swore an oath not to reveal their presence until they had time to get out of her neighborhood.[2]

The journey of thousands of escaped prisoners across the southern landscape in the last winter of the Civil War had personal as well as epic consequences. The fugitive Yankees interacted with slaves and white southerners under conditions very different from that of their comrades who marched across the land as part of invading Union armies. These Federals were vulnerable, disoriented, and totally reliant on the goodwill and aid of slaves, women, and children. They shared intimate moments with southerners of both races and faced daily challenges to their prejudices and stereotypes. The first wave of fugitive Federals to break over the South Carolina countryside in October and November 1864 navigated a complicated racial landscape that belied their simplistic views of blacks and their place. Although the Yankees developed a deep gratitude for the blacks who helped them, most of them were unable to see the nuances of the terrain over which they traveled.

African Americans, more than 400,000 living in South Carolina, foresaw the epic consequences of the aid they gave to escaped prisoners of war. Slaves in South Carolina were engaged, whenever and wherever they had opportunity, in a rebellion against their masters. Freedom was tantalizingly close. Federal forces had captured a chain of barrier islands on the Atlantic coast known as the Sea Islands, including Hilton Head, in November 1861, and took control of thousands of slaves and the cotton plantations they worked. Northeastern reformers descended on the islands to produce cotton using free-labor arrangements and to establish schools. Union gunboats periodically forayed a short distance upriver into the coastal lowlands. Male slaves working the rice plantations located there fled whenever possible to these boats or to the Union lines at Hilton Head. Some planters removed slaves to interior portions of the state, but many of these returned to the low country in 1864 because of their masters' financial hardships. Female slaves, who ran away in smaller numbers, slowed down work and showed increasing defiance to their mistresses, who were left to govern them while masters and their sons served in the Confederate army. Slavery remained more stable during the first three years of the war in the central and piedmont regions of the state, but that was about to change.[3]

The perceived Yankee plague that hit the countryside in October 1864 altered the equation for the first African Americans to be exposed, those in the environs of Columbia, where 11,000 slaves toiled on farms and plantations that produced cotton, corn, peas, and sweet potatoes. When escaped Yankee prisoners arrived on their doorsteps night after night, slaves recognized that the moment had come to escalate their operations against their masters' state. Running away was an act of self-liberation. Slowing down work and committing acts of defiance disrupted the daily operation of slavery. Now African Americans organized in new ways to help the Federal soldiers whose presence in the interior parts of the state signaled to them the last days of slavery. It was time to bring down the Confederacy.

The first Federals to escape in October had difficulty contacting African Americans, however. Journalist and fireman J. Madison Drake and his companions, who leapt from the moving train on its way from Charleston, traveled six days before they encountered a slave. They mistakenly took a road *toward* Columbia, the last place they wanted to go, and kept accidentally wandering onto farms and mills where white men and their dogs gave chase. Finally, while sneaking through an open wood on October 12, the party stumbled across a black man chopping wood, who assumed they were kidnappers. As they tried to convince him they were not, his master approached and they had to flee. The next day, the Yankees spotted a garden of corn and beans and crawled through a large cotton field to get there. As they shelled the beans, a group of slaves on their way to pick cotton stumbled upon them and ran away in a fright before the fugitives could say a word.[4]

But as escapes escalated throughout October and November, and the number of fugitive Federals in the countryside increased from dozens to several hundred, slaves and free blacks learned to recognize the Yankees. When Milton Russell and his companions knocked on the door of a slave cabin, they pretended to be Confederate soldiers on furlough and demanded food. The woman inside told them that they could not fool her. She knew they were Yankees because of the buttons on their jacket. She fed them and arranged for a series of pilots to guide them for the next several days.[5]

A slave chopping wood did not run away when the imperious Charlie Mattocks, Charles Hunt, and Julius Litchfield approached him their second night out, when they were but fifteen miles from Columbia on November 5. The three Maine officers planned to avoid all white men, but Litchfield had previous escape experience and told his companions that blacks as a race could be trusted. Mattocks was reluctant to do so, but hunger compelled them to make an appeal to the slave who came near their hiding place, so Litchfield approached the man and asked for help. Mattocks was an aristocrat who enjoyed asserting his social authority over the whites from the lowest social classes in New England in the two regiments he had commanded. He was nonchalant in his assumption that inferior blacks were delighted to serve him. "Boarded a darkey," he wrote in his diary. The Federals spent the evening in the slave's cabin talking with their host, toasting their feet by the fire and supping on chicken, corn bread, and potatoes.[6]

The irrepressible Indianans John Hadley and Homer Chisman, only a day behind the Mattocks party but still unsure of the ultimate route for their escape, implemented a system to obtain the help of slaves as part of the military discipline their party adopted for the journey. Every night at 10:00 P.M. the group would approach some slave quarters. Two men would stop 200 yards away, one man would stop at 100 yards, and the commander for that twenty-four hours would go alone to the huts and knock on the door. They memorized a speech to recite when the door opened. It went something like this: "I am a Yankee just escaped from a Rebel prison. I have three companions nearby and we are all nearly starved. Our only hope is your aid. There are no friends with white skins for us here. Your race caused the war and brought this calamity upon us. It is as much for your good as ours if you help us. Can you give us something? Only what you can spare and nothing more." After receiving whatever help the slaves offered, the Federals asked for the name of a black person they could contact who lived at least fifteen miles ahead on the road.[7]

Other fugitive Federals likewise implemented systematic methods to contact slaves once they had a better sense of the lay of the land. Lieutenant Edward Dickerson, a thirty-three-year-old Wisconsin mechanic who wore a beard so long it touched his belt, escaped from Camp Sorghum on October 28 and headed for Georgia. Four nights later, he and his companions had observed that male slaves made darkness the mask for their nightly movement off the plantations. These rovers visited the places where their wives lived or entered the woods to forage and hunt. Armed with this information, the Yankees waited for sunset on November 1, hid close to a plantation, and watched for its black men to disperse into the night. They picked one and stealthily followed until he was a safe distance from the plantation. Dickerson then jumped the man in his confidence that the slave would not fight back against a white attacker and that he would thus have time to convince the slave of his Yankee identity. The fugitives repeated this strategy nightly.[8]

Once contact was made, the Yankees' ingrained assumptions about racial superiority governed their initial encounters with slaves in South Carolina. The first slave Hadley's party met on the road tried to avoid the group of whites who suddenly came out of nowhere, but the Federals would have none of that. Confident in their ability to command and manipulate blacks as a prerogative of their whiteness, they complacently accepted his eventual offer of help. "The fellow was like all others of his race we afterward met," Hadley wrote later, "easily flattered and credulous, and when we once turned the key to his heart he was as completely in our service as if he had been a brother." It was comforting for the two Indiana Yankees to confirm that blacks in South Carolina were just as they had supposed them to be: innately loyal and generous to the whites who led them.[9]

The slave took Hadley, Chisman, Baker, and Good to his cabin, and soon twenty other African Americans crowded in to see the Yankees. The ensuing conversation surprised Hadley. The slaves knew who Abraham Lincoln was, were able to explain the political origins of the rebellion, and had full knowledge of the Emancipation Proclamation. They laughed behind the backs of their master, who tried to frighten them with stories that Yankees would enslave them in the North where they would freeze to death, or sell them to Cuba, and that Federals shot black soldiers out of their cannons. These slaves were giving Hadley an exhibition of their incredulity and distrust of whites, but the lesson did not sink in. What did dawn on his understanding was an appreciation for the remarkable knowledge and memory that African American slaves possessed of the human and physical geography of their neighborhoods. They knew the landscape down to individual trees, stones, and cow-paths, and could provide precise directions to the homes of whites and blacks within a fifteen-mile radius.[10]

A small door opened in Hadley's closed mind. The conversation convinced the Federals that they should seek more than food and shelter from the slaves. They should listen to their advice about where and how to proceed on their journey. Hadley and his companions submitted their disagreement about the two potential routes out of the Confederacy to the slaves' judgment. The slaves advised them to head north to Knoxville. The way to Georgia was filled with hazardous swamps, and they confirmed that whites in South Carolina spoke frequently of "Tories" in North Carolina, a word that meant loyalty to the United States. The Federals deferred to the slaves' judgment and the decision was made. Subsequent experience confirmed the reliability of African Americans' knowledge. "There was not an instance on the whole route where we were misled," Hadley later asserted.[11]

For the rest of the trip, Hadley and his companions jumbled together contradictory opinions about African Americans, mixing their prewar assumptions with glimmers of new knowledge. Yankees expected to find among slaves in the South, and thus did find, innocent sufferers and cunning tricksters, simpletons and superior intellects, passive victims and courageous heroes, Christian martyrs and superstitious heathens.[12] The Yankees recognized and described the individual personalities of the blacks they met yet saw them all as a variation on racial "types."

Despite perceptive distortions, the fugitives discerned some truths about southern slaves that historians and linguists would not rediscover until the twenty-first century. Recent research confirms what Willard Glazier heard: that regional dialects within the South varied considerably and that blacks and whites within a given region in the mid-nineteenth century spoke similar vernaculars that would have been difficult for outsiders to distinguish. Scholars who study slavery now assert what fugitives carefully described in their accounts: despite masters' efforts to constrict their movement, slaves were mobile, carved out neighborhoods for activity that crossed plantation boundaries, and possessed extensive communication networks across space.[13]

Talking and eating in the slave cabins of South Carolina both liberated Yankees from and bound them to their prejudices and stereotypes. The Federals' clouded vision of the slaves they met did not obscure the one stark truth of their experience, however. Blacks in South Carolina were true friends to them. Fugitives wrote the word over and over in the diaries kept during the journey and spoke the word again and again to the Union authorities who took their reports if they arrived safely in Union lines. The 344 fugitives who successfully reached the Union lines at Hilton Head universally gave credit where it was due. "The negroes did everything," James Morgan reported to the provost marshal who took his statement. "We trusted over a hundred and were not betrayed." J. L. Paston put it succinctly: "We could not have got along without them."[14]

Although the Federal fugitives paid the slaves at times (when they had money they offered it) and gave them heartfelt embraces to thank them for their services, the Yankees rarely reciprocated the risks that slaves took on their behalf. Captain Isaiah Conley recorded that a slave on one plantation "pled very hard for us to take him along, but we thought it would be unwise." Fugitives explained their refusal on the grounds that if prisoners of war were caught together with runaway slaves, they expected that all in the party would be executed. But occasionally prisoners of war and slaves—"the same victims of Rebel hate," as one fugitive put it—made common cause in the quest for freedom. A private in the Seventy-Sixth New York who jumped from the train on the way to Florence brought with him to Union lines a slave who guided him safely down the Pee Dee River, where they hailed the Federal gunboat *Flambeau*. Three Ohio fugitives and a slave traveled together from Georgia to the Florida coast and did not part until the freedman obtained employment with a doctor in New York.[15]

Escaped prisoners of war, although they nearly unanimously supported emancipation as a war goal, were primarily interested in their own survival and would not risk their own lives to free slaves they encountered. But their presence brought freedom nearer anyway. The fugitive brigade trudging through the countryside invaded a land already in the throes of racial and institutional upheaval. African Americans gathered information through their communication networks to assess the chances for Union military success in their area, and then acted to gain freedom at carefully chosen moments when the signs were favorable.[16] In the fall of 1864, South Carolina's slaves knew Sherman's army was marching unimpeded in Georgia, and they knew something was going wrong in their state or the Rebels would not have lost so many Yankee prisoners. They saw a chance to strike an effective blow and acted accordingly. Yankees weren't necessarily likeable—it is hard to imagine any slave thinking favorably of Hadley's speech that blamed them for the war—but slaves knew that helping the Yankees hurt the Confederacy. It was a military act to guide the Yankees back to the armies that would finish off the Confederacy and bring slavery to its final end.

It was also a religious act. Some Christians assisted Yankees simply because Jesus Christ commanded them to love those who were in need. When a Rhode Island lieutenant tried to pay for the food a slave provided, he was rebuffed. "This is the charity the Lord says must be given to those who suffer," the slave responded firmly.[17] The Christian faith of other slaves tied the aid they gave to escaped Federals to their vision of the coming jubilee: the time that God had ordained to free them from bondage. The Christian slaves the Federals met had deep faith that God was purposeful in history and active on their behalf. One elderly slave explained this to an escaped New Yorker she took into her cabin. Her mother raised her in the expectation that slavery would end one day because the Lord would deliver them just as He had delivered the Israelites from Egypt so long ago. When the war commenced, she told the Yankee, she knew the time had come. The arrival of Yankee soldiers in her home, even weak and hungry ones, was another sign to her that God's promise was being fulfilled. One fugitive hiding in a stack of cowpeas on the road between Columbia and Augusta overheard two slaves talking about God's sovereignty over current events. They expressed confidence that God smote America because of its wickedness. It was time for slaves to sprinkle the sides of their houses with blood, like the Israelites did in the days of old, for God was on the side of the Yankees and He would pass over the oppressed slaves as He destroyed their masters.[18]

The coming of jubilee required the defeat of the Confederacy. Time and again slaves expressed their conviction that the success of Union armies was necessary to their aspirations. Alonzo Jackson, who lived in the Georgetown District, hired his time from his master. When the war started, he worked at a livery stable owned by a free African American. His wife brought in income as a pastry cook and laundress. But Rebel cavalry plundered the stable and destroyed the business. So in February 1864, Jackson rented a flatboat and carried freight on the Pee Dee and Waccamaw Rivers, traveling for up to two weeks at a time in a sixty-mile radius from Georgetown. During his voyages, Jackson learned the location of Rebel pickets on the coast and the routes of Yankee gunboats. And he picked up fugitive Federals. He used his flatboat on two different occasions to ferry parties of Florence escapees to the safety of Union lines. "I knew what I needed most and looked to the [Union cause] certain! I wanted to be free and wanted my race to be free. I knew this could not be if the rebels had a government of their own," he later testified. Another stated simply, "I knew we could never be free if the Confederates were victorious. I always prayed for the Union Army to succeed."[19]

Simon Dufur, one of the 400 Yankees who fled from the open field in Florence, recorded just such a prayer in his diary during his several-night sojourn in a slave cabin. Slaves commonly held prayer meetings for the fugitives they shielded. Dufur's host, a slave named Johnson, invited fifteen other slaves to pray for Dufur and his companion. They asked the Lord to "assist these gentlemen who have fled from rebel affliction" and to "bamboozle" the hounds that would chase them. They prayed for the success of President Lincoln and all the Union generals engaged in battle. They asked God to watch over the Union soldiers who were chained up in the South and the slaves who were ground down and oppressed. "May the year of jubilee come and the rebels turn up their toes," they petitioned.[20]

Glazier and Lemon, hiding in a hut near Black Creek on their fourth day out of Columbia, participated in a prayer meeting led by the slave Zeb, whose petition was infused with the conviction that God governed military events and that He acted for the Yankees in judgment on the Rebels. Zeb asked God to be with Glazier and Lemon in their time of trouble and to lift them through all danger to the other side of the Jordan. He requested a Moses to lead them through the Red Sea of affliction to their promised land. "Send Mr. Sherman sweeping down through these parts to scare the rebels until they flee like the Midians, and slay themselves to save their lives," he prayed. Glazier, who knew his Bible, recognized this as a reference to the incident recorded in Judges, where 300 Israelites under the leadership of Gideon attacked an enemy camp with thousands of soldiers. All Christians knew the lesson: God sent home 31,700 Israelites before the battle so people would know that God and not human might brought victory. The book of Judges records that when Gideon's men approached the Midianite camp and blew trumpets, "the Lord caused the men through the camp to turn on each other with their swords." Trusting that God's sovereignty was timeless, Zeb asked for "heaven's best judgments" to rest on Abraham Lincoln and the "year of jubilee come for sure."[21]

Slaves offered a variety of services to the Yankees, from the covert to the overt, for the purpose of bringing on the jubilee and turning up the

Published narratives of escaped prisoners often featured an illustration of slaves providing food. This one appeared in Albert D. Richardson's *The Secret Service, the Field, the Dungeon, and the Escape* (1865).

Rebel toes. The two were inherently linked. Slaves funneled limited resources to their masters' enemies. When Yankees appeared on the roads at night and approached slaves at work in the fields or at rest in their cabins in October and early November, slaves offered food or provided it upon request. Given that provisions were scarce in many parts of South Carolina during the winter of 1864–65, the generosity of slaves in sharing their meager food stores was a tangible sign that they offered common cause to the Yankees. Slaves in the Georgetown area were on half-rations and low-country slaves received meat once a week if at all. Fugitives who made it to Union lines at Hilton Head reported that many slaves they encountered were almost starving yet "would divide their last mouthful with us."[22]

The Mattocks escape party quickly learned that the meal of chicken and corn bread they enjoyed on the night of November 5 was a special treat. Two nights later the Maine officers hid in some woods near a cornfield eight miles south of the village of Newberry. They obtained one potato each and some raw corn for dinner. The next night a slave brought them sorghum and baked sweet potatoes. For the next seven nights, they ate potatoes and shared a hunk of corn bread. Only two meals provided an exception to this monotonous fare: on the eleventh slaves brought cake and milk (as well as tobacco and grease for their boots and sore feet), and on the fifteenth an elderly woman prepared a hot meal for them in her cabin complete with a small slice of dried venison. One Yankee prisoner who traversed the same ground identified another problem besides scarcity with obtaining provisions from slaves. "The rations were issued to them every morning, and by night it was all eaten. We found all of the slaves friendly and anxious to see us, but [they] had nothing to give us."[23]

Food was not the most important aid that slaves provided to the fugitives, since many Yankees stole corn and sweet potatoes from the fields and killed hogs and geese to cook in their woodland hiding places. The slaves' greatest service in South Carolina was to operate as guides for Yankees en route to Knoxville or Augusta or to channel them down the rivers to Hilton Head. Fugitives encountered male slaves whose work as teamsters and freighters required interstate travel or whose journeys with low-country masters to upcountry summer resorts made them well acquainted with the roads to North Carolina and Tennessee. In rice-producing areas, masters on each plantation designated a slave crew to maintain and operate a fleet of boats. These men knew the state's waterways like the backs of their hands.

Slaves utilized their existing modes of resistance to slavery when they aided fugitive Federals in the capacity of guide. They already knew which paths and woods to use that gave them the best chance of moving from place to place without arousing the notice of patrols, and they already had established hiding places in woods, swamps, and quarters used before the war to shield runaways or truants who desired a temporary break from the rigors of slavery. Now they used the spatial infrastructure of prewar resistance to help the Yankees.[24]

When the first Federals escaped in September and October, individual slaves provided this type of guidance for short distances. Quickly the aid became more organized. When Hannibal Johnson of the Third Maine escaped from Camp Sorghum in late November, slaves guided him between prearranged stations in northwest South Carolina. Over the course of eight nights in that section of his journey, he was handed off between thirteen different guides who took him to established stops and hiding places in woods and cabins. One guide gave his Yankee cargo the code name "birdies."[25]

By December, with fugitives spreading across the land and news of Sherman's impending invasion traveling through every grapevine, slaves became more overt and more military in their assistance. At the same time that slaves in Jalapa formed the counter-picket to guide Yankees around their masters' trap, slaves in St. Matthew's Parish organized a paramilitary company in the wake of so many fugitives moving through their area. Anxious white community leaders in the district of Clarendon reported widespread stealing and disintegration of order, while portions of the low country descended into lawlessness and chaos when slaves no longer submitted to the old regime.[26]

The collapse of slavery in South Carolina, as elsewhere in the Confederacy, was a process that occurred unevenly across space and time. In Clarendon and St. Matthew's Parish, both located in the central section of the state, the slave regime was gone in December and slaves openly fought against their masters. In some districts of the piedmont, the arrival of fugitive Federals initiated the first significant tremors to an institution that still seemed stable. By late November and early December, the Yankees who escaped from the trains and from Columbia reached the upcountry region of western South Carolina in large numbers. Union armies had not yet threatened these interior districts, where refugees from Charleston congregated for safety and where slaves remained and labored on the farms and plantations. When unarmed escaped prisoners arrived on the scene, however, they destabilized the relationship between masters and slaves.

The Harris farm in Spartanburg District exemplified the change fugitive Yankees brought to the neighborhood. This district lay along one of the paths they took to Knoxville. Located in the foothills of the Appalachians, the region housed 9,000 slaves, about one-third of the total population. Ten of these belonged to David Golightly Harris and his wife Elizabeth, who farmed 100 of the 550 acres they owned. The disruptions of war increasingly plagued the couple and their seven children during 1864. In February, Harris complained that the Confederate draft took too many men out of the district for farms to produce their usual crop of corn. Shortages and inflation made the acquisition of nearly every needed item increasingly difficult. Harris worried about whether he would have enough to feed his family once he turned over a portion of his crop to the Confederate government as required by the tax-in-kind laws and once he paid the $581 of additional Confederate taxes he owed. Thieves, active in the neighborhood since 1862, stole six hogs from the couple between February and June.[27]

Although the Harris slaves still worked, plowed, cleared, and planted on the family's land throughout the summer and early fall of 1864, their behavior started to change. Elizabeth wondered if her slaves were doing some of the rampant stealing. A local slave was selling pork, and people in the neighborhood were so needy they bought it without question. Did this slave get his black market pork from her slaves? With Harris absent in June on duty with his cavalry regiment near Charleston, male relatives and neighbors of Elizabeth helped her interrogate the slaves, who denied stealing anything. A month later she caught one stealing eggs, and a month after that watermelons disappeared from the garden. In late October, thieves around the farm seemed bolder. Elizabeth bemoaned that she lived in a "lawless land." When Harris returned home on furlough in November, he wrote, "The thieves about me are troubling me as much as the war. It seems they will steal all we have got and leave us but little for my family." In late November and early December, thieves killed and skinned four more of the Harris hogs.[28]

The reason became clear on December 16, when Elizabeth discovered that her slaves were feeding and hiding escaped Yankee prisoners in the gin house. Yankees were responsible for the increased activity in the neighborhood during the past few weeks. She alerted her neighbors, who set up ambushes around the farm, guns in hand, but the prisoners slipped away. A search of the land indicated that the slaves had been hiding prisoners for many days past. They refused to answer any questions about the Yankees. A few days later, the slaves left the farm without permission and took a longer Christmas holiday than permitted. Although they returned, they were increasingly rebellious and none of the men in the neighborhood were willing to whip them for her. "It seems that people are getting afraid of the negroes," Elizabeth wrote in her journal.[29]

The Harris farm was safe from Union armies, but it was not safe from the escaped Yankee prisoners whose presence inspired slaves to further acts of resistance. When Elizabeth Harris entered her gin house and saw the evidence of Yankee inhabitation, she knew that her slaves had declared war against her. It could never be the same again. The Yankees signaled the jubilee, the signs were favorable, and in Spartanburg slaves escalated resistance against individual masters while slaves in St. Matthew's moved against the Confederate state.

Local, state, and Confederate authorities were powerless in some districts to govern the slaves who aided Yankees and formed military-style companies. The guards at Florence and Camp Sorghum loosed their prisoners into neighborhoods that no longer possessed the resources to govern the slaves if they proved rebellious. Before the Civil War, slave patrols policed the movement and behavior of slaves away from their home plantations. In South Carolina, slave patrols in the countryside were chosen from the local militia company, known as a beat company, composed of white males between the ages of eighteen and forty-five (with some exemptions), while villages and cities usually employed paid guards. Citizens also formed extralegal vigilante organizations to provide additional patrolling in times of threat or emergencies. This happened all over the state during the secession crisis in 1860–61.

The Confederate government disrupted slave patrols when it mobilized men for the army and depleted the countryside of military-age men. Older men and overseers of plantations, who were exempt from state service and the Confederate draft, continued to patrol in 1861–62, but when the state mobilized militia companies in a given district for service to defend Charleston and the coast from Union operations at various times in 1863, patrolling temporarily ceased in such places. The Confederate government dealt the death blow to effective slave patrols in February 1864, when a new conscription law drafted men between the ages of seventeen and fifty and reduced the exemptions allowed. This drained the South Carolina countryside of the men needed to police slavery.[30]

Petitions from citizens begging for the return of men for patrol duty flooded into the Confederate and state governments. Twenty-two citizens from a community in the Darlington District begged the secretary of war in March to release John B. Rhodes from the Twenty-First South Carolina Regiment. The male population of Swift Creek consisted of a small number of infirm elderly men. Slaves, "knowing we are not able to help ourselves," openly committed "depredations," broke into homes, robbed hen houses, and killed hogs. The petitioners asked for Rhodes because he was an experienced patroller who knew the bays and swamps where blacks regularly hid. Even more importantly, he owned a pack of bloodhounds that only he could manage. A man who could govern dogs, they asserted, was worth "ten other men." The flux of fugitive Federals across the countryside later in the year made the absence of men even more frightening. Fifty-five ladies living near Fort Motte, forty miles southeast of Columbia, asked the governor in November for their men back. A few "decrepid old men" were left to control 5,000 slaves and the "good many *escaped prisoners* 'strolling' about the vicinity." They were "at the mercy" of "*treacherous* negroes and *heartless* Yankees." It is significant that these women mentioned the fugitives in tandem with the slaves.

They perceived the alliance formed between the two groups and realized that the Confederate state did not protect them from this new menace.[31]

Even in districts where whites maintained relative control over the slave population, the disruption of patrols made their authority tenuous and fragile. The South Carolina General Assembly granted the Georgetown Police Court extraordinary wartime powers to govern slaves because the district was located close to Union forces operating on the coast. There were not enough men in any rural neighborhood to conduct slave patrols along the rivers, a favorite avenue for escaped slaves and escaped Yankees. The Police Court resorted to eleven executions and numerous other drastic punishments to suppress slaves' threatening behavior.[32]

The Georgetown Police Court may have temporarily suppressed overt acts of rebellion, but the dysfunctional patrol system opened the district to fugitive Federals. When Alonzo Jackson used his flatboat to ferry two parties of Florence escapees to the Union lines at North Island, he assured the Yankees they could get to Union lines "unmolested." Although there were Confederate pickets posted along the shoreline around the city of Georgetown, the rivers that flowed into the coast were empty of patrols. His knowledge of Union gunboat routes enabled him to deliver the fugitives safely.[33]

Dogs, not men, were the most effective police force left in South Carolina during the last three months of 1864 for governing slaves and recapturing escaped Federals. Before the Civil War, dogs were an essential tool slaveholders used to manage slaves and track runaways. Most slaveholders did not own bloodhounds but relied on ordinary farm dogs or on a specialist who trained and managed a pack that local officials called upon when the need arose. During the war, the Confederate army enlisted trainers and their animals to guard prisoners, track deserters, and hunt runaway slaves. Federal naval paymaster Luther Billings met such a man, named Baker, when bloodhounds pursued his escape party after they jumped from the trains ferrying prisoners from Charleston to Columbia. The Yankees headed for the coast, only thirty miles away from their jumping-off point, but this choice led them within fifteen miles of the camp of the Second South Carolina Cavalry stationed at Adams Run Station. After the mass escapes from the train, officials ordered Baker to use his dogs to track Yankees, and he received a graduated reward according to the rank of each Federal officer he captured. Baker received a private's pay and bragged that his dogs were also enlisted in the army and drew a regular ration. Although everyone classified his dogs as blood-hounds, Baker used English foxhounds bred in his family for genera-tions to hunt human quarry and bring them to bay. He trained two "catch dogs," part mastiff and part Irish deerhound, to attack the quarry at the end of the chase.[34]

Dogs located the bulk of the Federals who escaped from the trains in October. Indeed, more officers would have escaped from Camp Sorghum that month than actually did because of a dramatic display Confederate officials put on for the Yankees when they reached Columbia. When the officers arrived at the train station in the capital, before they marched to the open field, guards brought before them the wounded and mangled figure of a lieutenant who escaped from the train. The animals who cap-tured him tore his body so badly he died a few hours later. This sight made a deep impression on the shocked and outraged Federals. It also reinforced the image of the South that northern abolitionists had ex-pounded to the northern public for three decades: a land where savage and ferocious beasts hunted human prey. The prison guards at Camp Sor-ghum were hardly intimidating; the dogs who prowled the neighbor-hoods on the other side of the imaginary line bounding the camp certainly were.[35]

Slaves who aided Federals provided them with advice and tools to avoid bloodhounds. They rubbed pepper, green onion tops, and turpen-tine on the Yankees' shoes and legs. They told the Federals to travel in water whenever possible and to enter rather than avoid the swamps. Baker, the bloodhound trainer, laughed over these methods in a conver-sation with Billings after he captured the naval paymaster. He told Billings that there was only one hope for a fugitive once well-trained dogs had the trail: a heavy rain storm. But that only worked if the hunted party lay down right where he was when the downpour started and did not move until the pursuers gave up the hunt. Whether Baker accurately re-vealed the truth of his trade or lied to discourage the Federal from an-other escape attempt, Billings was unsure.[36]

Bloodhounds recaptured fugitives and policed slavery in the vicinity of Florence, Charleston, Columbia, and the railroad tracks, but the prob-lem for Federals in the South Carolina interior were the "mongrel" dogs who barked at them and chased them from every field and farmhouse along every road. These guard dogs were a constant annoyance to the Yankees and created logistical problems when they wanted to approach a slave cabin at night. One captain entered such cabins without knocking or speaking in order to avoid attracting the dogs' attention. By the time another Columbia escapee, Edward Dickerson, reached Georgia, he perfected a method to deal with the ubiquitous plantation dogs. "If you get on the place before dark when the people are about they make no fuss," he commented, "and will pay no attention to you after."[37]

Dogs were the bane of J. Madison Drake's journey. On October 15, his escape party was near Rock Hill, South Carolina, close to the North Carolina border. As usual, when they walked past a residence on the side of the road, dogs burst out of nowhere and set on them. The four Yankees ran for it, turning periodically to swipe at the dogs with clubs they made during the journey for just this reason. The dogs chased them through a small settlement and into a vault in the graveyard. The Yankees waited there half an hour before the dogs left and it was safe to emerge. Even when dogs did not give chase, fugitives ran at the sound of barking, knowing that the noise would awaken and alarm the sleeping households.[38]

Bloodhounds under the command of a knowledgeable trainer and ordinary guard dogs imbued with a zealous desire to protect their territory compensated to a small degree for the dearth of men to patrol slavery and to recapture fugitive Federals. But dogs could not prevent the collapse of slavery, already underway in South Carolina and accelerating under the joint maneuvers of runaway Yankees and rebellious slaves in November and December 1864. These operations coincided with the Confederate government's last-ditch attempt to impress slave labor for work on the fortifications around Charleston.

This effort starkly revealed that neither the Confederate nor the state government possessed effective authority over slaves *or* their masters. Although the vast majority of slaveholders in Virginia and North Carolina cooperated with impressment, this was not the case in South Carolina, where slaveholders impeded the process. Masters did so because they wanted to protect their personal property (slaves often sickened and died while working for the Confederacy), because impressment destabilized slavery on their plantations when it withdrew able-bodied male workers, and because masters were loath to hand over their personal sovereignty to a state entity. But when slaveholders undermined impressment, they ironically provided an important nail for slavery's coffin.[39]

South Carolina first impressed slaves to defend the state in December 1862. The Confederate military needed labor to build and fortify the defenses around Charleston. The General Assembly divided the state into four divisions, authorized the governor to issue calls for slave labor upon request of the Confederate States of America, gave local officials the duty of summoning owners to provide slaves, and imposed a fine on slave owners for noncompliance. Planters in South Carolina immediately balked at this unprecedented invasion of their claimed sovereign property rights and this threat to their personal control over slaves. The results were abysmal; after several calls for slaves in early 1863, the state received only 750 of the 3,000 needed. In April, the assembly penalized local officials who neglected to enforce the law. Federal operations against Charleston in July 1863 stimulated planters to provide 2,850 slaves for coastal labor, but the numbers dwindled down to 500 later that year. To address the pervasive evasion of the law on the part of both slave owners and local officials, the General Assembly passed additional legislation in September and December that made defaults on the part of planters a misdemeanor, required magistrates to issue warrants in such cases, and ordered sheriffs to arrest and deliver slaves that owners failed to produce.[40]

The state proved powerless to enforce the law. This was bluntly revealed in the summer of 1864, when Major General Samuel Jones, commander of the Department of South Carolina, Georgia, and Florida, wrote Governor Milledge Bonham that the state agent had furnished him with only nine slaves. In November, Bonham informed the General Assembly that not a single district in South Carolina had provided its quota of slaves. The governor frankly admitted that sheriffs refused to do their duty, and since state courts were virtually closed, it was impossible to compel them. In December, Confederate and state authorities combined to issue calls for more than 6,500 slaves, but under threat of imminent invasion from the dreaded Sherman, masters produced fewer than 2,000. Meanwhile, in the state capital of Columbia, the city council passed an ordinance asking city residents to lend the mayor slaves and tools so he could erect fortifications to defend the city. He received none of either.[41]

The unintended consequence of slaveholders' virtual nullification of state impressment laws was that male slaves were home to aid the Yankees who poured out of trains and the porous prisons the Confederate government created in October. Impressment agents were engaged in futile attempts to gather slaves in many of the counties flooded with fugitive Federals, such as Lexington and Spartanburg. Elizabeth Harris was hoisted on her own petard. Her slaves should have been working on the coast for the Confederate government rather than feeding Yankees in her gin house. She ignored repeated calls for them. "They shall not budge till they are literally compelled to go," she wrote in her diary. "I've sent my husband and that is enough for me to do." The state never compelled her.[42]

With local authorities unwilling and state authorities unable to enforce impressment because their attention was turned to the impending invasion of Sherman's army, the Confederate government tried to take command. On December 12, 1864, the Bureau of Conscription issued a circular instructing its officers to impress South Carolina's quota of 2,500 slaves and to cooperate with any terms established by state impressment laws. This circular was a paper tiger with no possibility of being implemented, as the bureau's head Brigadier General John S. Preston frankly informed the secretary of war. But the threat of losing control over the mechanism of raising slaves stimulated legislators in Columbia to pass on December 23 the state's first comprehensive impressment law, as strong on paper, and as weak on the ground, as the circular.[43]

South Carolina's state impressment agent R. B. Johnson bluntly informed Governor Magrath that citizen resistance would render the legislation useless: "The well affected are very reluctant to respond to any call, whilst the factious and unpatriotic, the lukewarm and the disaffected, now so numerous, are ready to interpose every possible hindrance to the execution of such impressment.... All attempts, therefore to impress by main caption would be futile." Sherman rendered the point moot on December 30, when he ordered a division of the Twentieth Corps to cross the Savannah River into South Carolina. His invasion of the state had begun, and the unenforceable law fell by the wayside.[44]

Threats to South Carolina and to Confederate authority there multiplied rapidly between October and December. During that time, Sherman marched through Georgia and captured Savannah. Federal armies occupying the Sea Islands conducted raids on the railroad that ran between Savannah and Charleston. The Federal navy tightened its siege of Charleston. In the face of these military maneuvers, Confederate and state authorities called for more than 6,500 slaves for defense at a time when their labor on farms and plantations was barely enough to feed the population and the armies.

In this context the Confederate government sent into South Carolina thousands of prisoners of war who escaped by the hundreds in the last three months of 1864. In sizeable portions of the state, slaves aided the enemy, formed networks to funnel Yankees to safety, organized militia companies, committed depredations against property, and disobeyed their masters. Confederate and state authorities were powerless to use slaves as a resource for state defense or to stop their subversive activities. There was a long and winding road ahead, with a few U-turns along the way, but the jubilee had come to South Carolina.

3

They Cover the Land like the Locusts of Egypt

The Collapse of the State

Charlie Mattocks, Charles Hunt, and Julius Litchfield snuck through the town of Newberry, South Carolina, located forty-three miles northwest of Columbia, at 2:00 A.M. on November 9, the eighth night of their journey from Camp Sorghum toward Knoxville. Just north of the village, the road forked in several directions. This had happened to them before, but outside of other towns there had been guideboards indicating the next village along each road. To read the signs in the dark, Hunt had climbed on the 6′2″ Litchfield's shoulders. But this time there were no signposts. Using Mattocks's compass, they took the road that seemed to head northwest, the general direction to Knoxville. After walking a couple of miles, the compass shifted and they feared they were wrong. So they backtracked and tried another road. And then another. Finally, they encountered a black man at a small railroad station six miles north of Newberry. While they talked to him, Captain Simeon Baker arrived on the scene and told them that John Hadley, Homer Chisman, and Thomas Good were hiding close by, and that they had just encountered another party of fugitive Federals. The slave chimed in with the unwelcome news that two other Yankees passed through the railroad station the day before and that seven others were recaptured just outside of Newberry on the same day. "It is getting to be quite a popular route," Mattocks commented dryly.[1]

He and Baker talked it over. A crowd of Yankees on the road increased the likelihood of discovery. They agreed to create separation between their parties. Baker returned to his Indiana friends to wait overnight while the scions of Maine moved on. Mattocks, Hunt, and Litchfield traveled ten more miles and then hid for the day in some woods near the pike. During the small hours of the night on November 10, they passed through the village of Clinton, which appeared to the Yankees as a small collection of houses on a single street. They walked past a structure that looked like a guardhouse and through the window saw that a recaptured fugitive was being held there. As they turned to move on, they came face to face with a white man. He looked hard at them but did not say a word.

The frightened Yankees ran as hard as they could for the next six miles, passing along the way three other fugitive Federals, before they found a piece of woods to hide in northwest of the village of Laurens. They hoped they were now safely distant from any other escaped prisoners.[2]

Throngs of Yankees converged on villages in South Carolina that lay along routes to Knoxville or to Augusta, Georgia, where fugitives traveled in the hopes of linking up with Sherman's army. Edgefield, located about thirty miles from Augusta, was one of these unfortunate communities. Townspeople captured eight fugitives in mid-October, and the editor of the local newspaper, the *Edgefield Advertiser*, prophetically advised citizens to be constantly alert "for we expect there are more of them prowling about through the country." By November 30, the paper proclaimed that Yankees "actually cover the land like the locusts of Egypt." Citizens in the district were vigilant and constant in their efforts to arrest the fugitive Federals, so much so that Edgefield became notorious among escaped prisoners. But the Yankee plague continued to multiply. In early December, the editor was stung into biting sarcasm when he read in a Columbia newspaper that 200 Federal prisoners had just been transferred to the city. "In all probability some fifty head of these same beasts will be in Edgefield jail before another week passes by; or at all events, prowling about the district," he commented. "On Wednesday, a squad of sixteen, after a four day sweet-potato carnival in our jail, departed from among us, to enter again into their house of bondage in Columbia—which by the by seems to be anything but a house of bondage." The writer suggested that if authorities in Columbia could not contain the prisoners, they should kill them all immediately.[3]

The problem for the citizens of Edgefield District was that no Confederate or state troops arrived to hunt the fugitives. It was clear they would have to handle the "wretched and unfriendly vagrants" on their own. In mid-December, the Confederate enrolling officer, in charge of conscription in the district, and two prominent citizens held a meeting to coordinate a "society for defense." The enrolling officer had already organized some citizens into "supporting forces" that helped him search for deserters. Now he planned to create squads of citizens who would cooperate with his supporting forces to patrol for escaped Yankees and to prepare to defend the city if Sherman marched in its direction.[4]

But citizens did not turn out as expected, and the *Edgefield Advertiser* chastised locals for their "lethargy and apathy." The editor acknowledged two reasons for their attitude: the general belief that the community was so weak it could never make an effective defense against a Yankee army and the objection that such a society was unable to make men do their duty without the authority of law to back it up. Although Edgefield's citizens refused to form a "society for defense," individuals acting on their own authority policed their neighborhoods and arrested the Yankees who nightly disturbed their peace and rest. Residents captured twenty-four fugitive Federals in the two weeks before the organizational meetings: the Confederate enrolling officer and his supporting forces nabbed a few of these, but most were brought in by "the people at large."[5]

The inhabitants of Edgefield faced multiple threats in the last three months of 1864, and they discovered that neither the state nor the Confederate government possessed the power to help them. The journey of escaped prisoners reveals the process through which Confederate authority dissolved across space and time in South Carolina. When Yankees jumped off trains and poured out of prisons, traveling the highways and byways, they exploited the ongoing disintegration of the Confederate and state infrastructure. Confederate authority ceased to function in significant portions of the state in the weeks before Sherman's army invaded. When that happened, protection from the prisoners devolved onto the people of South Carolina.

The story of fugitive Federals and the communities they invaded also reveals the role citizens took on as the Confederacy collapsed during the last few months of the war. The disintegration of Confederate and state authority facilitated a breakdown of order that left the public largely responsible for its own security. Families and individuals, rather than Confederate officials, made decisions on the ground about when, if, and how they would handle threats to the state. Once that occurred, citizens were no longer willing to contribute their manpower or their resources to a government that no longer functioned. When Confederate authorities proved unable to respond to the threat of fugitive Federals, effective control reverted to local agency.

The Confederate States of America controlled most troops in South Carolina and never considered sparing any of them to address the Yankee fugitive problem. Military officials in South Carolina were consumed with three external threats to the state: the siege of Charleston conducted by the Union's South Atlantic Blockading Squadron, raids against the railroad that connected Charleston and Savannah conducted by Union armies that occupied the coastal islands, and Sherman's movements in

Georgia. Lieutenant General William J. Hardee, commander of the Department of South Carolina, Georgia, and Florida, had only 11,136 men present in his command at the end of October to defend the cities of Charleston and Savannah and to garrison the prisons at Columbia and Florence. That total included Confederate Reserves, composed of youths between the ages of sixteen and seventeen and men between the ages of forty-five and fifty. In the entire state of South Carolina, the Confederate Conscription Bureau had only 219 officers and soldiers on duty; the point of highest concentration for its forces was the Fifth Congressional District with its nine officers and thirty soldiers. Every other district had fewer than twenty-one soldiers present.[6] When the Federal prisoners arrived in South Carolina, the reserves and conscription officials were already stretched thin in a losing battle against deserters and brigands in the mountains, and anxious state officials in Columbia were learning that conscription had so decimated the state militia that it had effectively ceased to exist.

The Confederate military's main concern about internal security in the months leading up to the transfer of prisoners into South Carolina was the activity of brigands in the region that encompassed Greenville, Anderson, Pickens, and Spartanburg. Greenville District was a particular point of anxiety because it was a vital agricultural and manufacturing center that served as a refuge for families who fled Charleston during the Union navy's bombardment of the city. On the eve of the Civil War, the district produced 2,984 bales of cotton and 623,288 bushels of corn. Its yeomen, who individually owned fewer than five slaves and collectively possessed 70 percent of the farms, also planted wheat. Wives and daughters shared the hard farm work with slaves and the occasional hired laborer, as well as weaving and dyeing cloth for the family's use. The town of Greenville, with a population of 1,800 people, possessed thriving paper and cotton mills, several carriage factories, tinworks, and three institutions of higher education, including a female college. After the war started, the Confederate government commandeered the local textile mills to produce shirts for the army, with one day's output per week reserved for the civilian population. One of the carriage factories supplied its entire output of wagons, more than $140,000 worth, to the Confederacy. In 1862, South Carolina located its State Military Works in Greenville. Superintendent David Lopez brought machinery and skilled workers to the village from Charleston and Nashville. Employees manufactured and repaired a variety of weapons, including the Morse carbine, a breech-loading rifle.

For all its contributions to the Confederate cause, the district was volatile. A strong tradition of Unionism, dating back to the nullification crisis in the 1830s, undergirded the reluctant secessionism of its leading political figures, most notably Benjamin F. Perry. Although Greenville District furnished fifteen companies to the Confederate army, few volunteers emerged from the upper portions of the county, nicknamed the "Dark Corner." And the commitment of those who served proved shaky. Entire companies of soldiers from the district deserted and returned home in 1863. The suffering of their families was certainly one factor in their decision. High inflation rates, diminished production on the farms, and the drain of foodstuffs to Confederate armies left many soldiers' wives and children hungry. The state established welfare programs to address the problem. On the first Monday of each month, what locals called Draw Day, officials distributed corn obtained through a tax-in-kind to the hundreds of needy persons who descended on the village.[7]

The deserters posed a serious threat to the security of loyal Confederates who lived in Greenville. When Major John D. Ashmore assumed command of the district as chief enrolling officer on June 29, 1863, he found to his horror that the region was infested. More than 500 deserters had formed bands of twenty and thirty men each that roamed over 150 miles of inaccessible mountain terrain. Local citizens sustained them with supplies, alerted them with signals when strangers approached, and openly defended their conduct. The bands fired on two officers sent to reconnoiter, robbed the property of loyal Confederate citizens, and fortified buildings to mount an organized defense in case of attempts to capture them.

Ashmore organized a small detachment of conscripts to meet the threat, but they were too afraid to perform the duty. Confederate military officials could not spare any troops at that time, so in August 1863, Governor Milledge Bonham ordered one company of mounted state militia troops to the region. With national authorities providing such minimal force, the state looked to county agencies to perform the Confederate government's function. At the end of September, the South Carolina Assembly passed a law that required sheriffs and deputy sheriffs to arrest deserters and to summon a posse comitatus for that purpose. Those who refused to perform such duty were fined $1,000 for each offense.[8]

In a region where its loyal citizens were under siege, neither the national nor the state government could summon the means to provide effective internal security. This void in effective control widened in February 1864, when Ashmore had to recruit local residents to help repel a rumored invasion from East Tennessee. With reports in hand that 600 Federal cavalry with artillery were moving toward Walhalla, Ashmore immediately sent detachments of ten to twenty men from the mounted state troops to round up inhabitants of Walhalla, Greenville, Anderson, Pendleton, and Pickens. Although this effort produced "numerous" volunteers in Greenville, one captain reported from Pendleton that he expected little result from the signal he sent calling on all men to meet in the village. There were few around and even fewer weapons and ammunition. Although the purported Federal raid never materialized, the incident starkly highlighted the region's inadequate defenses.[9] Consequently, deserters and marauders amplified their activities and established contact with Union forces in Knoxville.

When Union officers appeared in company with deserter gangs in the mountains around Greenville, military authorities finally acknowledged they had lost control of the district. At the end of March 1864, a detachment of twenty men scoping out caves and ravines thirty miles from Greenville surprised a party of deserters in the company of a Federal officer "in full uniform." By this point Ashmore also distrusted the women who surrounded him, claiming to his superiors that they were "all disloyal." He begged for troops to suppress the "brigands," but his superiors had none to send. All troops in the vicinity were tied up against numerous and ongoing Union operations on the coasts of the Carolinas and Florida, or against the chaos and anarchy that reigned in the mountains of western North Carolina. In April, the newly appointed Confederate commander for the department, Major General Samuel S. Jones, determined to assert some measure of authority over the "ruffians" who defied the government. He sent a lieutenant with instructions to gather available cavalry from the enrolling officers of Anderson District. This yielded a force of thirteen that captured fewer than thirty deserters. Jones tried again in June with thirty hand-picked soldiers and a pack of well-trained bloodhounds, but his meager effort was equally ineffective.[10]

If the Confederate States of America did not control the South Carolina upcountry, neither did the state. In a confusing netherworld between Confederate and state authority stood the reserves, a body raised in each state under the authority of the Confederate government, composed of seventeen-year-olds who would be conscripted into Confederate regiments upon turning eighteen, and men between the ages of forty-five and fifty. The Confederate Congress created the reserves through the February 17, 1864, Conscription Act and intended them to provide local defense and detail duty within their states in order to free eighteen- to forty-five-year-old males for service on the frontline battlefields where Union armies threatened. The commander of the reserves in South Carolina was Brigadier General James Chesnut Jr., who organized the state's youths and older men during June and July 1864.

Chesnut believed his force was an auxiliary to be called into the field only in emergencies and assumed its primary purpose was to defend the state under his own bailiwick. During August and September he began distributing companies as camp, post, provost, and railroad guards. The Confederate departmental commanders believed the reserves were at their disposal. The complicated and overlapping Confederate command structure distorted any clear lines of authority; Chesnut often acted on his own, but also received a bewildering array of orders regarding his troops from the governor, the Confederate departmental commander, and the War Department in Richmond, all of whom interfered and bickered with each other over using the reserves. Chesnut gave priority in August to establishing order in the upcountry and posted a battalion, divided into four infantry and two mounted companies, at points on road junctions and mountain gaps around Greenville, Anderson, and Spartanburg.[11]

Then the Yankee prisoner crisis shattered any illusion that the reserve forces were the answer to the state's security problems. Without warning or previous arrangement, Chesnut received a telegram from Adjutant General Cooper on September 6, ordering him to provide guards for an unspecified number of prisoners on their way to South Carolina from Andersonville. Chesnut offered 800 men for the duty, but insisted that reserve forces stationed in the mountains remain there. "The presence of an organized force is required to give a sense of security to the inhabitants and to protect them from the active depredations of marauders, deserters, and tories," he wrote. His men had not yet established order; they had just begun to "worry" these internal threats.[12]

For the next three weeks, Chesnut negotiated a quagmire of contradictory orders from Cooper in Richmond and Jones in Charleston, last-minute information about the location and timing of the prisoners' arrival in the state, and an escalating personnel crisis. A "large proportion" of the reserve force did not turn out when the general issued the call, and the inadequate and poorly trained numbers who did respond could not prevent mass escapes from the trains or from the initial installment of the prisoners at Florence. Chesnut had to use some of his reserve forces to round up delinquents from the service and had to pull some of his troops from the mountains, but by October 5, he had 1,500 reserves guarding the 12,362 prisoners at Florence. On October 11, he removed another company out of the upcountry when Jones unexpectedly dumped the 1,400 Federal officers on Columbia. Chesnut considered the presence of the remaining 500 reserves in the mountain regions "indispensable" to the safety of its inhabitants, but a month later he withdrew all reserve forces as both Confederate and state authorities scrambled to assemble a force to confront Sherman's movements in northeast Georgia.[13]

Ironically, the use of reserves to guard prisoners at Florence and Columbia removed the only organized official Confederate forces from the very region that escaped prisoners would target as their escape route. Fugitives frequently passed through Anderson, Spartanburg, Pickens, and Greenville. Because the Confederate government had not suppressed the deserter bands that effectively held sway in the region, deserters and their wives continually aided the hundreds of Federal fugitives who traveled through the South Carolina upcountry. Black South Carolinians who guided the Yankees had contacts among the brigands and handed fugitives off to them.

Cooperation between black guides and white deserters was especially effective in Spartanburg District, which had a tradition of extralegal fraternization between whites and blacks in taverns and secret gambling venues. Despite laws against it and a penalty of forty lashes if caught, slaves in Spartanburg Village distilled and sold alcohol to neighbors of both races. Slave patrols lapsed in the late 1850s, but after the onset of secession and war, white district residents feared slave rebellion and tried to clamp down on such activities. Patrols stopped and questioned white and black travelers in the district. The Court of Magistrates and Freeholders inflicted increasingly severe punishments on slaves who violated laws against interracial gambling and drinking. But local authorities never established control, and by 1864 the deserters who infested the district joined with slaves in a rampage of stealing and lawlessness. They also cooperated when fugitive Federals arrived in the district.[14]

Escaped Yankees wanted to avoid white faces in South Carolina, and their experience with deserters justified their caution, even though they received help. A typical encounter involved three captains from the 101st Pennsylvania who escaped from the train ferrying officers from Charleston to Columbia on October 5. Two weeks later, on October 19, Captain Isaiah Conley and his companions reached the outskirts of Spartanburg, where they enlisted the aid of a free black named Henry Martin. Martin sharecropped for a Confederate sympathizer and could not leave home without arousing suspicion, but that night he visited the wife of a deserter named Ray and enlisted her aid. Martin moved the Federals to the woods near his brother-in-law's farm while they waited for Ray to come in from his hideout.

Making contact with deserters, for those fugitive Federals who did so, was one of the most dangerous moments of their journey. Deserters were suspicious of anyone they did not know, and the fugitives were equally reluctant to reveal their identity. Mutual distrust did not make for an easy or safe exchange of information, even when the parties expected each other, as Conley discovered when he walked from the fugitive's hideout to a nearby stream. A man in Confederate uniform sitting on a log brought his rifle to the ready, pointed it at Conley, and called out, "Halt! Who are you?"

"Who are you?" Conley replied, anxious not to betray any information.

"I want to know who you are first," the man in Rebel gray replied.

"What's your name?" Conley insisted.

"My name's Ray."

"I guess you are the man I'm looking for," Conley replied.

"Are you one of the Yankees?"

"Yes," Conley stated, and began to walk forward. Ray immediately returned his gun to the ready and told Conley, "Just keep a little distance away." Conley invited Ray to meet the other fugitives, and as the two men walked, Ray enforced distance between them with his weapon. When they arrived at the hideout, Ray trained his gun on the other two Federals and told them not to come any closer. During the ensuing conversation, Ray's wife arrived, and Ray then agreed to pilot the fugitives the next fifty miles of their journey in exchange for Conley's silver-cased watch. Before the party left the hiding place, Ray's wife begged Conley to convince her husband to accompany the Yankees all the way to Union lines. By the time the party crossed the North Carolina border, Ray was convinced. He traveled all the way to Knoxville with the Federals.[15]

Deserters like Ray have been something of an enigma. Because few left written accounts, it is difficult to uncover what desertion meant to the men who committed the act. Southerners possessed multiple loyalties—to family, to God, to state, to Confederacy—that shifted in priority depending on circumstances. Thus desertion did not necessarily indicate disloyalty to the Confederacy, because a soldier's loyalty to his needy family at home might momentarily supersede his continuing loyalty to the nation. Whatever motive prompted the initial act, encounters with fugitive Yankees revealed that deserters in South Carolina were willing to aid the enemy. They generally responded, when given the opportunity, with active assistance to the hundreds of U.S. soldiers they met. Deserters hid Yankees in their mountain caves or swampy lairs, their wives fed, provisioned, and guided the escapees, and their children were sent on errands to warn fugitives when danger approached. Because fugitives openly expressed to deserter families their desire to escape in order to return to their regiments and fight, aiding the Federals toward that goal was a clear act of disloyalty. Deserters and their wives in South Carolina did not just temporarily withdraw from state authority for the sake of their families; during the last three months of 1864, they worked to undermine it.[16]

Slaves and deserters turned the South Carolina upcountry into a pipeline for Yankees moving between Columbia and Knoxville. Inhabitants of the region who supported the Confederacy found that the national government provided no security against the increasing amounts of disorder in their neighborhoods during the waning months of 1864. Deserters and Yankees robbed their crops, and Yankees continually moved across and hid on their property. The state offered no effective protection, either, because the South Carolina Militia no longer functioned in the fall of 1864. Governor Bonham was unable to mobilize the state's forces in October to guard prisoners, or in November to defend the state against Sherman's threatened invasion.

A high rate of volunteering for Confederate armies combined with conscription decimated South Carolina's state forces. Ironically, the state's exceptional contribution to the Confederate cause contributed directly to the failure of its internal security and its collapse under external threats during the last three months of 1864. In 1860, there were 60,000 men between the ages of eighteen and forty-five in the state, and by January 1864, conscription reports showed that South Carolina achieved nearly full enlistment. The figures for individual districts told the tale: 925 of the 1,000 military-aged white men from Horry District were Confederate soldiers; 88 percent of upcountry Lancaster's white males were in uniform. Although South Carolina passed state laws to exempt men from military duty to oversee slave labor, the General Assembly did not, as did the legislatures of Georgia and North Carolina, exempt state militia officers and local magistrates from Confederate service.[17] The Confederate government sent the majority of South Carolina's soldiers to Virginia or Tennessee and left a limited number to serve the defense of Charleston.

With South Carolina's white males between the ages of eighteen and forty-five "almost to a man in the field," according to the state's governor, the Confederate government further dipped into the state's male population in February 1864 when it drafted all seventeen- and forty-five- to fifty-year-olds for the Confederate Reserves. This conscription did not impact the state until June, when Brigadier General Chesnut began the process of organizing the forces and assigning them to duty. Bonham panicked, with good reason. Exclusive of the members of the South Carolina General Assembly, only 3,168 men between the ages of seventeen and fifty were exempt from the Confederate Conscription Act of February 17, 1864. He requested that the Confederate government send some of the South Carolina troops back to the state to provide internal security in the mountain districts. The governor reminded the secretary of war that no state provided a larger portion of its arms-bearing population to the Confederate service. The manpower situation in the state was so dire that there were not enough men in some districts to provide even subsistence for its population and food had to be imported to those regions. Bonham predicted that mobilizing the reserves would possibly cause starvation in portions of the state. His request was denied; Robert E. Lee needed South Carolina soldiers for his desperate fight against Grant in Virginia.[18]

This left youths of sixteen and men over the age of fifty as the pool for the state militia force, the only body of troops under the control of the governor and the state's adjutant general. South Carolina's militia laws distinguished between men who were liable to serve outside of the boundaries of their own district and those who only served within the confines of their residence. All men, even those who were ordinarily exempt from duty because of special occupations, were required to turn out for local defense in times of alarm, insurrection, or invasion, and likewise had to serve as part of a posse comitatus if summoned.[19] Bonham assumed that he had the authority to mobilize on behalf of the state every able-bodied male over the age of sixteen, whether enrolled in the militia or not, and in August 1863, he issued such a call for the men of the state to "organize themselves."[20] In another effort to bolster state defense, the South Carolina Assembly passed an act requesting that citizens form volunteer companies of mounted infantry as a permanent force for local defense and to help arrest deserters. On paper, the state had a militia structure that encompassed all undrafted men between the ages of sixteen and sixty for the performance of local defense. In reality, according to Chesnut, the militia was "too inconsiderable to be counted."[21]

Incompetence and disorganization on the part of the state government further frustrated any effort to provide for internal defense. As late as August 1864, the state adjutant general's office was deluged with questions regarding the composition of the militia. Militia officers had no idea who was supposed to serve in their regiments. In response, Adjutant General Albert C. Garlington issued a circular with information that contradicted published state laws.[22] After the fall of Atlanta, Bonham issued a flurry of orders in September and October to ready the militia for active service. When the governor called up the militia to defend the state on November 18, the hollowness of the state's security was starkly exposed. Officers had not executed the September and October orders correctly, and the colonel of the Thirty-Third South Carolina Militia (SCM) had accidentally turned over his forces to the Confederate commandant at Florence rather than having the unit rendezvous at Florence as ordered. The Confederate army refused to give the men back. An untold number of men who were liable to militia duty had not enrolled or reported when called, but the numbers were unclear because Garlington had no accurate rolls for the state troops. Two of the state's regiments had organized no companies. After three months of effort, by December 2, with Sherman's army threatening the state's border, the adjutant general had pulled together only 1,300 men who were eligible to serve beyond their own district, and some of the companies had no arms. He admitted to Bonham that the militia was incapable even of local defense.[23]

The state had left a "handful" of its militia forces in their home districts to continue the battle against the deserters and "lawless" men who controlled increasing portions of the state, Garlington told the governor, but the numbers were inadequate to maintain order. In the problematic upcountry districts, in December 1864, only one company, the volunteer Pendleton Mounted Infantry, patrolled the Anderson district, and a single company attached to the Thirty-Sixth SCM served in Spartanburg. Elsewhere, merely twenty-five men from the Eighth SCM in Marion District, twenty-two miles east of Florence, sought to restore order over the bands who were "taking the lives of citizens, terrifying the defenseless people, and committing depredations upon property." And the juvenile appearance of the state militia units did not inspire South Carolina's loyal citizens with confidence. The spectacle of "little boys" who looked no older than twelve being armed for war with guns too big for their size was demoralizing and painted a vivid picture of a government on its last legs.[24]

Frightened citizens petitioned state authorities to return some military-age men to their home districts. Their language reveals their total lack of security and their sense that the Confederate government had abandoned them. Citizens from Horry District, a coastal county 100 miles north of Charleston, were "at the mercy" of deserters and claimed that enrolling officers were "powerless" because deserters outnumbered the Confederate presence in the region. A resident accused Confederate authorities of being "unconcerned for the fate of the people of this *out of the way* section."[25]

Fugitives exploited the emptiness of the South Carolina countryside. Confederate, reserve, and state troops guarded the environs of Columbia, Florence, Charleston, Georgetown, Branchville, and the railroad lines but had little to no presence elsewhere. Yankees who traveled between Columbia and the coast found that if they avoided these areas, they encountered no official resistance to their escape. There were "no guards on the rivers except at the railroad bridges" and these were "not strong in any resistance." Fugitives "met no pickets" along the roads. One of the guards at Camp Sorghum actively assisted Federals to escape and advised them to steal a boat. There were only two pickets along the entire 250-mile length of the Edisto River. One Yankee who arrived safely in Hilton Head commented, "The country there is left entirely unprotected."[26]

Fugitives who headed toward Knoxville likewise encountered minimal trouble from organized forces. Drake and his party had only one scare while they traveled in South Carolina. In the rural environs of Columbia on October 11, they spotted a small house and observed it for half an hour to ascertain that there were no men about. When they were confident that the women inside were without male protection, Todd and

Lewis knocked on the door and asked for food while Drake and Grant looked out. As the woman and her two daughters prepared some applesauce, bacon, and sweet potatoes, two men in Confederate uniform, who somehow evaded Drake and Grant's notice, walked right into the house. Todd invented a plausible lie, unrecorded to posterity, and the Yankees got out of the house with a quart of sweet potatoes and a piece of corn bread. Those two Rebels would be the last that the party encountered in South Carolina. For the next nine nights, they traveled a route that took them through Winnsboro, Rock Hill, and Yorkville before they crossed into North Carolina on October 20. Along the way they spotted a few older white men and were chased by dogs, but never chanced upon any companies of state militia.[27]

The Maine trio of Yankees, traveling on a more westerly route than the Drake party, experienced more traffic on the roads but avoided state security forces. Mattocks, Hunt, and Litchfield reached Greenville, South Carolina, on the night of November 13. They rested in some woods near a house and were startled when a "perfect avalanche of young damsels" poured out of the house and walked down a path only thirty feet away from their hiding place. They snuck through the main streets of Greenville at 4:00 in the morning and ran into a "wagon park," the campfire of teamsters who halted their wagons alongside the road for the night. They flanked it, but Mattocks fainted twice along the way. He had a lame leg, and the exhaustion of the escape and the cross-country march finally got to him. The Yankees hid among some oaks on the outskirts of town to give him time to recuperate, but daylight revealed they were in an open growth with no place to conceal themselves.

A young black woman walked by on a nearby path, and the tall, gaunt Litchfield, in his ragged clothes with a gray blanket wrapped around his shoulders, approached her to ask if she would lead them to a better hiding place. The terrified woman ran away and they feared the game was up. "Frightened almost to death all day," Mattocks recorded. Wagons and men on foot passed up and down a road not far away from them and they heard the barking of dogs. They moved on the next day and flanked another wagon park near Traveler's Rest. The Yankees obtained food, tobacco, and advice from some slaves on the Elias Montgomery plantation, who informed them that there were guards posted on the roads ahead who hunted for deserters. They avoided these Rebels, most likely one of the handful of small state militia companies still posted in the mountains, and flanked three more wagon parks before they reached the North Carolina border on November 17.[28]

Traveling a day behind Mattocks after agreeing to separate at Newberry, John Hadley and his comrades also encountered a whiff of trouble around Greenville. The Yankees marched a few miles north of the town in a pleasant stupor after participating in a meal with some slaves that Hadley likened to a party. The leader of their military organization for that twenty-four hours was asleep on his feet and allowed two horsemen to ride within 200 yards before he gave the "hiss" that signaled danger. All four fugitives broke for the open forest at the side of the road, which lacked bushes or undergrowth, and fell flat onto their faces. The two horsemen reined in their animals, and the Yankees heard them asking each other if they had seen anyone run into the woods. They decided the man they had glimpsed was probably a slave and rode on. "We always thought they were afraid," Hadley commented, "or they would have ridden a little way into the woods." As other fugitives would discover, many would-be pursuers were intimidated by slaves and deserters and were reluctant to chase unknown parties through the countryside.[29]

Despite the absence or ineffectiveness of official forces, getting out of South Carolina was anything but an uneventful stroll for the Yankees. Two days before he safely crossed the border, slaves told Mattocks that Rebel citizens had captured three escaped prisoners near the base of the Blue Ridge Mountains and warned him to be vigilant. Mattocks did well to heed that warning; unlike him and his friends, most fugitive Federals in the fall of 1864 never made it out of South Carolina. Only 144 of the 373 officers who escaped from Camp Sorghum and only 168 of the Yankees who escaped from other locations in South Carolina between September and December safely reported to Union lines.[30]

These figures tell their own story. Despite the fact that Confederate and state officials provided minimal to no internal security in areas threatened with deserters and an influx of escaped prisoners during the last three months of 1864, fugitive Yankees faced long odds. Every noncombatant left at home, from the little boys and "decrepid old men" to the "helpless" ladies, took over local defense and was diligent in meeting the threat of the escaped prisoners. Families provided their own security and made personal decisions about whether to comply with the demands of state and Confederate authorities that no longer possessed the resources to compel duty. Individuals acting on their own capacity, and usually within the boundaries of their own property, recaptured the bulk of the fugitives in South Carolina.[31]

Two neighbors followed footprints in the snow from slave cabins to the woods and found Colonel M. A. Cochran's party of five escaped prisoners. They sent for more neighbors, nine of whom arrived on horseback two hours later. These "old men and boys" were "timid" until they discovered their quarry were unarmed Yankees rather than a band of deserters.[32] In the vicinity of Greenville, Lieutenant Francis Murphy of the Ninety-Seventh New York stumbled upon a white man chopping wood. The snap of rotten wood when Murphy stepped on a fallen limb alerted the man's hounds, who gave chase and cornered him. The man questioned Murphy about his identity and travel plans, pretended to buy his story that he was a traveling citizen of Columbia, and invited him to supper. Murphy declined, knowing that the man suspected him but could not capture him without help. Murphy returned to the woods, found his hidden companion, and took off running. The baying of dogs in the distance signaled that the man had gathered his neighbors for the hunt. "Every man in the Confederacy," Murphy commented, "is a soldier authorized to arrest any suspicious persons."[33] Murphy misunderstood the situation. While Confederate and state authorities wished that every man was a soldier who acted on their behalf, in reality, Murphy's pursuer was a citizen, who likely wished that some Confederate soldiers were around to protect him.

Because state-sponsored security forces were minuscule or absent, citizens, rather than Confederate or state power, made decisions on the ground in South Carolina about what the individual's obligation was to the state. On the plantation of Alexander Taylor, near Black Creek, about thirty miles southeast of Columbia, dogs alerted Mrs. Taylor that Willard Worcester Glazier and his comrade were hiding on her property. Glazier admitted who they were and asked for food. She told Glazier that her heart belonged to the southern people and that it was wrong to aid a Yankee. He then appealed to her sympathies with a catalog of their misfortunes as prisoners and asked her to let them go. She supplied them with corn bread, bacon, and sweet potatoes, and promised not to betray their presence in the neighborhood.

A widow and her three daughters under the age of sixteen found Daniel Langworthy and his party in the woods on her plantation. The men painted verbal pictures of their wives and sisters waiting for them at home, just as the widow and her daughters now waited for their sons and brothers to return. They conceded to the widow that she was required to report them, "but if you have a true mother's heart, please wait until tomorrow." The daughters began to cry, but the widow stood silent. Finally, she said, "Mister, we will not tell on you uns today."[34]

Confederate authorities proscribed the actions taken by these loyal Confederate women. Confederate detectives infiltrated secret societies in southwest Virginia and North Carolina in September 1864, and determined that among other subversive activities, its members sought to liberate prisoners of war and aid their travels across the Confederacy. The Confederate Congress authorized President Davis to suspend the writ of habeas corpus under certain specific conditions that included giving "aid and comfort" to the enemy, having communication with the enemy "without necessity and without permission of the Confederate states," and helping to "liberate prisoners of war." Davis requested and received permission on November 9 to make arrests in such cases.[35] But if the Confederacy was powerless to arrest escaped prisoners and deserters in South Carolina, how could it reach those who aided them? The Confederate security presence in South Carolina had dissipated in portions of the countryside after September, and distant laws did not guide the women who confronted the enemy. Instead, they assessed the immediate threat and balanced their humanity against their loyalty.

Individuals who stumbled upon Yankees were disconcerted and frightened and had to make snap decisions about the level of danger they faced and how to respond. But most fugitives were also afraid, unarmed, and weak from exhaustion. Escaped prisoners preferred to run away rather than engage with white men they encountered and to plead for help from women if they could not avoid them. Fugitives did not know until hindsight enlightened them that their main danger came from unorganized citizens, and they assumed that authorities were on their trail and that every campfire they saw was a Rebel picket. They generally surrendered when cornered and did not offer resistance to any armed person who arrested them. Fugitives stole from inhabitants and disturbed their property but rarely threatened their lives.

A few Yankees were ready to kill men who discovered them. Drake and his comrades were among that number. Six days after their escape from the train, they were hiding in some woods when a white man carrying ears of corn approached along a nearby path. He kept his eyes fixed on the ground and seemed to be in a reverie. The Yankees grabbed clubs they had fashioned out of fallen branches to fight off dogs. "We made up our minds that if he discovered us, that moment would be his last on earth," Drake later admitted. "The cold sweat covered my face and body, and I felt sorry that the poor man had entered the woods. But self-preservation is the first law of nature." Like other Federals on the loose, the bold and brash Drake was reluctant to harm a noncombatant. Fortunately, the man never observed them, or as Drake pondered, "if he did, he had wonderful presence of mind, for he never winked as he passed around the butt of the tree, in front of which we were crouched." As the man walked out of sight, the Yankees breathed a sigh of relief. "He had saved his own life," Drake thankfully recalled.[36]

Whether or not fugitive Federals threatened life and limb, they were an enemy in league with slaves and deserters to spread theft and disorder across the countryside. Citizens diligently and successfully captured Yankees who encroached on their property, but each incident starkly reminded South Carolinians that their neighborhoods were not secure. By early December 1864, a significant portion of South Carolina's male population refused to serve the state and Confederate governments any longer. Both entities had proved too weak to protect their loyal citizens, who preferred to secure order at home rather than fight Union armies on behalf of a collapsing nation.

South Carolina and Confederate authorities discovered this stark reality when they made a last-ditch effort to assemble literally every last man they could find during the month of December, when Federal threats materialized and multiplied at various locations along the railroad that ran between Charleston and Savannah and along the South Carolina and Georgia border between Augusta and Savannah. Unfortunately for Willard Glazier, his chosen route took him through this chaotic movement.

Trying to reach Augusta in the belief that a portion of Sherman's army would occupy the city, Glazier and Lemon left their hiding place in the slave huts near Black Creek, South Carolina, where Uncle Zeb held the prayer meeting for them, on November 29. They crossed the North Edisto River and encountered another slave, who piloted them to a road leading to Aiken, a community about twenty miles from Augusta, where local citizens had just formed a company for home defense. While crossing one of the bridges over the South Edisto River, they met another party of fugitives from Columbia, who agreed to take a different route. During the day on November 30, Glazier and Lemon hid in the swampy bayous on either side of the Aiken road to avoid the wagon park of agents for the Confederate quartermaster, who were impressing supplies in the area.[37]

The Yankees had no idea that they were headed directly for the rendezvous point of the South Carolina Militia. Two days before, Governor Bonham ordered all men eligible for service beyond their district to rendezvous at Hamburg, where the South Carolina Railroad from Charleston terminated directly across the Savannah River from Augusta. The militia would supplement nearly 10,000 Confederate troops collecting in Augusta under the assumption that Sherman wanted to destroy the city and its Confederate gunpowder and textile factories.

But the situation changed quickly. Federal commanders at Hilton Head, without precise knowledge of Sherman's movements and locations but hoping to aid his advance, wanted to disperse Confederate forces in Georgia stationed on the north side of the Savannah River. On November 28, Brigadier General John P. Hatch launched a raid against the Charleston & Savannah Railroad in South Carolina that supplied the Rebels guarding Savannah's environs, numbering fewer than 1,000 men of all arms on that date. Hatch's troops steamed up the Broad River toward Pocotaligo, a depot on the railway.

Orders poured forth from every direction within the Confederacy's broken command structure, which was nebulous and constantly shifting. There was no plan and no coordination, only reaction to Federal initiative. Two Confederate generals competed for the 12,466 Confederate troops present in the Department of South Carolina, Georgia, and Florida. Lieutenant General Hardee commanded the department and his subordinate Major General Jones, assigned to the District of South Carolina. But also present on the scene was General Braxton Bragg, who outranked Hardee and served as President Davis's special "military advisor." He was in Augusta to arrange the defense of the city and also issued orders to Jones. Hardee and Bragg dispensed competing and contradictory orders to the commander of the South Carolina Reserves, Brigadier General James Chesnut Jr., and to officers in the state militia.

Hardee was in Savannah when he heard about the Federal raid and sent 1,200 men from the Georgia militia to cross into South Carolina to defend the railroad. Bragg ordered Chesnut and 1,000 South Carolina Reserves to report to Hardee, who then had to forward them to the scene of action, and sent 2,000 North Carolina troops to Jones in Charleston, who was trying to move all his troops out of the city to defend the railroad. Governor Bonham proclaimed that any state militia troops not already at Hamburg should report to Charleston instead. When the Federal troops disembarked and marched inland, Confederate units already guarding the railroad and the Georgia militia units had occupied entrenched positions near Grahamville with five pieces of artillery. The Federals launched several futile assaults down a narrow road bordered by swampy ground covered with trees and brush. The 1,400 Rebels defeated the 5,000 Federals at the Battle of Honey Hill on November 30 while the troops from Augusta and Charleston were still en route to Grahamville.[38]

Glazier and Lemon, like other Yankee fugitives trying to link up with Sherman's army, moved among these constantly shifting troop movements. The morning after the battle that took place nearly 100 miles to the east, they moved out of their hiding place and spent a thirst-crazed day seeking a drink. The swamp water was nauseating, and in the afternoon they traveled over a barren, sandy high ground covered with stunted oaks. In the late afternoon of December 1, a ravine, over 100 feet deep, opened before them, with a clear refreshing stream running through with beautiful stands of pine trees on its banks. They rested in the wild and romantic spot until the next day, then continued on the road toward Aiken. During the predawn hours of December 3, they flanked the village and ran into Captain James Bryant, Fifth New York Cavalry, another fugitive from Camp Sorghum, and his African American guide.[39]

The slave convinced Glazier and Lemon as he had Bryant the day before that Sherman was not going to strike Augusta. The guide was correct, and he knew it as soon as Confederate commanders did. Couriers reported to Bragg in Augusta on December 1 that portions of Sherman's army were headed that way, but the next day Bragg realized that Sherman had veered for the Georgia coast, and he left Augusta that evening with 10,000 troops for Savannah. The 1,300 members of the South Carolina Militia, all the state was able to pull together, followed the next day and were stationed at Grahamville near the Charleston & Savannah Railroad. Almost half of them were unarmed, a circumstance that caused a flurry of telegrams between state and Confederate authorities trying to figure out what happened to more than 2,500 Enfield rifles intended for the militia that had disappeared.[40]

Meanwhile, Glazier and Lemon discussed with Bryant and his slave guide how to navigate the unfolding military movements in the region. The guide told the Yankees that it would not be possible for them to cross the Savannah River south of Augusta. The Rebels had destroyed all the boats. After a short conference, Glazier and Lemon decided to move on to Augusta and cross the river there, then move fifty miles southeast toward Millen, Georgia, in hopes of catching Sherman's rear guard. They parted from Bryant and immediately lost their sense of direction. They found another slave, who held a prayer meeting over them and gave them directions to the tracks of the South Carolina Railroad that ran between Augusta and Charleston. They could then follow the tracks west to Augusta. But the confused Yankees, moving through the dark with stars overhead that seemed unfamiliar, unknowingly headed east when they struck the track.

Not only were the unwitting fugitives going the wrong way, they were walking along a busy but slow-moving freeway still in the process of transporting Confederate troops out of Augusta to Charleston, and thence to Savannah with stops at Pocotaligo and Coosawhatchie to repel Federal raiders from Hilton Head trying to break the Charleston & Savannah Railroad. As December 4 dawned, a passenger train filled with Rebel soldiers passed the plodding Yankees. The soldiers shouted at them, and the fugitives ran into the scrub oak woods lining the track. Glazier and Lemon heard heavy cannonading off to the southeast and began to wonder why they had not reached Augusta. Lemon found some slaves chopping wood who informed them of their mistake but told them where they could cross the Savannah River south of their present location. One of the slaves guided them a few miles and left them alone to "undertake the voluminous directions of our colored friends," the ever-lost Glazier noted. Sherman was somewhere out there, and the New Yorker was determined to find him.[41]

At this point Glazier and Lemon, the slaves in South Carolina, and Confederate authorities finally realized that Sherman's target was Savannah. On December 5, Governor Bonham issued a proclamation informing South Carolinians that Sherman was rapidly moving on the city and that possibly Sherman intended to cross the Savannah River and make Port Royal his base of operations. He urged citizens along Sherman's potential path to tear up or obstruct all roads that led away from ferries on the river and to remove all livestock and provisions. He then called upon all men who were capable of bearing arms to report to the commanding officer of the nearest state militia troops.[42]

Three days later, General P. G. T. Beauregard arrived in Charleston to organize Confederate defenses. He was commander of the Military Division of the West, which encompassed six states, including portions of Georgia, but not South Carolina. He had no formal authority over one of the states he was sent to protect and no operational authority over any army in the field unless he joined them in person. He was one of two full generals now issuing orders to subordinates in Georgia and South Carolina. No single commander was in charge of stopping Sherman. Organizational disaster and complete bureaucratic incompetence contributed their share to the ongoing collapses within South Carolina.[43]

Federal threats evolved rapidly around Savannah during the next two weeks, highlighting for anxious South Carolinians their vulnerable position. On December 11, Hardee reported that Federal troops developed in strong force along his entire front around Savannah. The advance units of Sherman's juggernaut had arrived. Hardee and Beauregard agreed on one thing at least: save the army rather than the city. When Federal troops from Hilton Head again landed on the South Carolina coast and threatened to break Hardee's communications, Hardee evacuated Savannah. During the night of December 20, his 9,000 men crossed the Savannah River on pontoon bridges and rendezvoused the next day at Hardeeville, South Carolina. Thirty miles to the north, at the Pocotaligo station on the Charleston & Savannah Railroad, Jones had 5,500 men of all arms. Hardee immediately sent 2,000 of the Georgia militia troops back to Augusta and a Confederate division to Charleston. He dispersed the rest of his and Jones's forces along a sixty-mile defensive line that stretched the length of the Salkehatchie River from its origin near the village of Barnwell, South Carolina, to its drainage point into the Atlantic Ocean. Hardee ordered Major General Joseph Wheeler's Confederate cavalry troopers to guard the country between the border of the state and the river, and to protect the right flank of the defensive line located at Barnwell Court House.[44]

The next few days revealed that citizens had not augmented the state's forces as Bonham requested at the beginning of the month. On December 25, newly elected Governor Andrew G. Magrath wrote Jefferson Davis that South Carolinians were afflicted with "a chilling apprehension of the futility" of opposing the enemy. A petition that thirty-five prominent state citizens sent to Secretary of War Seddon underscored the sense of helplessness. They requested one corps from Lee's army in Virginia to save their state. Sherman would lay waste to South Carolina without it. "There is no force here to prevent it," they wrote in dismissal of Hardee's troops. "Half-trained citizens" needed a more impressive army to rally around or their efforts "will amount to nothing."[45]

The new governor promised to reorganize the militia once again, but was unable to estimate its effective force, a shocking statement considering that the state had spent the last two months organizing and calling its forces into the field. Magrath and Chesnut issued order after order in late December and early January for militia and reserve officers to round up delinquents and forward them for service. But with the minuscule forces at their command, authorities could no longer compel service, and the results of their efforts starkly revealed that most citizens had decided not to participate in state-sponsored efforts for defense but instead operated under their own bailiwick. With Sherman's powerful invasion of the state well underway, South Carolina produced for the field by February less than half of the state's paper-strength militia force: only 2,959 of the potential 6,202.[46]

Residents of South Carolina and state authorities openly acknowledged the effective collapse of state-sponsored security and called upon *every* loyal Confederate to transform into a combatant to defend himself, his family, and his property against whatever threat manifested on his doorstep, whether it be deserters, brigands, slaves, fugitive Federals, or Sherman's forces. L. B. Beckwith wrote in the *Daily South Carolinian*, "Arm yourselves, fellow citizens, and shoot down every one of these thieves on any provocation—it is our only mode of redress." Unable to organize an effective militia, Governor Magrath proclaimed that every man should rise up and fight on behalf of the state. "In every quarter of the State, in every district, Village, and Town, let the men stand with their arms in their hands." Magrath asked his male citizens to resist and kill when he met the foe, and to "repress disorder and put down all violence" until Sherman arrived. The state asked women, too, to defend themselves; they should give Yankees "resistance unto death."[47]

The collapse of South Carolina and of any tangible Confederate authority within portions of its borders was effected *before* Sherman's army entered the state. Confederate troops operated within the state, but the regime they were there to defend was already lost. On December 30, when Sherman ordered a division of his Twentieth Corps to cross the Savannah River and begin the invasion, there were 7,030 men from Confederate and state forces (both South Carolina and Georgia) stationed south of the Salkehatchie River at three points along the Charleston & Savannah Railroad south.[48] This modest and dispersed force was one of the few indicators that Confederate authority still functioned in South Carolina. In other portions of the state, the Confederacy could not mobilize manpower or command the movement of people and resources on its behalf.

This explains something that historians have narrated without grasping the significance of what they described: the utter lack of resistance to Sherman's invasion in a state where the white population remained rhetorically defiant and ideologically committed to Confederate independence. The reason was not simply that Confederate and state forces in the region lacked the numbers to engage Sherman's veterans, or that Confederate commanders did not properly deploy the troops they had available, although these were certainly factors.[49] Confederate conscription had sapped the state's strength and disorganized its security; deserters, slaves, and fugitive Federals had exposed and exploited the state's weakness; and the citizens who took over the functions of authority had disengaged from the state's defense to secure order in their neighborhoods. By January 1865, the state functioned mainly in a handful of enclaves, authorities in Columbia issued laws and orders that could not be enforced, and more than half of both Confederate and state forces were absent from their commands.

The open fields for prisoners in Florence and Columbia, guarded by undisciplined and unmotivated youths and old men, who themselves had to be guarded, symbolized the breakdown of South Carolina's security infrastructure in the months before Sherman's invasion of the state and his capture of Columbia. Confederate and state officials failed to handle either the movement of large bodies of prisoners of war or the defense of the state. When the trains and open fields spewed out the Yankee runaways, South Carolina's residents were left to fend for themselves.

4

Guardian Angels

The Collapse of the Home Front

By October 29, J. Madison Drake and his three intrepid comrades were
in the mountains of Caldwell County, North Carolina. As they walked
along a mountain ravine, they came across two women cutting sorghum
grass. A fifteen-year-old boy used a sled to deliver it to a small mill a short
distance away. Pretending to be Confederate deserters on the way to their
homes in Kentucky, the fugitives offered the women a ring in exchange
for rations. The women agreed, and the boy Joseph rode off to get his
mother.

Joseph returned quickly with a large and powerful woman whose bold
and fearless demeanor was so unlike what he expected from her sex that
she appeared masculine to Drake. She walked right up to the fugitives
and demanded, "What are you doing here?" When Drake launched
into the story about Kentucky, the woman firmly but politely told him
that she did not believe a word. She knew they were Yankees and assured them she hated the Confederacy and all those who supported it.
"I am not afraid of *you*, be you Yankee or rebel," she said. "For I can by
lifting my hand have you killed where you are now standing. A dozen
true rifles are at this very instant leveled upon you." She demanded proof
that Drake and his friends were not Rebel spies. "We had met a great
many women in our time, but none like this one before us. She was
the bravest woman I had ever seen," Drake recorded in his diary. When
Drake produced his commission, his travel diary, and sketches made
in prison, Mary Estes shook his hand and introduced herself. She then
waved a white handkerchief around her head three times. At that signal,
more than twenty men dressed in Confederate uniform and carrying
rifles descended from the mountain and surrounded the Yankees.[1]

Mary Estes was a forty-one-year-old wife and mother with five
children between the ages of six and fifteen. Her husband, a much
younger man, owned no real estate of his own, but possessed $300 worth
of personal property. William Estes led a gang of deserters who defied
Confederate authority, but officials considered his wife to be just as dangerous to their cause. Like other women married to deserters or guerrillas

J. Madison Drake's initial encounter with Mary Estes. Sketch from *Fast and Loose in Dixie* (1880).

that the fugitive Federals encountered in the Appalachian Mountains, she did not carry arms herself, but it was clear that without her, the men hiding in the mountains could not continue the fight. She supplied the men with food and clothes, she carried messages between companies of deserters with information that they needed to conduct raids and ambushes, and she piloted men through remote mountain areas. Her activities were so important that North Carolina Guard for Home Defense units watched her for days at a time, periodically conducted searches of her house, and targeted her children. They tortured Joseph in front of her to no avail. "I taught him the value of his father's safety and Joe would have died sooner than reveal his father's hiding place," she told Drake.[2]

Drake and his party stayed with the Estes family for two days while Bill made preparations to lead the Yankees into Tennessee. During this interlude, neighbors and Mary's female relatives brought copious amounts of food and the fugitives feasted on chicken, pork, biscuits, and potatoes. After dark, Mary and two young girls led the fugitives by the hand to a deep ravine. The three women left briefly, and returned with their own feather beds and heavy quilts, which they spread upon a flat rock and duly tucked in the men. This kind of motherly care reminded the Yankees of their host's femininity, which had been a bit obscured in their minds by her earlier display of physical prowess in leading them across steep, rocky terrain and wide streams of water. They slept soundly for the first time since their escape, confident in the care of the women they now termed their "guardian angels."[3]

Yankees traveling to Knoxville were exhilarated when they crossed the border into North Carolina. It was their "Rubicon," and they believed the most dangerous part of the journey was behind them. Charlie Mattocks, scribbling in his diary as he did every night, was filled with optimism on November 17. After two weeks without speaking to a white man, they had reached the Blue Ridge Mountains where "plenty of Union men will help us along." John Hadley believed he had penetrated an invisible barrier that "marked the division between friends and foes." He turned and spat on the South Carolina side. His party was still 140 miles from Knoxville, but they were "almost home."[4]

They were deluded, as all Yankees found to their sorrow. There were plenty of Union men who did help the Federals, but there were also plenty of Rebels. The most hazardous leg of the Knoxville route was in western North Carolina. It was a terror-filled journey. Before reaching the mountains, Yankees constantly evaded Guard for Home Defense units tasked with arresting disloyal citizens and deserters from the Confederate army. The Unionists they met were secretive and afraid, the true face of any person they encountered obscured beneath a mask. Evasion and lying governed nearly every interaction. The mountains were worse, a guerrilla-infested no-man's land—neither the Union nor the Confederacy had effective control—where entire families and neighborhoods were mobilized to fight. Western North Carolina was not a safe zone; it was a place where the home front collapsed in the winter of 1864–65. Neighborhoods and houses were battlefields; families, women, and children sustained the violence. The process occurred at different times and places in different mountain counties, but escaped prisoners spread into the region as the home front faded away.

Women and children were a vital part of the chaotic combat in western North Carolina. Wives, sisters, daughters, and little boys served as the supply line, as messengers, and as spies for the men engaged in guerrilla warfare and in resistance to the Confederate draft. Drake and his party were the vanguard of the fugitive invasion that moved through the district in November and December 1864. The stream of escaped prisoners provided a new constituency to the conflict. Women and children who fought against the Confederacy now provisioned and guided fugitive

Federals and warned them of danger. The shocked fugitives learned that women had become coleaders of their families and were protecting, instead of being protected by, men.

Before they reached the region, fugitives stereotyped western North Carolina and its 130,000 residents as an isolated bastion of Unionism peopled almost uniformly with white subsistence farmers, when in fact it was a collection of dissimilar communities with varied societies, economies, and political sentiments. Planters with their slaves settled in the fertile river valleys, dominated the political scene across the region, and invested in mercantile and industrial pursuits. A prosperous middle class practiced diversified agriculture and engaged in the professions. Farmers living in higher elevations foraged their hogs in the vast woods and drove them by the hundreds of thousands to markets in South Carolina and Georgia. Tenant farmers and landless laborers scratched out livings where they could. Every year in the late spring, tourists and low-country South Carolina and Georgia elites occupied the towns of Asheville, Hendersonville, and Flat Rock to enjoy the breathtaking scenery and take up residence in opulent hotels and summer estates.

During the secession crisis, western North Carolinians were cautious and debated whether secession or Union best protected slavery and their region's economic ties to markets in the Deep South. Once President Lincoln called for volunteers to put down the rebellion, the majority of citizens supported secession and volunteered for the Confederate army in greater proportion than their eastern Carolina counterparts. However, disaffection and division emerged quickly as the pains of war began to impact the region. The high number of men in service disrupted market trade and the cycle of agricultural production. A drought and a hog cholera epidemic hit in the summer and fall of 1862. That winter, families consumed the surplus food farmers always set aside for such emergencies. There was no margin of safety for the ensuing years of war. Shortages and inflation (the price of corn increased 3,000 percent) hit such families hard. Danger loomed on the western border of the state, in eastern Tennessee, a true stronghold of Unionism whose citizens defied the Confederate government and launched an insurrection. The violence there frightened residents of the Carolina mountains, and men wanted to protect their communities from raids across the border.

Defying the Confederate draft that required their service for the duration of the war, Carolina highlanders deserted the army at a rate of 24 percent, the highest in the Confederacy. By the summer of 1863, there were thousands of deserters hiding out in the mountains, many of them citizens of other Confederate states. Governor Zebulon Vance reported to the War Department in Richmond that he "found it impossible to get them out." In the fall, a Confederate inspector sent to the region requested help from armies in the field. Deserters escaped the army with their weapons and overpowered guards at bridges and ferries on their way to the mountains. While many deserters hid in the woods close to their homes, others formed bands numbering fifty to 500, drilled regularly, patrolled for and fired upon Confederate conscription officials and state Guard for Home Defense units, and robbed loyal Confederate citizens. They killed to avoid capture and to revenge the death of one of their own. Conscripts no longer reported when drafted because they saw how helpless the Confederate government was against the deserter gangs. The Confederate secretary of war endorsed this report and others like it with the terse comment, "The condition of things in the mountain districts of North Carolina, South Carolina, Georgia, and Alabama menaces the existence of the Confederacy as fatally as either of the armies of the United States." Robert E. Lee obligingly dispatched Brigadier General Robert F. Hoke with two infantry and one cavalry regiment for a two-month campaign in October and November 1863 that arrested over 3,000. A month later, it was as if they had never been there.[5]

Deserters and recusant conscripts worked with genuine Unionists, who conducted subversive activities in response to an aggressive military regime in North Carolina that repressed them and denied them civil liberties. Most threatening to authorities was a secret society, the Order of the Heroes of America, or the Red Strings, that originated in the North Carolina piedmont region and spread throughout the mountains in southwest Virginia, western North Carolina, and portions of Georgia and Alabama during 1864. Initiates took solemn oaths to encourage desertion from the Confederate army, to harbor all deserters and escaped Federal prisoners of war (the Red Strings recognized and took advantage of the Confederate prison transfer debacle), and to provide Union armies with intelligence. The initiation ceremony was intimidating and the oaths infused with threats of retribution. In western North Carolina, ten men with fixed bayonets surrounded the initiates, who swore the oath of the order with hands on the Bible, and then the master of ceremonies said, "May your hearts be pierced by bayonets should you reveal any of the secrets of this order." Upon these words, the guards charged the bayonets and pressed the tips into the initiates' chests.[6]

Members, both male and female, identified themselves to each other in the course of daily business through a series of hand signals and passwords that revealed their disillusionment with war and a desire for the stability of the old Union. "These are gloomy times here," a member would say. "Yes, but we are looking for better," was the response. "What are you looking for?" The answer was a red and white cord "because it is safe for us and our families." Members of a similar society in Alabama used a secret handshake they called "the constitutional peace grip." Their passwords began with the observation, "I dreamed that the boys are all coming home."[7]

The geographic scale and the impressive numbers of Unionist secret societies in the mountains were a substantial threat to conscription efforts in the fall of 1864. Members infiltrated the state militia and Guard for Home Defense and alerted recusant conscripts and deserters about patrols and raids. They served as sheriffs, justices of the peace, and local magistrates, making prosecution under state and Confederate treason laws impossible. They fed deserter bands and encouraged them to terrorize loyal citizens. Earlier in the year, President Jefferson Davis asked the Confederate Congress to suspend the writ of habeas corpus and to authorize mass arrests of suspicious persons because of the threat that deserters and secret societies posed. "Without suspending the writ, we cannot enroll in the army at this time," he proclaimed. "We shall not be able to retain those already in service. Must independence be put in peril for the sake of conformity to the technicalities of the law of treason?" Congress gave him what he wanted, but a report from the secretary of war in November 1864 indicated the problem had spread rather than abated.[8]

Unionists were not a majority anywhere in western North Carolina, were never safe, and never assumed control of any county. But their militant resistance and participation in irregular warfare at the local level destabilized and ultimately eroded Confederate authority, which collapsed in counties across the state due to the activities of Unionists, deserters, and recusant conscripts. The Confederate and state governments effectively controlled less than 60 percent of North Carolina in early 1864. When fugitive Federals arrived, portions of the Blue Ridge Mountains and the piedmont district were already immersed in two types of irregular warfare being waged against the Confederacy. One was a "people's war of resistance and self-defense" fought by self-constituted bands of Unionists. Another was the "raiding warfare" of Union army units recruited from the dissident population in North Carolina that launched attacks from bases in East Tennessee.[9]

Because women sustained and supplied both deserter bands and Unionist guerrillas, they were the target of reprisal and mistreatment from state troops. Governor Zebulon Vance subjected women to arrest in his orders and proclamations. Families of such women launched retaliatory strikes and targeted loyal women for abuse. Vigorous Confederate counter-irregular operations escalated rather than suppressed the violence. Companies of the Guard for Home Defense destroyed the property of Unionists, arrested dissidents and held them indefinitely, intimidated women and children, and killed suspected guerrillas. A variety of groups and individuals contributed to the collapse of the home front in western North Carolina. And when they arrived in the region, fugitive Federals did too.[10]

Civil War Americans initially envisioned the home front as a place separate from the battlefront, where families lived apart from soldiers and where violence was absent. White southerners hoped it would remain a protected sphere where most of the daily routines of peacetime continued amid the economic and personal sacrifices families made for the cause. The experience of escaped prisoners and the actions they took to survive in the region reveal places within the Confederacy where this idealized home front no longer existed. When the Yankees arrived in October 1864, a critical mass of the public, including women and children, provided direct support for violence targeting those perceived as enemies; armed companies representing the state conducted constant patrols and raids into neighborhoods and homes; political and military leaders who operated in the region were targets for assassination; and because no one was safe from violence, suspicion and distrust characterized daily interaction between people, who adopted masks and survival lying to cope with the situation.[11]

As soon as they crossed the border into North Carolina, fugitive Federals realized the game had changed. They had entered a battlefront. Drake, Todd, Lewis, and Grant learned the lesson immediately after entering the state south of Gastonia on October 20. The next night, the Yankees crossed a covered bridge, and when they reached the other side they heard the pounding of hooves. The Federals dashed into a swamp adjoining the bridge and observed a small force of cavalry patrolling the road. This was a company of the Home Guard for Gaston County, headquartered in the small town of Dallas located about two miles from the bridge. North Carolina, unlike its southern neighbor, exempted officers in the state troops from the Confederate draft and maintained a more active security presence in the countryside. In a marked contrast to their experience in South Carolina, where no state troops haunted the Yankees' progress, from this point on Drake's party worked hard to avoid pursuit. They lay in a hiding place in the woods and listened to the sound of the Home Guard passing up and down the road.[12]

A month later, Hadley, Chisman, Baker, and Good entered North Carolina just south of Saluda, about seventy-five miles west of Drake's point of entry. They ran into an African American teamster who offered to hide them in his wagon and take them to Asheville. Baker and Good leapt at the rare chance. Hadley and Chisman wanted nothing to do with the scheme. They thought it too risky: foraging parties might seize the wagon and there were Confederate troops at Asheville. The discussion escalated and they threw out the rules they established at the outset of the journey to resolve disputes. Hadley honestly but ashamedly admitted that the argument "culminated in blows." The party almost split, but after they calmed down, they continued the journey together. It was fitting that the Yankees fought among themselves when they stepped into such a divided land. They had begun, Hadley wrote, "a chapter of troubles."[13]

The next night they walked past a farm house set very close to the road. A pack of dogs burst from beneath the porch and attacked. The Yankees formed a circle and swung at the animals with their clubs. The door of the house opened and a white man stared at them. The Federals fled, but they knew they were in deep trouble. They were spotted and dogs had their scent. They left the road and hit the woods, attempting to cover their tracks as they moved by walking backward and forward and dragging a wet blanket behind them. Eight miles from Saluda they came to a crossroads. Nearby was a mansion and a long row of huts. They made contact with the slave Reuben at 10:00 P.M. He informed them a captain and twenty members of the Guard for Home Defense were posted along the road watching for them. Reuben advised against further movement and hid them for the night and next day.

Reuben gave them locations and instructions for avoiding the Guard for Home Defense pickets posted along the roads and in the communities between Saluda and Hendersonville. They left their hiding place after dark. Just past the crossroads, a white man suddenly appeared in front of them. He and the Yankees were equally startled. "Who are you?" he stammered. Hadley stretched out his hand and stick "like a specter" and spoke in a "ghostly, guttural tone": "M-o-v-e o-n." The man scooted off. The lone guard at a narrow pass was asleep, and the Yankees snuck right past him. When the Federals approached the spa resort of Flat Rock with its Confederate storehouses and company of soldiers, they remembered Reuben's guideline that all pickets were posted within a mile and a half semicircle of the community. But they entered the road too soon, and an officer and four soldiers stopped them. Reuben told them if that happened, "run to the mountains." They broke from the road and ran to the top of the adjacent mountain. Sunlight revealed woody hills in every direction but open fields and numerous houses between the Yankees and cover. To move and to stay put seemed impossible. It started to rain, then sleet, then snow. "This day culminated our troubles, and it seemed that one feather more would have broken the camel's back," Hadley recalled. "There are no words in the language that can convey a correct idea of our anguish of mind and real suffering of body, on that Sunday, on that North Carolina mountain."[14]

Active and constant patrols were the first sign Yankees had entered something more akin to a battle zone than a home front. In South Carolina, security collapsed without state troops to patrol the countryside, but ironically, because there were no effective forces to battle deserters and rebellious slaves, Yankees thought the home front was intact there. In North Carolina, where desertion and disloyalty were more pervasive earlier in the war than in South Carolina, state troops were constantly in the field and regularly engaged Unionist irregulars. Rather than securing the home front, however, state forces precipitated skirmishes and incidents that undermined it. Yankees entered North Carolina through a corridor of counties where the state was at war with its own citizens.[15]

The frontline troops for North Carolina were the Guard for Home Defense, a force created in July 1863 out of men exempt from the Confederate draft who were between the ages of eighteen and fifty. The state legislature tasked the guard with defense from invasion, suppressing insurrection, and arresting Confederate conscripts and deserters. In 1864, there were 9,196 officers and men in the guard and nearly 10,000 Confederate Reserves available to operate against deserters in the state. In August, the state placed the guard in the western district of North Carolina under Confederate Brigadier General James G. Martin. For the duration of 1864, the guard served continuously in a cluster of battle-zone counties: all counties west of the Blue Ridge; Ashe, Alleghany, Surry, and Wilkes on the northwest border; Randolph, Union, and their contiguous counties in the central piedmont; and Polk and Rutherford counties on the southwest border. They had orders "to intercept parties attempting to make their way to East Tennessee," to "clear out, capture, or destroy deserters, bushwhackers, and tories," and to "aid the civil authorities in preserving order."[16]

The guard's activities in the fall of 1864 succeeded in destroying the home front but not in clearing out disloyal elements, despite the fact that 1,287 deserters and recusant conscripts returned to the army during that period. The guard captured 421 of these and the rest surrendered under Governor Vance's proclamation that guaranteed them pardon. But thousands of deserters remained and the violence escalated. In late November, the governor informed the state assembly about the "deplorable and distressing condition of inhabitants in the western border of the state," where raids and lawlessness were a way of life. Throughout the state, deserters infested swamps and mountains, and continued to "muster in such force as to almost suspend civil authority as they are aided and protected by friends and relatives." Vance requested "unrestrained control" of the guard and new laws to make it easier to convict those who harbored and aided deserters. In December, the General Assembly passed an act for local defense that in effect acknowledged the battle-zone conditions in portions of the state and authorized citizens to form paramilitary organizations. Any time more than ten persons "associate themselves as a military company" to conserve the peace, they "shall be considered as belonging to the state troops of North Carolina, serving without pay or allowance."[17]

When the state sanctioned military companies whose relation to state authorities was tenuous at best, the home front no longer existed. Yankees witnessed this through the behavior of the residents they encountered. It was obvious to them that Carolinians distrusted their neighbors and never felt safe. It was no wonder. Unionists risked arrest from authorities and death at the hands of the state forces and vigilantes who waged irregular warfare. Confederates knew that secret societies infiltrated the ranks of state troops and local officials. People wore masks to hide their true loyalties and identities; conversations were fencing matches where contestants sought to conceal themselves and uncover the other.

The Yankees too were deceivers. And they had many opportunities to practice in western North Carolina. Drake and his companions evaded the Gaston County Guard for Home Defense their first night in the state. The Federals emerged from their swampy hiding place and continued down the road at 1:00 A.M. on October 21. Soon they heard singing and observed a black woman with a male companion approaching. Drake was not an admirer of African American music. "She made a terrible noise with her mouth," he recorded. Assuming the man was black and hoping for help, the four Yankees with their clubs emerged from some bushes and commanded the pair to halt. The woman screamed and ran away. The man, who proved to be white, pulled a revolver and pointed it at them. He demanded to know who they were and what their business was.

They were prepared for this eventuality. Some slaves they had met right after they crossed the border told them that conscripts for the Rebel armies rendezvoused at Morganton, a city about fifty miles northwest of Dallas. Harry Todd, from New Jersey like Drake, had a talent for imitating a southern accent and was a bold and accomplished liar. Todd told the man they were conscripts who had lost their way. The man dropped the revolver to his side and eyed the Yankees closely. He invited them to walk home with him where he would show them something to their advantage.

As the group sauntered down the road, the southerner, clearly suspicious these were Yankees, and the Yankees, suspicious their companion was a genuine Unionist, probed each other cautiously. Such conversations usually followed the same thread. The man said he was tired of the war—a safe statement to strangers, since even loyal Confederates expressed such sentiments from time to time. Todd said he was too. The man hoped the war ended soon. Oh, yes, Todd agreed. The man grew bolder. The government in Richmond grossly mismanaged the country's affairs. Todd assured him no set of politicians was more incompetent. But opposing Confederate policies did not necessarily indicate loyalty to the United States and treason to the Confederate government. Someone had to risk a statement that crossed the line. The Yankees with their clubs outnumbered the southerner with his gun, so they chanced the first move. Todd admitted he was a Union man. Then Drake stepped in and confessed they were escaped Yankee prisoners and showed the man his commission and his diary. The man handed Drake his revolver and embraced each of the fugitives. He took them home and his wife fed them while they rested until daylight. The Yankees were disappointed to learn that this loyal patriot was an isolated minority who feared discovery of his true feelings. When Drake published his diary in 1866, he refused to name this man in case he was still in danger from his neighbors. The southerner guided them around Dallas, gave them directions to the Tennessee border, and provided them with the names of Unionist families along the way.[18]

The Yankees continued on their journey, passing through Lincolnton and then crossing a railroad track four miles from Morganton, the headquarters of Brigadier General Martin, commanding the Confederate District of Western North Carolina. Marching in single file, the party entered a dense pine wood. Immediately before them was a Confederate colonel in full uniform astride a fine horse. Todd walked right up to the officer and in his best southern slang asked for directions to the conscript rendezvous at Morganton. The colonel burst out laughing. The Federal officers were not daunted. Their manhood—the ability to act unconcerned and nonchalant in the face of danger—had been tested numerous times on battlefields and in prisons. Drake stepped forward and asked for a "chawterbacker." The keen-eyed southerner handed him a plug and watched as Drake broke it in two and handed half to Todd.

"That's damned cool, anyway," the colonel said smilingly. "You fellows do not want to go to Morganton. But if you do, that's the way." And he pointed in the direction from which the Yankees had just come.

"Well, boys, let's lie down and rest awhile—then we'll go back to Morganton," Todd said, and his comrades sat down and stretched out.

The colonel started to ride off, but halted and beckoned the Yankees to approach. They got up and did so. "Boys, you cannot deceive me," he said. "I have seen and met too many of your kind. Nevertheless I will befriend you. You want to reach the mountains yonder—this I know." Two companies of his troops were near. He gave them directions to find a small scow that would carry them across the Catawba River. "You have my hearty wishes for success. *Run*."[19] They did, and eventually found their way to Mary and Bill Estes.

The uniform of the enemy covered the heart of a friend. Other Yankees learned that even family members cloaked their true selves from each other. Although kinship solidarity was the rule in western North Carolina and even contributed to the bitter local fighting, divided households existed. Fugitives benefited from families that contained a hidden wolf or two in the fold, none more than Hadley, Chisman, Baker, and Good.

Fighting despair at the top of the mountain, the Yankees watched all day for signs of a search party. Seeing none, they walked down to a cabbage patch and Good snuck in to steal dinner. Unbeknownst to the

Yankees, they were on the Flat Rock estate of Christopher G. Memminger, who had resigned as secretary of the treasury for the Confederacy five months before. The cabbage patch was on land Memminger rented to Josiah Holinsworth, a farmer and occasional day-laborer with a wife, eight children, and two carpenters for the estate living in his household.

Suddenly, four of the young Holinsworth sisters—Delitha, Elizabeth, Martha, and Alice—who initially mistook Good for a troublesome neighbor boy, chased him into the laurel bushes where the other Yankees were hiding. The fugitives pretended to be Confederate soldiers, but the sisters knew otherwise and nipped that ruse in the bud. They spoke bitter and harsh words against the Confederacy and proclaimed their support for Federal arms. But the Yankees presented a problem for them. Two of their older sisters were married to soldiers in the Confederate army. The captain of the local Guard for Home Defense, who had no idea of the true sentiments of the various members of the family, regularly ate dinner at their house, and the night before he told them that his company was searching for escaped Yankees who had run up the mountain. The girls considered. Seventeen-year-old Alice ran back to the house to get food while twenty-one-year-old Martha decided how to handle the men in the bushes.

Martha decided to hide the Yankees in the upstairs garret and procure a guide to take them to Knoxville. She informed the bemused men of her decision but proffered a caveat. They must submit to her authority in all matters. Neighboring Rebels suspected her family of disloyalty and constantly watched the house. She would undertake nothing without a guarantee that the men "would not exercise any will of their own." She offered to shake hands on it. The Federals did so. They had no particular reason to trust her, but Hadley made much of her sympathetic expression, which he believed no woman could truly counterfeit, and the feel of her hand. "There is a language in shaking of hands that carries with it more meaning and less deceit than any articulate sounds," he assured himself. Besides, the girls possessed rustic and simple manners, and were not "full of show" like "better-educated folks."[20]

Martha and Alice snuck the party upstairs one at a time behind the back of their father while their sisters sung a hymn to distract him and some visiting Rebel neighbors. They told Hadley that their father must never know Yankees were hidden in the house. He loved the Union, Martha assured Hadley, but had already been arrested once. The sisters wanted their father to be able to swear truthfully that he knew nothing if he were questioned. Later in his journey, another Unionist told Hadley that Josiah Holinsworth was in fact a bitter Rebel. Hadley believed Martha at the time, and later his other informant. Perhaps Holinsworth was loyal to the old flag but played the part of the Rebel so well that he fooled all his neighbors in order to keep his position on the Memminger estate. Perhaps the Holinsworth household was divided between a Union mother and her teenage daughters and a Rebel father and the two sisters married to Confederate soldiers. Perhaps Martha told the Yankees her father was a Unionist to conceal the risk they took from entering the house of a Rebel. The real faces under the masks were hard to read. Whatever the truth of the father's loyalties, his wife and daughters hid four Yankees from him for four days and nights.

Martha Holinsworth was as intrepid and brave as Mary Estes, who harbored Drake and his friends. When Martha's brother Isaac deserted the Confederate army, she constructed and concealed a scuttle hole from the upstairs bedroom to a small garret. Isaac hid there for more than two months but could not stand such close confinement. When the governor proclaimed a general amnesty for any deserter who surrendered, the young man did so. After placing the Yankees in the garret, well after midnight, Martha and Alice walked six miles round-trip through the woods to find guides. They contacted two outlaws, Jack and Jerry Vance, who robbed and killed among Union folk and Rebels alike. But the brothers frequently traveled over the mountains to Knoxville and would do anything for money. The Yankees were willing to pay.

In the meantime, Martha, her sisters, and her mother perfected the lying that the war zone around them made necessary. As the Yankees waited for the Vance brothers to get ready for the journey, Josiah left the house and Hadley briefly came downstairs. As the midwesterner returned up the stairs, Josiah walked in the house and saw him. "Alice, what man was that I saw going upstairs?" Holinsworth asked. Alice and her mother broke out laughing. Oh father, she said. It was only Martha, who put on Isaac's clothes to haul wood and ran upstairs when you came in. As Alice and her mother continued to laugh, the old man smiled and accepted the story. Whether he really believed it cannot be known. But Hadley took the incident as an example of the women's "ready sagacity and invention."[21]

Fugitives learned that under the pressure of constant danger, mountain parents trained their children to lie. An African American guide led fugitive Daniel Langworthy and his four companions to the home of a county sheriff who used his position to protect local Unionists and aid escaped Yankee prisoners. Upon the barking of dogs, the sheriff came out to his porch and called out, "Who is there?" The guide stepped forward and responded, "A friend." A little boy, seven years old, ran outside and joined his father while he conversed with the Yankees. The sheriff sighed. "We have endeavored to bring him up to be a good religious, strictly honest and truthful boy, yet if anyone should come here tomorrow and ask him if there had been any strangers here, no matter what they did to him they could not get a word out of him. Isn't that a terrible way to bring up children?" Two days later, another party of five fugitives from Camp Sorghum arrived, three of whom had served with Langworthy in the same brigade of the Union army. The sheriff procured a guide to take the ten Yankees, three white Unionists, and an African American man to Union lines in Tennessee.[22]

Lying was necessary because daily life was life-threatening. A critical mass of citizens, including women and children, engaged in activities that directly supported violent actions against local enemies. Some women sustained local resistance to Confederate authority without contributing to warfare. Martha Holinsworth was such a one; she fed and hid deserters and escaped Yankees. Other women, like Mary Estes, enabled violence. She provided intelligence and carried messages to gangs that conducted raids and ambushes. Fugitive Yankees encountered both sorts of women but did not recognize any of them as combatants.[23]

At the beginning of the Civil War, Americans on both sides assumed that women would not directly participate in the violence of war. Armies and governments would protect women and make a distinction between enemy soldiers in uniform and noncombatants. Women would support the war effort, of course, by giving up their men to the army, by managing the family while their husbands were away, by encouraging soldiers emotionally, by joining voluntary organizations that made and sent supplies to the front lines, and by holding fairs and bazaars to raise money for the cause.

It did not take Americans long to see that women's activities blurred the supposedly rigid line between combatant and noncombatant. Federal military officials figured out that Confederate guerrillas could not operate without the aid of southern women who protected, uniformed, and fed them. In military terms, women were the supply line of the irregular warfare that emerged wherever Union armies marched and occupied. Confederate authorities experienced a similar revelation. Without the actions of women who hid, clothed, fed, guided, and spied for deserters, draft-dodgers, and Unionist guerrillas, there would not be such widespread and effective resistance to the Confederate government.[24]

As these epiphanies spread through the armies, government bureaucracies, and the general population, Americans in the Union and the Confederacy developed two categories to describe people's role in the war: they were either loyal or disloyal. The disloyal were enemies of the state even if they were not combatants; the war continued because of their support. Governments therefore targeted the disloyal, male and female. Confederate officials moved against women who collaborated with deserters, Union guerrilla bands, and escaped prisoners of war. State legislatures made it a crime to harbor deserters and draft dodgers. Governor Vance ordered the arrest of women and children who violated the law. The Confederate government commanded military authorities to arrest without warrant citizens who gave "aid and comfort" to the enemy, who harbored deserters, who communicated with the enemy "without necessity and without the permission of the Confederate states," and who attempted to "liberate prisoners of war."[25]

Government authorities treated disloyal women as criminals under civil law, but Confederate and state troops in the Carolinas terrorized them. Squads of infantry and cavalry monitored their movement, searched and destroyed their homes, and occasionally tortured them in the quest for information. During the same time that escaped Yankees moved through the countryside, Guard for Home Defense officers in three North Carolina counties arrested fifty women, some of them pregnant, and kept them in close confinement under military guard for several weeks. Confederate Reserve units in Anderson, South Carolina, a key station on the fugitive route to Augusta, whipped two women. Colonel Alfred Pike and his squad, hunting deserters in Randolph County, North Carolina, slapped a woman while she held her baby in her arms, tied her hands behind her back, and hung her from a tree by the thumbs, then pressed her fingers between fence rails. The officer was unrepentant. "If I have not the right to treat Bill Owens, his wife, & the like in this manner I want to know it," he told the district solicitor who investigated, "& I will go to the Yankees or to anywhere else before I will live in a country in which I cannot treat such people in this manner."[26]

When the general population heard about such incidents, they reported them to the government with outraged demands that the perpetrators be punished. Equally horrified superiors ordered courts-martial and reiterated that women were liable to arrest but not to physical abuse. But crushing women's activities remained a vital part of military strategy on the battle fronts within the Confederacy, and daily practice belied official policy. Officers and troops in western North Carolina conducted operations in a region where the home front no longer existed. They could not fight women in the same way they fought men, but to win the war they had to defeat women. They terrorized disloyal women because it was the only way they could wage war against disloyal men.[27]

The Yankees were not blind to the political nature of the southern women who helped them, and they generally believed that all women who endured danger for their sake did so because they were brave and heroic patriots of the United States. The Yankees knew that these women cursed the Confederacy and worked against it, and it never occurred to them that their guardian angels might have been secessionists when the war began. Considering the long hours that fugitives spent in close conversation with these women, however, and the lasting friendships they developed with mountain families, it is only fair to credit the fugitives when they claimed that they and their guardian angels were on the same political page in the fall of 1864.

Disloyal women, for their part, expanded the hostilities they waged against the Confederacy when fugitive Federals entered the fray during the last three months of 1864. They did not do anything for the Yankees that they did not already do for their husbands and brothers, but when they scouted and spied for Federal soldiers who were strangers to them, no one could claim that their actions were purely domestic. It was an overt act of war against the Confederate state that promoted the collapse of the home front in western North Carolina.

Charlie Mattocks, Charles Hunt, and Julius Litchfield arrived on the battlefield of Transylvania County in late November. After they crossed into North Carolina on the seventeenth, they passed through Hendersonville, and then got lost. They generally stuck to the roads, but they took a wrong turn, and their path ended in a barnyard. They backtracked, wandered aimlessly for two nights, and finally entered a valley of the French Broad River, where they contacted an elderly slave woman and her daughter, who welcomed the Yankees into their small cabin and fed them applesauce and boiled potatoes. She told them they were in Transylvania County, near the small community of Brevard, the "Land of the Waterfalls." There were more than 250 cascades within twenty miles of their location.[28]

In conversation with the two slave women, Mattocks and his party learned that slavery was still relatively intact in western North Carolina. Slaves were 10 percent of the population when the war began, but their ranks increased when low-country masters removed slaves to interior regions and when mountain masters purchased slaves from coastal areas threatened by the Union army. The region's active slave trade continued, the value of slave property in the area was high, and first-time investors were confident enough to move into the slaveholding ranks during the last few months of 1864. But the initial symptoms of the institution's collapse had begun. Masters had problems disciplining their increasingly defiant slaves. Slaves cooperated with and aided deserters, and when fugitive Federals arrived, they organized to aid them in the same ways and used the same knowledge they had in South Carolina.[29]

The slaves provided names of many Unionist white men and gave the Federals directions to the home of Jack Loftis, who lived six miles away and was famous for his applejack. The women were intimately acquainted with the human geography of their neighborhood. They ticked off the names of every family whose house the Yankees would have to pass; Loftis lived in the sixth house after a particular bridge. But when the Yankees stood in front of the sixth house, some hours later, it was abandoned. They did not know what to do. Mattocks and Litchfield wanted to move on. But Hunt smelled a storm brewing and wanted to get beneath a roof. Probably the women did not include this house in the count since it was abandoned. He offered to take the risk. He would knock on the door of the seventh house while the other two hid at a safe distance. If he did not return after a reasonable time, Hunt gave his friends permission to continue the journey without him.

Hunt knocked on the door, a sick feeling in the pit of his stomach. He had not spoken to a white person in two weeks. He saw no light come on inside the house, but heard a rustling sound. The door opened and a gray-haired man stood outlined in the frame. Hunt asked about the roads to Asheville, stalling for time in order to gain courage. As the man answered, Hunt blurted out, "Are you Loftis?" It was. As Hunt tried to explain his identity, and before he knew what was happening, Loftis reached underneath the blanket the Yankee wore over his shoulders and pulled off a brass button to confirm it belonged to a Federal uniform. "I guess you are all right, then," Loftis said. "I did not know but that it was a trap set for me." Hunt said he had two companions with him. "Well, go and get them," Loftis replied. "I will take care of you."[30]

The three Yankees were exuberant. Loftis informed them that numerous parties of fugitives from Camp Sorghum were hiding in nearby houses, including friends of theirs, Captain Edward Chase and Lieutenant James Fales. Loftis produced an autograph book with the signatures of all the escaped prisoners of war he had helped during the last month. The Maine trio added theirs. Loftis was afraid to have the Yankees in his house because his Rebel neighbors suspected and closely watched for him. He hid them in a small building where he kept his cider press. They munched on apples and listened to rain pound on the roof, unable to sleep because they were so happy. The next morning Loftis brought them breakfast. "Boys, that is Rebel beef," he said. He meant he got it in a raid against his neighbors. He and they shot at each other on sight. "I have never anywhere else known such bitterness, as existed between neighbors here," another fugitive who traveled through the area wrote. "It was not unusual for persons to be waylaid, and assassinated when passing along the public highways."[31]

Women directly participated in this violence between neighbors. Unionists cut holes between the logs composing the outer walls of their homes. When Rebels or companies of the Home Guard surrounded a house, the family bolted the door, and the women loaded weapons and handed them to the men, who fired through the holes in the wall. After a recent shoot-out in the vicinity, Unionists found seven dead Rebels in their yard. "Every man, even every boy about 12 years of age is thoroughly armed," Mattocks wrote in wonder. It was common for a man to carry on his person two rifles and two revolvers. Families posted pickets on the road twenty-four hours a day to watch for Rebel raiding parties and units sent to arrest deserters. Women took the day shift; men stood guard at night.[32]

The fugitives remained with Loftis two days, entertaining visitors who called to congratulate them on their escape, and partaking of applejack. The containers were underground, but the old man showed the Yankees how to find the hiding place, stick a long straw through a nearly invisible hole in the earth, and suck the brandy down. "These people are the strongest for the Union question of any persons I ever saw," Mattocks remarked. He met women who were prepared for agents of the Confederate state to torture them for information. Rebecca Havil, or "Aunt

Becky" to Loftis and his family, brought the Yankees some chicken for dinner. "I ain't afraid of these rebels," she told them. "I tell them 'you may hang old Becky if you want to, but with the last breath I draw I will shout, Hurrah for the Union!'"[33]

The Yankees enjoyed treatment that went beyond simple hospitality. "They are doing everything for us," Mattocks recorded in his diary. He did not exaggerate. At Litchfield's request, Loftis's daughter, married to a man living in the mountains to avoid the draft, named her infant son after him. The young woman also gave Mattocks the stockings off her feet, all she had left after supplying so many other fugitives with footwear, so he would have a pair for the trek over the mountains to Knoxville.[34]

Loftis arranged for Mattocks, Hunt, and Litchfield to rendezvous with seventeen other escaped Yankees at the home of Robert Hamilton, the deputy-sheriff and a justice of the peace for Transylvania County. Hamilton used his position as an officer in the Guard for Home Defense to protect deserters, sending word ahead when his unit conducted patrols or raids. Once his squad surrounded a house while he and three others searched it. Hamilton found the deserter hiding under a bed, but told the captain the room was empty. By November 1864, the sheriff was busy funneling to Knoxville large parties of fugitive Federals and southern mountaineers who decided to join the Union army. Three weeks earlier, he hid and organized thirty future Federal soldiers and thirty fugitive Federals, several of whom escaped from the train between Charleston and Columbia on October 5, and who arrived in Transylvania County in clusters around November 3. Three of the Yankees, veterans of the 101st Pennsylvania, nicknamed one of Hamilton's hiding places, a deserted cabin in the mountains, "The Pennsylvania House." After dispatching that particular party, Hamilton prepared to send out another on November 21.[35]

The Maine trio arrived at Hamilton's house a little before daylight. Jack Loftis's seventeen-year-old nephew was with them. Home Guard troops shot the young draft-dodger in the forearm right before the Yankees arrived, and Loftis wanted the boy out of danger. They found three friends—Edward Chase, Asa Goodrich, and James Fales—and a dozen other Yankees already there. Fales credited women and children for his party's safe arrival at the rendezvous. A twelve-year-old served as their guide at one point, and a shoemaker and his wife hid them in a cave for three days while the couple mended their boots and clothes. The Yankees joined the shoemaker on a raid for "Rebel beef."

The five officers pictured here were in the party of sixty men that Sheriff Robert Hamilton dispatched to Knoxville just before Charles Porter Mattocks arrived in Transylvania County. Notice the clubs they carried to ward off dogs and to help them cross the mountain terrain. Photograph in Daniel Avery Langworthy, *Reminiscences of a Prisoner of War and His Escape* (1915).

Hamilton procured the party a guide named Gilbert Semple, a Confederate deserter. Semple seemed reluctant to undertake the trip, but he agreed when the Yankees told him they would pool their resources and pay him $500 when they arrived in Knoxville. They left Semple's house at 10:00 A.M. on November 22 and made sixteen miles that day. It seemed to Mattocks that every time they approached a house, two or three young men leapt out of windows and ran for the woods. Only when the women of the family positively ascertained that the group was composed of Yankees did the men come back. Then the Federal officers and the mountain resisters ate apples together and shared their wartime adventures. The fugitives told of their escape from Confederate prison. The southerners told of bushwhacking and their bloody battles with the Guard for Home Defense.[36]

Semple acquired another guide on November 23 who helped him navigate through a portion of the Balsam Mountains that was unfamiliar to him. Twenty-three exhausting miles later, the entire party took refuge in a one-room cabin. The family consisted of an elderly couple, what seemed to be scores of boys and small children, and two daughters at the right age for flirtation. There were five beds in the room, and the young women remained in theirs while they kept up a stream of conversation with the twenty Yankees scattered across the floor of their home. "To our New England ideas of propriety this seems horrible, but here every night we have had similar experiences," Mattocks scribbled into his diary.[37]

The scion of a wealthy Maine family was titillated. Normally reserved and class conscious, he had been confined in prison for several months, and the sight of a bare foot was worthy of mention in his journal. "I was gently aroused from my slumbers by a gentle damsel who very naively informed me that she was hunting for her stocking which had been lost during the night. Taking pity on the fat, plump foot, which I could not fail to see peeping out from a dress not too long according to Paris styles, I at once rallied myself and tried to find the missing article." For Mattocks, the entire scene with the ladies was romantic. "What a theme for a poet!!" he exclaimed. Hunt was more prosaic. To him, it was annoying to have a "strapping" young woman poking around looking for her socks while he was trying to sleep. "Here, you uns, get up!" she commanded him. "One of my stocking is down here under you somewhar."[38]

The guardian angels fascinated the fugitives. They were unlike any other women the Yankees had ever known. So Federal officers drew on the conventions of the literary culture with which they were familiar. For the most part they were avid readers whose immersion in the stories of others made them self-conscious about their own. They enjoyed thinking about what was happening to them as a narrator would, using the plot and character elements from the tales they loved. Mattocks's imagination had been formed around the chivalric Waverly novels of Sir Walter Scott, the sentimentality of the popular Charles Dickens, and the sublimity of the romantic poets. Thus he spoke in flowery language of a "gentle damsel" who was to him a "fair Terpsichore," the muse of dance in Greek mythology. To find language to express his feelings, he condensed some lines from *Macbeth*: "Can such things be and not excite our special wonder." He did not remember the source of the quotation, however. "As Shakespeare or somebody else has said—who, it is hard to remember among the unliterary associations of these mountains."[39]

Intimate encounters with southern women cultivated the fugitives' sense that they were living out an epic Romance. Tired, sick, and on edge as they were, they were also conscious that their quest was a grand adventure worthy of immortalization. And everyone knew that such a story needed a Heroine. Thus when fugitives encountered a woman who en-

gaged in valiant feats on his behalf or provided him with special attention, he idolized her according to Victorian literary conventions. When J.
Madison Drake later reworked his diary for publication, he drew on
courtly language to describe Mary Estes. She had a "comely form" and
was "robed in a green dress." She offered them food "with a gracious
smile, worthy of a queen." Before he parted from her, he gave her the
heavy gold ring that he always wore on his finger.[40]

Fugitive Federals deeply admired the Appalachian women whose
loyalty and devotion to their families epitomized the feminine virtues,
even if such virtues were displayed in the unconventional manner of
supplying food to heavily armed gangs lying out in mountain caves. Fugitives extolled the assertiveness, resourcefulness, and courage of the
women who aided them. When Federal troops encountered such
qualities in loyal Confederate women, they denigrated them as "she-
devils." Drake called a group of outspoken female Rebels that he met "tar-
tars" and "Amazons." But fugitive Yankees who depended on southern
women for their survival were grateful for these qualities. Their unique
experience enabled them to reconcile their angels' femininity with behaviors they normally reserved for men: independence and militancy.[41]

But conflicting with their tendency to idealize the mountain women
who ensured their survival was a deep disdain for southern culture in
nearly all its facets. Prejudices surfaced and infused their reaction to the
intimate moments they shared with these southern women, whose lack
of education and hardscrabble life fit within stereotypes they held of the
South. Running through their diaries and narratives was commentary on
the ignorance and laziness of southerners. Although one fugitive thought
Sheriff Hamilton and his family were of above-average intelligence, Hunt
was disgusted that they chopped only enough wood to last each day. "This
was not the way we Yankees were brought up, and someone proposed
that we go into the woods and get up a good stock of fuel," he later told a
northern audience. "We spent the largest part of one of the days we were
there in cutting, splitting, and piling up in Hamilton's back yard more
wood than, probably, was ever there at one time before or since." Midwesterner Hadley spent much of his time with the Holinsworth sisters
reading and writing letters for them, since no member of the family
was literate.[42]

Many fugitives filtered their experience of the world through the lens
of civilization, a term that encapsulated the pinnacle of human achieve-
ment. Civilized societies, according to many of the Federal officers and

soldiers who escaped from Confederate prisons, produced refined and literate women with artistic taste and sensibilities. In contrast, the mountain regions of the South were barbaric, places where people were generous and kind, but "ignorant in the conventionalisms of life," as New York fugitive John Collins Welch put it.[43]

Such thinking ended one Yankee's intimate encounter with the heroine of his story. Junius Henri Browne was a captured war correspondent for the *New York Tribune* who escaped from Salisbury prison in North Carolina on December 18, 1864. Witty, self-consciously sardonic, and a womanizer who distrusted women and scorned marriage, he was a member of the self-styled Bohemian set of journalists who valued skepticism and a literary sensibility over conventional thinking and behavior. Browne wrote articles early in the war about the barbarous condition of Arkansas and Missouri, whose "brown and brawny women offended his taste . . . chilled his gallantry . . . and repressed his chivalrous sentiment."[44]

Three years later he was in the mountains of western North Carolina, hiding in a small cabin with Confederate guerrillas hot on the trail of his escape party. When riders on horseback approached the cabin, Browne and a sixteen-year-old girl ran out the back door and into the woods. A lightning storm blazed around them, but the girl would not leave him, despite his pleas for her to do so. Overcome by her bravery and loyalty to him, Browne kissed her as she clung to him. Later that night, in the one-room cabin filled with sleeping family members and fugitive Federals, Browne had a memorable dream. The girl turned out to be a princess in disguise. A magician provided a winged dragon who flew Browne and his princess to New York City for an elegant supper at a refined French restaurant.

He awoke to the sight of the mountain girl in her homespun dress sitting in the chimney corner preparing a plain breakfast of corn bread. As he watched her, reality hit. Of course one such as her "was no princess," he later wrote, and his dream left him "longing after the Ideal" that could never be fulfilled in the uncivilized girl before him.[45]

Browne, like Mattocks before him, left his guardian angel and traveled across the mountain ranges that bordered western North Carolina and eastern Tennessee with a large and varied party of escaped prisoners, deserters from the Confederate army, and recruits for the Union army. Five hundred and sixty-six fugitive Federals from Confederate prisons in the Carolinas, Virginia, Georgia, and other states reported to Union authorities in the Knoxville area after the fall of 1863. They journeyed in company with unknown thousands of southern refugees who were likewise moving across landscapes that were marked with clear borders on a map. But as the next stage of the trip would reveal to Mattocks, Drake, and Hadley, in and around the collapsing Confederacy, borders were distorted and constantly shifting, and the lines on a map held no real meaning.

5

God's Country

The Collapse of Borders

Crossing the Blue Ridge Mountains brought both Charlie Mattocks and J. Madison Drake to a point of deep despair. Danger surrounded them on all sides and survival required them to push the boundaries of their physical and mental stamina. The sleepless hours Drake spent battling the natural elements on Grandfather Mountain was "the most terrible night" the battle-hardened veteran ever experienced. Two days before, November 1, 1864, Drake and his companions had been optimistic when they set out toward Knoxville with Bill Estes and a party of thirteen well-armed men. "We felt like a standing army," Drake wrote. "*We* were soldiers once more." But the climb up Grandfather Mountain, elevation 5,946 feet, with strong winds swirling about him, exhausted Drake. Snow fell in blinding sheets. A Baptist clergyman who lived in a rude log cabin sent the party to "Rock House," a well-known shelter for men lying out to escape Rebel patrols. It was hardly a house; merely a giant leaning boulder that provided some cover from the elements. The party built a fire and others stretched out to sleep, but rest eluded Drake. He was covered with body lice, and when his skin warmed up, the lice became an active torment, drawing blood with their fangs. He scratched until his flesh was raw and bleeding. If he moved away from the fire, he froze. He had no hat, his shirt was threadbare, and the brambles and bushes of the mountain had torn his pants off below the knees. He was barefoot. In his misery, Drake became convinced that the Carolinians he traveled with would desert him in the morning to a cruel fate of death in the wilderness.[1]

Later that harsh November, on the twenty-fourth, Mattocks climbed a mountain within the Great Balsam range of the Blue Ridge. "The ascent was hard but the descent was actually perpendicular," he recorded in his diary. Laurel formed an undergrowth of "impassable thickets." Pushing through the laurel was "the hardest labor I ever undertook." Since it completely covered the ground, Mattocks and his friends had to carefully find a foothold in the branches of the shrub with each step they took. After the party crossed and recrossed the same stream, the eighteen

Portrait of William Estes from *Fast and Loose in Dixie* (1880).

Yankees and two Carolinians suspected that their guide, Gilbert Semple, was lost. They were out of food. After three days of tramping through the laurel, and listening to panther screams during the night, Mattocks wrote, "Worse and worse!!" Semple had finally admitted he was lost and the party decided to follow a stream in hopes of coming across a house, but its banks were covered with impenetrable laurel and its rocks with ice. Mattocks fell into the water and was drenched up to his armpits. After eight fruitless hours, the travelers voted to leave the stream and head northwest by the compass. Mattocks was proud to discover that he was "improving on starvation," but Charles Hunt's feet were covered with painful blisters, and both James Fales and Edward Chase nearly fainted with exhaustion. They nibbled on crinkle root and ivy leaves.[2]

Despite the inhospitable and seemingly inaccessible environment, humans by the thousands were on the move in the Blue Ridge during the winter of 1864–65. Escaped prisoners, refugees, recruits for the Union army from South Carolina, North Carolina, and Georgia, Confederate deserters seeking sanctuary in Union lines, guerrillas on the prowl, U.S. and Confederate raiders, and state militia units crossed over the physical and political borders that supposedly demarcated the sovereign states within the Confederacy. On the final phase of the journey to Knoxville, each fugitive personally encountered hundreds of men and women on an exodus out of the Carolinas and Georgia. As the Confederacy disintegrated across time, the motion of people across space facilitated its collapse.[3]

In order to win the war and achieve independence, the Confederacy endeavored to restrict the movement of external and internal enemies across its borders. Persons living in the Confederacy who wished to travel within or beyond its claimed boundaries had to obtain permission and a pass from military authorities. The goal, according to Secretary of War James Seddon, was to "preclude the passage of dangerous and disaffected persons." The permit system guarded against spies, smugglers, subversives, and men who sought to evade conscription. By the fall of 1864, however, the borders of the Confederacy were open to all of these elements. In the region that comprised western North and South Carolina, East Tennessee, and southwest Virginia, states and military authorities could not prevent the movement of Federal recruiters into their territory and the subsequent departure of thousands of men whose military service the Confederacy demanded. Southerners who joined the Union army engaged in continual raids across the borders of the Carolinas in the winter of 1864–65. The Federal enemy built a portion of its forces out of southern men who broke the borders of the Confederacy when they left as "disaffected persons" and when they returned as raiders wearing the uniform of the U.S. Army.[4]

Protection of a state's borders in the Confederate federal system was the responsibility of two organizations: the state itself, using the state militias that were legally bound to remain within its borders, and whatever Confederate military department was superimposed over that state, using Confederate forces assigned to the department. By 1864, the Confederacy had no clearly established boundaries to its various military departments that crossed over the Appalachians. As pressures on state borders multiplied in the form of guerrilla raids, Federal recruiting excursions, and Federal invasions, the confused Confederate military departments hampered an effective response. State officials and commanders of Confederate units stationed within the various military departments, in order to meet immediate emergencies, created ad hoc alliances with entities in other states and departments, often bypassing completely the official Confederate military departments within which they supposedly operated. By the end of the year, state militia units were crossing state borders to meet threats and Confederate military units were ignoring the commands of immediate superiors. The lack of clear jurisdictions made it more difficult to contain the movement of people and armies that threatened the Confederacy's existence. Fugitive Federals traveled through a land with increasingly unfeasible and meaningless borders.

After being lost for four days in the wilderness of laurel, Mattocks's party chanced upon an organization that represented the confused jurisdictions within the Confederacy. On November 28, the travelers found a well-marked trail that led northwest into Tennessee. The state line was just over a mile away. As the party started down the trail, they spotted a house at the base of a mountain. A heated debate ensued. Three men were willing to risk recapture and wanted to approach the house to obtain food, considering that several in the party were on the brink of complete physical breakdown, and the lost guide was unsure whether it was seven miles or twenty miles to the nearest Union settlement; the others desired to press forward considering that help in Tennessee must be in reach within twenty-four hours. The party split, with Mattocks, Hunt, and Litchfield joining the larger group that moved on. After a short distance, however, the guide decided to go back to the house. Five men refused to go backward, and the party split again, with the Maine trio following the guide. The house turned out to be deserted, so the fugitives followed an old road that led away from it in the hope of finding another dwelling.

Their exhaustion and confusion undermined their caution. They straggled along in small groups at different paces. Hunt fell behind the entire group because of an injured foot and lost sight of any of his companions. Suddenly, he heard two shots. He limped to a clearing, saw an abandoned mill, and tried to climb through the window. A juvenile voice ordered him to come down. He obeyed the fifteen-year-old with the long rifle; Hunt quickly assessed the boy knew how to use it. Meanwhile, Mattocks and two other men were caught completely unaware when two white men and a Lufty Indian jumped from a hiding place at a bend in the road, leveled weapons at the Yankees, and demanded surrender. The unfortunate captives complied immediately, without resistance. "We thought we were fortunate not to be killed by the blood-thirsty 'Yahoos,'" Mattocks remarked. His captors led him to the house of a man named Joe Gunter, where Mattocks found the rest of the fugitives who had returned to the house being guarded by Indians, and as he put it, "worse than Indians—just such aborations of humanity as had captured us." At 2:00 in the afternoon, their Indian captors marched them under guard to Quallatown, the headquarters of the Lufty who were members of Thomas's Legion, a unique Confederate military unit whose operations within the Appalachian Mountains defied political and military boundaries.[5]

The legion was the brainchild of William Holland Thomas, an antebellum merchant, land speculator, and railroad promoter who understood the regional trade connections between western North Carolina, East Tennessee, western South Carolina, and northern Georgia. A band of Cherokees in western North Carolina, the Lufty, adopted him and chose him to represent them in Washington, D.C., during the 1830s. He advocated for them effectively and secured their protection from removal to Oklahoma. In May 1861, Thomas organized 200 of the Lufty into a two-company battalion for local defense and inaugurated plans to create a legion—a unit that contained artillery, cavalry, and infantry and thus could function as a small army—to protect the region where portions of different states connected within the Appalachian Mountains. In this rugged terrain, Thomas believed, fighting would not involve large field armies and set-piece battles, but rather skirmishes to control mountain passes, communication lines, and crossroad villages. When Confederate authorities nixed his initial plans, the entrepreneur traveled to South Carolina in February 1862 and obtained the governor and Executive Council's approval to use his proposed unit to protect the passes between the Carolinas and Georgia. During the summer of 1862, with permission of the Confederate government, Thomas organized the "Highland Rangers," a unit comprising companies of Lufty Indians and companies of whites recruited from western North Carolina, East Tennessee, and Virginia. The companies were scattered; some guarded the vital East Tennessee & Virginia Railroad near Knoxville, while others protected mountain passes in North Carolina. Although the command evolved into the designation Thomas's Legion, and eventually comprised an infantry regiment that served in the Shenandoah Valley in the fall of 1864, detached companies in North Carolina and East Tennessee, and an artillery battery, it was never a real legion and never did its component parts serve together.[6]

At the time that Lufty members of Thomas's Legion were marching Charlie Mattocks to Quallatown, the unit was emblematic of the broken Confederate command structure and the hopelessly tangled political and military jurisdictions that operated across the Carolinas, East Tennessee, and southwest Virginia. Obtaining food for the Lufty members of the legion was a convoluted process that bypassed North Carolina authorities. Earlier in the year, Lufty families were living on weeds and bark. Thomas did not have a quartermaster or commissary and could not draw supplies through available military channels in the state. He wrote

Governor Milledge Bonham of South Carolina with a reminder that the Lufty forces were necessary for the defense of the entire region and with a request that South Carolina would provide subsistence for the legion and for Lufty families in North Carolina. Bonham forwarded the letter to General P. G. T. Beauregard, then in command of the Department of South Carolina, Georgia, and Florida, who transferred stores from a commissary in Anderson to Walhalla. Thomas bought this grain, rice, and other foodstuffs with his private funds and transported them by wagon from Walhalla to Quallatown.[7]

A military department with no jurisdiction over the legion supplied the unit's companies in North Carolina, and it was unclear to authorities in Richmond what military department in fact governed the legion. From the start of the war, President Jefferson Davis had struggled to create effective regional military departments and to unite them under a coherent chain of command. Davis initially appointed Samuel Cooper, the highest-ranking general in the Confederate army in 1861, as adjutant and inspector general, a position Davis intended to function as chief of staff for the army. Before the Union did, Davis established the rudiments of a modern command system, but he appointed as head a man incapable of fulfilling his role. By 1864, Cooper's office was bogged down in trivialities, and the various Confederate military departments were still operating independently of surrounding departments. Davis often coordinated movement across departmental lines, but he issued discretionary instructions rather than direct orders, which enabled military commanders to debate or simply to ignore requests to send troops to another military department. Davis, Cooper, and Secretary of War Seddon regularly received reports from and issued orders to subordinate officers in military departments without informing the overall commander of the department.[8]

The problem of divided responsibility was evident when Richmond authorities confronted complaints in November 1864 that Thomas's Legion was not under the proper control of any department commander. The legion was in the District of Western North Carolina, and for months no one had been sure whether the district was part of the Department of North Carolina and Southern Virginia or the Department of East Tennessee and West Virginia. To make matters more complicated, Beauregard commanded the Military Division of the West, which supposedly encompassed all of Tennessee, yet the commander of the Department of East Tennessee and West Virginia issued orders regardless of

Beauregard. General Robert E. Lee, commander of the Department of Northern Virginia, also issued orders to officers in the Department of East Tennessee and West Virginia. His correspondence at the time indicated that he was utterly confused about the troops stationed in the region and whose command they were under.[9]

The Lufty Indians of the legion were caught in the quagmire of competing military departments in the Appalachians. Colonel John B. Palmer, who commanded the mountain subdistrict of the District of Western North Carolina, complained to the War Department that Thomas repeatedly defied his orders. Palmer requested control over the legion. Governor Zebulon Vance likewise wrote Seddon that Thomas was "worse than useless" and "a positive injury to that country." Vance was furious that Thomas undermined the state's attempt to control the deserter problem in the mountains. Thomas recruited deserters from other Confederate units for the legion, enrolled them in his companies, and allowed them to stay and defend their homes. Vance wanted Palmer replaced with someone who could control the troops in the district and who was better fitted for field service. Seddon forwarded Vance's letter to Davis for consideration with the comment that he was surprised to hear these complaints, as he considered both Palmer and Thomas to be particularly efficient. Davis returned Seddon's letter with the simple question, "Is not Brig-Gen Martin in command of the District of Western North Carolina?" Four days later, Seddon shamefacedly replied that James G. Martin was indeed in command. The Confederate secretary of war was unaware of who was really in charge amid the muddled boundaries of Confederate military jurisdictions in the region. The legion, as did other forces in the Appalachians, moved in and out of the boundaries of these confused jurisdictions without orders from the top and under the authority of company commanders. Lufty scouts regularly raided East Tennessee on their own impetus.[10]

Federal zones of occupation and recruitment overlay the Confederacy's claimed regions of dominion, further complicating the landscape through which fugitives moved and presenting another threat to state borders within the Confederacy. J. Madison Drake's escape party encountered the gamut of Union scouts, guides, and recruiters who ranged across portions of northwest South Carolina, western North Carolina, north Georgia, East Tennessee, and southwest Virginia from their bases in central and East Tennessee and southwest Kentucky. Loyalists from East Tennessee instigated the Union army's interest in recruiting soldiers from the region. In the first year of the war, an estimated 12,000 of them made a hazardous journey to Kentucky rather than submit to Confederate governance in Tennessee. An increasingly organized and complex network of Unionists during the first two years of the war smuggled thousands of recruits from Tennessee and North Carolina to Union lines in Kentucky, where they joined Tennessee, Kentucky, or other state regiments. A class of professional pilots emerged who earned a living guiding recruits; the most famous of these, Daniel Ellis, claimed he personally escorted more than 4,000 men, a figure accepted by those who witnessed his activities. After the Union army occupied Knoxville in September 1863, Major General Ambrose Burnside launched efforts to create and recruit regiments with North Carolina state designations. Officers and scouts on the Federal payroll spread into the western counties of that state and down into South Carolina and Georgia. Eventually 10,000 white and black men from North Carolina joined the Union army.[11]

These recruiting efforts successfully brought hundreds of southerners through the collapsing borders of this part of the Confederacy during the last winter of the war. Fugitive Federals who traveled through western North Carolina and East Tennessee in November and December encountered Federal officers collecting men for Companies F and H of the Third North Carolina Mounted Infantry, commanded by Greene County, Tennessee, native Lieutenant Colonel George W. Kirk. All fourteen of North Carolina's mountain counties contributed men to the regiment, and its roster boasted enlistees from South Carolina, Virginia, and Tennessee. For several months Kirk's men had effectively demonstrated that North Carolina could not protect its western border. In June, a couple hundred of them rode into Morganton, set fire to the conscript rendezvous located there, wrecked the railroad depot, and recruited forty men for the regiment. During the rest of the year, the Third North Carolina continually harassed the weak Confederate forces in the region. Cross-border raids contributed to the spiraling irregular wars within western North Carolina and the breakdown of Confederate control in the counties there.[12]

Escaped prisoners traveling to Knoxville banded together with recruits for the regiment. Federals met them along the roads or inside the homes of the loyalist network that incorporated fugitive Yankees into the system of guides, safe-houses, and alarms established to funnel recruits to East Tennessee. A woman in the Pickens District of South Carolina escorted fugitive Hannibal Johnson and his three companions to an outlier camp. Confederate deserters and loyal Union men living in the caves there had told her to bring any escaped Yankees their way; they wanted to join the Union army and hoped to travel with some of its officers to Knoxville. They formed a party of forty-six well-armed men, although fourteen of the South Carolinians turned back a few days later in North Carolina, frightened at the snow and the rumors that Lufty companies of Thomas's Legion were on the prowl.[13]

Drake, Todd, Grant, and Lewis joined with a larger group of recruits. After surviving his terrible night on Grandfather Mountain, Drake was relieved to find that his thirteen Carolina companions did not abandon him. Two days later, the party reached the valley of Crab Orchard, Tennessee, where they met Lieutenant James Hartley of the Third North Carolina, who counseled them to wait until the snow melted before traveling further. Here the fugitives joined fortunes with sixty-three men and women from the mountain counties of North Carolina and Tennessee on their way to enlist the men in the Union army. All seventy-six travelers found shelter and food with local residents. When the journey resumed, the party met two boys armed with carbines and dressed in the full uniform of the Thirteenth Tennessee Cavalry (Union), who advised them on current troop movements in East Tennessee. Based on that information, the group decided to head for Union lines at Bull's Gap, Tennessee. That night, the fugitives found more residents of the valley willing to aid them. On the morning of November 7, as Drake was shaving for the first time in six months, he heard the horn warning that Rebel guerrillas were approaching. Regardless of a badly swollen knee, Drake ran out the back door, jumped a rail fence, and ran up the mountain behind the house. Soon Lewis, Grant, Todd, and Estes joined him on the summit. They hid in caves while the armed mountain men deployed as guards. Once again "the ravages of the merciless lice" kept Drake awake all night. He quipped that lice from just one state would not have been such a bother, but he was visited by large delegations from Virginia, South Carolina, Georgia, North Carolina, and Tennessee. The lice crossed state borders as easily as Federal raiders.[14]

When the Yankees and their southern mountain companions reached the end of the valley the next morning, they halted and debated the best route. Fortuitously, at just that moment, Ephraim A. Davis, an officer from the Thirteenth Tennessee Cavalry who had recently joined the Third North Carolina, arrived on the scene in his fatigue uniform of the Union army. Davis had just left Knoxville on a recruiting expedition into western North Carolina and was happy to turn back and guide the recruits who had unexpectedly fallen into his lap. He led them through a fearfully dangerous crossing of the Nolichucky River at a place where the torrent dashed down a steep mountain. The party climbed the mountain on the right bank of the river in single file, each member compelled to follow exactly in the tracks of the one before, using roots of trees for balance on the narrow projecting crags that served as the only foothold. Drake was terrified of falling into the "seething cauldron" of water below. At the top, a flat-bottomed boat attached to a rope ferried the party across in small groups. That night, they slept in the home of another officer of the Third North Carolina, whose family surrendered their only bed to the Yankees.[15]

The next morning the party resumed its trek toward Bull's Gap. Unbeknownst to them, they were headed right into the middle of a Confederate offensive originating from southwest Virginia. Major General John C. Breckinridge, commander of the Confederate Department of East Tennessee and West Virginia, advanced from Virginia with about 2,500 troops and surprised a brigade of inexperienced Tennesseans under Brigadier General Alvan C. Gillem at Bull's Gap on November 11. That afternoon, Drake stood on a ridge looking down at Greeneville, Tennessee, in the valley below. Suddenly, Confederate cavalry appeared on a parallel ridge two miles away. Lieutenant Davis and the armed men sprinted ahead, took up positions along the road, and checked the Rebels. After climbing another mountain, and gazing across another beautiful valley, Drake saw Bull's Gap in the distance. He also saw smoke rising from the valley and heard the roar of musketry and cannon. These were ominous signs. When the party reached a small village, a young woman who lived there volunteered to reconnoiter. By this point in their experience with mountain women, the fugitives did not blink at the sight of one of them riding her filly toward the sounds of battle. She returned at dusk with bad news. Gillem's forces were shattered and streaming back toward Knoxville. The Confederates possessed the bridges and other approaches to Bull's Gap.[16]

Drake described the next two days as "constant mental torment." They stayed in the little village, hearing news that Confederate forces now controlled the railroad between Strawberry Plains, Tennessee, and Bristol, Virginia. Confederate partisans from North Carolina massacred Unionists three miles from the village, plundered houses, and drove away herds of cattle and horses. It was clear the travelers could not remain where they were, so on November 13 they marched on and took shelter that night in a small ravine. At 3:00 in the morning, Rebel guerrillas charged into the pitch-dark camp. Drake heard "demonic yells" and saw flashes when the Rebels fired their guns. It was every man for himself. Drake ran, fell, and crashed into trees that he could not see. Daylight found him alone in an eerie silence. He waited. Lieutenant Davis and a few others appeared, including Lewis. Eventually thirty-seven men gathered. Todd and Grant were missing. The depressed and exhausted voyagers, after a lengthy debate, decided to risk the journey to Knoxville.[17]

Rebel guerrillas from North Carolina and northern Georgia were a real danger to fugitives on the journey through East Tennessee, a landscape infested with internal violence exacerbated by frequent raids across the border. The final leg of the expedition for escaped prisoners of war was through a place that had never fit neatly into designated borders, inhabited by people who had a history of wanting to redraw political lines. Immediately after the American Revolution, settlers on the Nolichucky and Holston Rivers, who lived in areas claimed by North Carolina, tried and failed to create the state of Franklin. They became part of Tennessee in 1796, but East Tennessee had little in common with the rest of the state. Trade, and eventually railroads, tied East Tennessee to western North Carolina, northern Georgia, and southwest Virginia rather than to Middle Tennessee. Its residents were poorer and a smaller percentage were slaveholders than the rest of the state. The majority in East Tennessee viewed secession as a conspiracy of slaveholders, felt alienated from the rest of the South, and remained staunchly and ideologically loyal to the Union. A convention at Greeneville in June 1861 petitioned the Tennessee legislature for permission to form a separate state. Unionists formed military companies, seized control of many counties, escaped to the Union army in Kentucky, and fomented a brief rebellion against Confederate rule in November that required 10,000 troops to suppress. Partisan and guerrilla violence for the next two years turned East Tennessee counties into battle zones. When the Federal army captured Knoxville in September 1863, military commanders faced the monumental tasks of protecting East Tennessee from conventional Confederate forces operating out of Georgia, North Carolina, and Virginia, coming to grips with the guerrilla violence that infested rural areas, and suppressing the activities of Confederate supporters.[18]

The office of the provost marshal general was the centerpiece of Federal efforts to restore order in the region. Brigadier General Samuel P.

Carter, a native East Tennessean, possessed broad governing powers, including jurisdiction in all civil matters. His agency, with deputy marshals in each county, executed Union occupation policies, including administering loyalty oaths and arresting men and women suspected of Confederate sympathies. Through Carter's initiative, the Federal department commander created the "National Guard of Tennessee," self-defense units that were armed by the United States and that acted as a police force in East Tennessee counties. Members were empowered to arrest "suspicious characters" and citizens who committed "acts of oppression and cruelty" against Unionists. Carter, on the theory that "self-defense is a law of nature," authorized any citizen to shoot on sight guerrillas and horse thieves. Although Carter reined in the worst abuses of the "National Guard," Union policy ultimately encouraged rather than suppressed continual partisan violence in East Tennessee, as fugitive Federals such as Drake discovered during their dangerous journey through the area.[19]

Unionist guerrillas from East Tennessee were no more static than their Rebel counterparts. Their continual raids into the Confederacy were among the multiple threats to state borders in the winter of 1864–65, another being the movements of Sherman's army in Georgia. Because the Confederate military departments did not adequately safeguard the borders between East Tennessee and the Carolinas, or effectively obstruct the Federal force threatening South Carolina, both North and South Carolina retracted their legislation that prohibited state militia units and the forces of the Junior and Senior Confederate Reserves from crossing over state lines. On November 23, 1864, the Confederate government suspended for a period of sixty days the law that restricted reserves to service within their state. South Carolina authorized the governor to send militia units out of state on December 6. North Carolina Home Guard and reserve units crossed into southwest Virginia to meet a Federal advance the same month.[20]

States were willing to cross the lines they drew at the beginning of the war because conventional Federal invasions broke through borders and required an ad hoc regional response cobbled together out of parts taken from the various dysfunctional Confederate departments. Willard Worcester Glazier, in his desperate attempt to catch up with Sherman's army in Georgia, continually crossed paths with the Confederate and state troops being shifted across the increasingly futile state and departmental borders. When he and Lemon had approached Augusta, they saw a train full of South Carolina militia troops on their way to Grahamville, South Carolina, located near the Charleston & Savannah Railroad, where a few days earlier units of the Georgia militia fought the Battle of Honey Hill, on November 30. The Yankees' journey then took them across the Savannah River. Confederate officials had patched together a defense of the Georgia–South Carolina border out of Confederate troops and reserves culled from two separate Confederate military departments (the Department of North Carolina and Southern Virginia and the Department of South Carolina, Georgia, and Florida), and state militia units from Georgia and South Carolina that had permission to move back and forth across the state line as needed to meet the military emergency.[21]

Sherman's operations after the fall of Atlanta ultimately pierced the borders of three states and three Confederate military departments. Glazier's journey to Savannah punctured the boundaries of his physical and mental endurance. Just as the natural elements in the Appalachian Mountains pushed Drake and Mattocks to their limits, the swamps of Georgia nearly defeated Glazier, and he too encountered multitudes on the move through the inhospitable environment. On December 7, Glazier and Lemon reached a hut belonging to African American fishermen who lived on the Savannah River near Point Comfort. One of them retrieved an old canoe and spent several hours caulking it while the Yankees hid in a hollow cypress log. At midnight the three men pushed off, but within a few hours the boat sank. The fugitives parted with their guide and headed into the cypress swamp that extended for three miles in width on either side of the river. Bayous, small streams, cypress stumps ten feet tall, and trailing Spanish moss interspersed in the landscape. They wandered all day in the swamps, frightened to see alligators dropping off logs into the water as they approached.[22]

Escaped Yankees hated southern swamps for both physical and cultural reasons. The discomfort was intense: wading through filthy water and sticky mud that reached to the chest, tripping over submerged logs and plunging face first into the water, enduring the constant pricks of briars, annoyed by gnats, mosquitoes, and small stinging flies, afraid every moment of the alligators and water moccasins. At night, the "nameless horrors of our own imaginations" tormented them. Miasma theory taught mid-nineteenth-century Americans that swamps emitted harmful vapors. Soldiers in the Civil War associated the putrid smell with malaria and other fevers. And a swamp's very wildness reminded them that they traveled through a hostile and uncivilized land. Northerners believed that science and technology allowed civilized humans to control and improve nature through cultivation. But southerners practiced shifting cultivation, which abandoned large plots of land to their natural state, and free-ranged their stock rather than enclose them in fences. Union soldiers in the South saw "wilderness" wherever they looked around them, an unimproved landscape that savage southerners did not control properly. Lieutenant Colonel Aaron M. Flory of the Forty-Sixth Indiana, who escaped in November from Camp Ford in Texas, put into apt words what his compatriots in the east experienced. After traveling hundreds of miles through swamps, tangled growths of timber, and twelve-foot-high blackberry briers, he reached a cornfield, or as he put it, "the limit of civilization."[23]

Glazier soon discovered that the Georgia swamps were a wilderness teeming with human beings. He and Lemon finally reached a cornfield skirting the swamp and found a slave possessing helpful information. They were only a few miles from Waynesboro, the scene of a fight eight days before between Federal and Confederate cavalry. Major General Joseph Wheeler's Rebels were now patrolling the roads. The slave procured them a guide who knew where Wheeler's pickets were located. They barely avoided one of the patrols but safely reached a hiding place in another swamp. The fugitives waded across three large streams and got soaked to the bone. On December 11, Glazier and Lemon reached a road that ran between Station No. 1 and Millen. The Federal Fourteenth Army Corps had marched along that road only a week before. "There were evident traces of their passage," Glazier remarked in an understatement. Smoke rose from charred and blackened buildings. Torn haversacks, blankets, hardtack, broken muskets, and dead mules littered the ground around them. It was, the veteran soldiers recognized, "the debris which may always be found in the desolating track of a large army." To these Yankees it was a welcome sight. They now had the track of Sherman's army and a clear path to follow.[24]

For the next few days, Glazier and Lemon encountered other travelers on the same trail through the swamps. Smoke drew them to the camp of two "interesting contrabands," a husband and wife who had followed Sherman from Burke County, Georgia, and joined a colony of 500 freedmen living on an island in Big Ebenezer Creek. Rebels shelled the island, so the couple fled into the swamps. They had decided to head back home, confident that slavery was dead, and that the old plantation was safer than the vicinity of Sherman's army. Glazier and Lemon callously forced

"Sambo" to seek food. He objected to the risk, but the Yankees detained his wife "as a hostage for his safe return." When the man brought back sweet potatoes, the masterly white men made it clear the couple was no longer welcome, and the Georgians left the fire and the food in the Yankees' possession. They were sixty miles from the city of Savannah.[25]

The movement of freedmen behind Sherman's army ultimately deprived the fugitives of the help they had come to rely upon. As they traveled, the countryside was increasingly stripped of food. "There are very few negroes left to befriend us," Glazier recorded mournfully. He and Lemon followed the corduroy roads that Sherman's pioneers had built through the swamps. They had to flank the pickets of Wheeler's cavalry to do so, at one point wading through water up to the armpit and taking two hours to move just 200 yards. They crossed Big Ebenezer Creek and found an island with garments and blankets strewn around the charred remains of a fire. After a good night's sleep at the abandoned camp and the fortuitous discovery of a boat, they paddled downstream, past the body of a dead Federal cavalryman lying on the bank. When they saw two horses tied to a tree, they swapped modes of transportation, and enjoyed the freedom of a brisk ride. When the countryside became too open, they let the horses go and paddled across Little Ebenezer Creek on two broken planks. The Yankees were twenty miles from Savannah and feeling confident in their ultimate success when they heard the dreaded words, "Who comes there?" spoken from the shade of some cypress trees. One of Wheeler's picket guards stepped forward, and they were captives once more.[26]

The moment of recapture, especially when so close to the destination, was an emotional one. Reactions varied according to personality and circumstance. One Wisconsin captain, whose family thought he had died at the Battle of the Wilderness, threw his cap to the ground, burst into tears, and replied to the demand for surrender, "My God, what do you expect us to do?" Another fugitive calmly asked, "Have you Johnnies anything to eat and any tobacco about you?" Charlie Mattocks worked himself into a towering rage. He filled his diary with sarcastic observations about the "yahoos" and "aborations" who guarded him, and bitterly mulled over the decision to turn back to the house rather than proceed forward. As one member of the party put it, "All our hardship and suffering had been lost for want of only two hours more endurance." The Maine trio had ample time to indulge their regret. They spent three days imprisoned in Quallatown and then marched to Asheville under strict Lufty Indian guards. There Mattocks enjoyed a respite because he was a Freemason. Local members of his order visited him with food, clothes, and money. The prisoners marched another sixty miles to Morganton, where they were put on a train for the prison at Danville, Virginia. They arrived on December 11, and Mattocks wrote, "By my table of distances we have marched 413 miles & ridden by cars 140 miles—all for nothing!" His bitterness increased when he later learned that his name had been called for exchange in Columbia two days after his escape. He would have been home in November if he had stayed put.[27]

Glazier, like so many other fugitives in his situation, refused to concede defeat. He was determined to escape again. "I should never return to South Carolina, a prisoner," he told Lemon. "It was quite as well to be hung by bushwhackers or torn to pieces by hounds in Georgia, as to return to South Carolina to meet a miserable death from starvation and exposure." Glazier misidentified the immediate threat, however, which became clear when the picket accused the Yankees of being spies rather than escaped prisoners of war, a charge that carried the death penalty. The officer of the picket guard sent Glazier and Lemon to Wheeler's headquarters at Springfield. Glazier faked a foot injury and pretended he could walk no farther so that he was allowed a mount. At the first opportunity, he made a break for it, but unluckily the horse ran right through the camp of Terry's Texas Rangers. The western horsemen easily chased Glazier down. When he and Lemon reached Springfield, Wheeler sent the Yankees to the county jail, then tried them before a military commission on charges of spying. The trial was no farce. The officers, members of Wheeler's staff, asked the fugitives where they were captured and where they escaped, found them not guilty of spying, and ordered the Yankees to Waynesboro along with fifteen recently captured prisoners from Sherman's Fourteenth Army Corps. Along the way, Glazier escaped with Lieutenant John W. Wright of the Tenth Iowa, another recaptured escapee from Columbia. Wright led his new partner to the hut of a slave who had helped him before. Of this man Glazier remarked, "His heart was as white as his skin was black."[28]

For the next four days, Glazier and Wright trudged through swamps and skirted pickets of Confederate cavalry. The big Iowan was wearing a sturdy pair of shoes he had obtained from slaves during his first escape journey, and at points he carried the weak and fainting Glazier, who now weighed less than ninety pounds. On December 22, they met a slave who informed them they had passed the last of the Rebel outposts. The

Yankees possessed a hill only eight miles away. The slave took them to the home of a free black family named Jones. The husband was out on a scout, but the wife volunteered the services of her eight- and six-year-old sons. Glazier posted the older on the road and ordered the younger to serve as lookout. When Jones returned, he procured the Yankees a reliable guide named March Dasher, who knew the exact location of every Yankee picket in the area. The next morning, December 23, Dasher took them straight to the pickets of the 101st Illinois, Twentieth Army Corps, who welcomed the fugitives with open arms and open haversacks. When they got to Savannah, Glazier and Wright were put under guard until their identity could be corroborated. Fortunately, Wright's old regiment, the Tenth Iowa, was there, and after his comrades confirmed his story, he and Glazier enjoyed a "reception almost equal to Caesar's triumph in Rome, after his brilliant campaign in North Africa."[29]

In the end, as Glazier knew on his day of triumph, and as Mattocks learned to his sorrow, the competence of a guide mattered to the fortunes of escaped prisoners, especially when the party grew to incorporate recruits for the Union army and other wanderers. John V. Hadley and his humorous friend Homer Chisman ultimately hit the jackpot in that regard, although the Holinsworth sisters made a disastrous first choice. After four days with the young women in Flat Rock, North Carolina, who "rebuilt us with new life and new hope," Hadley, Chisman, Baker, and Good started for Tennessee with Jack and Jerry Vance, deserters and outlaws, who told the Yankees they had "resolved to turn the war to their advantage." Their gang of eight men plundered, looted, and terrorized the countryside. The night before they met up with the Yankees, they stole $102 in silver from a local doctor. "As cruel as was the treatment, it was hard to prevent a smile to hear those wild men talk about how they made the negroes dance for their lives," Hadley wrote.[30]

Hadley and Chisman were among the Yankees traveling in the Appalachians who were unsure what posed the greatest threat to them: the environment, the Rebels, or their mountain companions. They made a dangerous crossing of the French Broad River over the remains of an old bridge. When they reached Mount Pisgah, located where the boundaries of Buncombe, Henderson, and Transylvania Counties cross, they spotted a number of fires in the distance. The Vance brothers refused to go any farther. The fugitives begged and offered more money. But the outlaws left them alone on the mountain and returned home. The Yankees had no compass and no way of figuring out the direction once the sun went down. Knowing they could not survive without a guide, they walked to the nearest settlement, South Hominy Creek, in Buncombe County. Just a few hours before, a company of Lufty Indians had attacked the village and arrested two men who sheltered deserters. An old man sitting alone outside his cabin told the Yankees about the skirmish and informed them that Henry "Kim" Davis was the man they needed. Davis had been through the mountains to Knoxville twice and was looking to travel north for good if he could get some company. The Yankees met Davis and two members of his gang in a gorge, where the fugitives endured a "cunning and sagacious" questioning. When Davis was satisfied, he made his proposition. He did not want to join the Union army because he was tired of war and killing. He had endured enough to excuse him from doing anything more. He wanted the Yankees to promise that once they got to Knoxville, they would conduct him north of the Ohio River and protect him from the army. They promised. Seven days later, on December 10, Davis delivered them safely to Knoxville. He never made a mistake on the 160-mile route.[31]

If Hadley was more fortunate than Mattocks in his guide through the mountains, he was also more fortunate than Drake in how the timing of his movement converged with the movement of guerrillas and armies across the landscape with porous borders. Exactly one month earlier in November, when Drake and his party were on the road, companies of Confederate forces from the District of Western North Carolina were skirmishing in East Tennessee against the Third North Carolina, Major General John C. Breckinridge and his small Confederate army were moving toward Knoxville from southwest Virginia, and Confederate partisans were raiding through two East Tennessee counties. In early December, when Hadley's party made it through, Union major general George Stoneman launched a major raid from Knoxville toward southwest Virginia. Union troops from southern Kentucky under Major General Stephen Burbridge also advanced. The tandem movements drove Breckinridge out of East Tennessee and drew most Confederate forces from the District of Western North Carolina to the northeast of the fugitive Yankees' path. The Federals proceeded into southwest Virginia, tore up the railroad for over twenty miles beyond the state line, and destroyed important lead mines and saltworks.[32]

The closest action to Hadley's escape party was at Paint Rock, North Carolina, some sixty-two miles north of them. On December 6, Stoneman sent the Fourth Tennessee and the Third North Carolina to hold the mountain passes into western North Carolina during the advance against Breckinridge. Rebel cavalry who were part of John C. Vaughn's command harassed these units and roamed the countryside between Paint Rock and Newport, Tennessee. Confederate forces from Asheville attacked the Federals at Paint Rock on December 7 and forced their retreat. During the rest of the month, Confederate troops stationed at Asheville, North Carolina Guard for Home Defense units from the mountain counties, and portions of Thomas's Legion fought, raided, and foraged against the Third North Carolina back and forth across the permeable line between western North Carolina and East Tennessee.[33]

The ever-present combination of divided responsibility and a broken command structure hampered Confederate defense in the region. To meet the threat of Federal forces moving into Virginia from East Tennessee, Confederate military authorities needed to coordinate forces stationed both in southwest Virginia and in western North Carolina, but these forces were not in the same military department. Breckinridge had not left clear orders to his subordinates holding positions in southwest Virginia, and they were not sure whether to advance to his aid or to maintain defensive positions. One of them telegraphed Robert E. Lee, who ordered that troops erect defensive works and hold the line at New River, Virginia. But the colonel commanding the forces at New River disputed the authority of the officer who issued the orders and telegraphed Breckinridge that he was ready to advance. Meanwhile, other officers in the Department of East Tennessee and West Virginia fretted over the question of whether to communicate with Lee or Breckinridge and dithered for three days rather than taking action. Breckinridge ordered a forward movement on December 20, but the delay meant that it was too late. Federal forces captured Saltville, Virginia, that day. Meanwhile, Colonel John B. Palmer of the District of Western North Carolina had the typical discretionary orders from Richmond to cooperate with Breckinridge "as much as possible." The orders did not give Breckinridge command over Palmer's troops even though they would be operating in Breckinridge's department. Palmer moved a portion of his forces into East Tennessee with the intention of hitting the main Federal army from behind, but by the time he arrived, Stoneman was already in Virginia. Palmer chose to chase the Third North Carolina back to Knoxville, but as he did so, a segment of his command returned to North Carolina without his permission or that of Breckinridge.[34]

When Federal troop movements threatened multiple Confederate military departments, commanders in the respective jurisdictions were supposed to voluntarily cooperate with each other. But in the winter of 1864–65, in the region comprising the western Carolinas, East Tennessee, and southwest Virginia, these efforts broke down. As borders collapsed, and the swirling movement of armies, stragglers, refugees, recruits, guerrillas, deserters, and escaped prisoners revealed how porous state lines really were, ordinary soldiers from western North Carolina returned to their local counties to defend the only boundary they had left: the one around their homes.

On their own quest to return home, Yankee fugitives found that the final few miles presented the ultimate test of their physical endurance. Their bodies were on the brink of collapse. Because most of them had been several months in Confederate prisons before their escape, they did not begin the journey in peak physical health. Exposure to the elements, hard marching over challenging terrain, and long periods without nutrition, punctuated by orgies of eating if food was available, produced a variety of illnesses and physical disabilities. Civil War soldiers believed that certain environments were hostile to their health, and they developed "self-care" routines to prevent illness, including eradicating pests, drinking fresh water, supplementing rations, and finding creative ways to remain clean. Prisoners of war and fugitives on the run were rarely able to do any of these things. Their biggest problem was lack of clothing. Fugitives were most often incapacitated by blistered, raw, and bleeding feet. The shoes they were wearing in prison, if they had any, did not last long on the journey. One fugitive subtitled the book describing his escape as "The Time That Tried Men's Soles."[35]

As Drake trudged along after the guerrilla attack in the ravine, his shoeless feet were in agony. One of the Carolinians wrapped them in rabbit skins. Then Lieutenant Davis conversationally remarked that the party was near the home of a Rebel who had shot and killed one of his men from the Third North Carolina. Drake determined to steal a pair of shoes from the murderer. Davis handed Drake a revolver. Drake went alone to the man's home and was rather proud of the scene that followed. He lingered over it when he published his narrative. When Drake leveled the revolver at the man and demanded his shoes, a pretty eighteen-year-old girl flung herself between Drake and her father. She begged the Yankee not to take her father's only pair of shoes and promised to give him a different pair. When a search of the house revealed no other shoes, she pathetically and dramatically exclaimed that he could have her own. "She showed true grief, and a spunk worthy of a better cause," Drake remarked. He pulled a shoe off her foot and attempted to put it on. She sobbed aloud, and he told her to "dry up." Drake walked off with the man's shoes, swinging the revolver "in a careless and independent sort of manner." "I would have tipped my hat to the lady," he wrote, "but I didn't happen to have such an article of wear about me." The shoes were much too big for Drake, and after an attempt to stuff them with hay did not work, he gave them to another member of the party.[36]

The next day, still shoeless, Drake feared that he would have to give up. The weather was cold and frosty. His feet were so lacerated he doubted he could wear shoes should any that fit be found. His companions ribbed him as he hobbled along awkwardly, telling him that he "was much better than a dozen dead men." On November 16, the party flanked Sevierville, Tennessee, just as it was being sacked by Confederate cavalry. They spent that night at the home of a Unionist named Thomas who was packing his family to leave for Knoxville in the morning. The stop was Drake's salvation. At the moment when Drake's feet could endure no more, Thomas provided the Yankee with a horse. "I had not felt so much confidence in myself in a long while," Drake said. "Mounted thus, I felt I was 'myself again.'"[37]

The next morning the fugitives, the recruits, and a large number of men, women, and children from Thomas's neighborhood set out for the short journey that would put them in Knoxville by the end of the day. Drake galloped ahead of his party, savoring the feeling of freedom. Suddenly he spotted blue-coated soldiers from a Pennsylvania cavalry regiment standing in the roadway. They demanded that Drake dismount. He showed them his commission and announced he was an escaped prisoner. The men embraced him, slapped him on the back, and jostled him with joy. Drake had reached "God's Country," the phrase escaped prisoners of war used to describe Union lines that divided "Freedom, Enlightenment, Loyalty" from "Slavery, Bigotry, Treachery." Shortly afterward, Lewis and the rest of the party arrived. The officer of the guard provided an escort across the Holston River to Knoxville for the fugitive Yankees, and an hour later Drake and Lewis, along with twelve other escaped prisoners of war, stood before the provost marshal general of that occupied city. Four of them were enlisted men who escaped from Florence on September 17 during the mutiny. Todd and Grant, the companions Drake lost in the ravine, reported in two weeks later.[38]

Drake did not record what he thought and felt at his first glimpse of God's Country. Perhaps he found those feelings to be anticlimactic. Nearly one month later, when Hadley gazed down upon the fortifications of Knoxville from the crest of a hill and saw Federal soldiers drilling on a lawn, he and his companions simply stood in silence. "We looked congratulations at each other. We did not fall down and give up the ghost. We did not go into ecstasies. We did not hug each other as some have done. We did not cry. We simply felt good and went on," he later wrote. Perhaps Drake was suffused with the same sense of fantasy that overcame Glazier in Savannah. "The first days of liberation after a protracted captivity are veiled in the misty atmosphere of unreality," Glazier quoted from the work of Lieutenant Colonel F. F. Cavada, a Federal officer who penned a famous memoir of life in Richmond's Libby Prison. "And thus it was with me. I could scarcely recognize the identity of my own being.... It seemed as though I had traversed the impassable gulf, the dreadful chasm of a dream,—but at length I became convinced that *I was I myself*."[39]

Escaped prisoners of war who made it to Knoxville in November met personally with Brigadier General Carter, whose overburdened office added a new function during the winter of 1864–65: processing escaped prisoners of war. Ten had reported in October and the number increased to thirty-five in November. In this early phase, talking to an escaped prisoner and hearing the tale of his marvelous adventure was still a novelty. Carter professed amazement at Drake and Lewis's extraordinary feat. "Our story exceeded any romance of which he had ever read," Drake proudly recalled. After a shave, haircut, and bath at a local barber's shop, Drake and Lewis were fêted by the Federals staying at the Bell House Hotel in Knoxville. The former fugitives, smoking imported cigars, told their story for two hours to a large crowd in the reception hall. They dined with Brigadier General Gillem. An officer in a Tennessee cavalry regiment bought Drake a pair of shoes, soft kid gloves, silk socks, a necktie, a handkerchief, and several linen collars; another man paid for his hotel room. Several newspaper correspondents interviewed the pair. "We were the lions of the place," Drake boasted.[40]

Not every reception was so warm and welcoming, as Hadley and party discovered when they arrived in Knoxville on December 10. Like so many other successful escapees, they were attired in an array of startling and indecent outfits. Some fugitives had spent nearly two years in Confederate prisons without receiving any issue of clothing, and the uniforms

Three of these Union officers escaped from Camp Sorghum on November 10, 1864. As was typical, once they reached the mountains of North Carolina, they joined with six others who escaped from Columbia at other times. This photograph was taken when they arrived in Knoxville on July 1, 1865, and includes the party's three guides: two Confederate deserters and a fourteen-year-old boy named Tom Zachary (top row, far right). Courtesy of the Library of Congress.

they were wearing when they were captured had disintegrated. Simon Dufur, who escaped from Florence in September, said that the amount of clothing he had on was not enough to make up a gun wad. Federal officers had more resources to supplement their wardrobe through purchase and trade while they were in prison. Many of them wore one item from their Federal uniform, such as the jacket or pants, with civilian clothes. A few of them were in full Confederate uniforms they had bribed guards to obtain. Some of the outfits they cobbled together often astounded observers. In this case, Homer Chisman had bound the uppers of a pair of southern army brogans to his feet with bark. His pants were cobbled together from his Federal blue uniform, brown jeans, and linsey-woolsey he picked up in North Carolina, and were shredded below the knee, so he had bound them to give the effect of knickerbockers.

Thomas Good had swaddled a pair of trousers around his feet. He wore Confederate gray pants with patched material on his rear and a jacket two inches too short with no elbows.[41]

The men marched single file, as they had throughout their journey, down the streets of Knoxville. "Our debut was not made eminently agreeable by the loitering soldiers," Hadley recalled. "They, as a rule, never are scrupulously severe in their practice of politeness when in the field. On this occasion they ruthlessly roasted us from start to finish." One shouted at Chisman, "Say, uncle, your calves are out!" Another yelled, "It's the last of the Mohicans!" Still another, "It's a menagerie." "There were no replies," Hadley wrote. "For we all knew too well the end of a soldier's tongue to make retort."[42]

As the number of escapees arriving in Knoxville increased over the following months, this kind of individual attention, from soldiers on the streets and from Federal officials, became rare. The provost marshal general, first Carter and then after mid-January Lieutenant Colonel Luther S. Trowbridge, was too busy finding rations, quarters, and transportation for the returned prisoners. Eighty-five reported in December, 46 in January, 86 in February, 171 in March, 48 in April, and 17 in May. The office eventually developed special printed forms with blanks for clerks to indicate the escaped prisoner's name, his regiment, his company, his point of capture and escape, the date of arrival in Knoxville, and where his regiment was located so that he could be forwarded there. Once news of the number of escaped prisoners arriving in Knoxville reached the northern population, northern families wrote to the provost marshal's office asking for information about loved ones. Clerks responded when there was something to report. Otherwise, they spent their time putting together the special orders and other paperwork necessary to send the returned prisoners back to their regiments, or in the case of officers, to the headquarters of the adjutant general of the U.S. Army in Washington, D.C.[43]

Knoxville ended one lengthy journey for escaped prisoners and began another. Their journey out of the Confederacy took them through a landscape with collapsing borders that teemed with people on the move. Their journey home would take them through battle zones, a maze of War Department bureaucracy, and the worst physical suffering of their lives.

A Futile Attempt at Imprisonment

The Collapse of Military Defense

Back in the open field in Columbia, recaptured fugitives returned to regale the prisoners of war with tales of their adventures. Not surprisingly, these men who failed in their quest discouraged their comrades from making an attempt. One officer who was caught after four days told his intrigued audience that the people were hospitable, but the intricate roads and rivers made it too difficult to find a passage out of the state. Duncan McKercher, the major of the Tenth Wisconsin, talked to as many of the returned prisoners as he could and recorded their observations in gray pencil on a small unlined notepad. Like the other officers in the prison, he wanted to know where Sherman's army was. On November 26, some fugitives who got close to Augusta reported that they heard artillery in the direction of the city. On the morning of December 3, the guard brought in thirty recaptured prisoners who informed McKercher that Sherman never came within eight miles of Augusta and was headed for Savannah instead. Five days later, the guards brought in nineteen more who confirmed Sherman's destination. That same day, two bloodhounds used to track escaped prisoners got loose and ran into the camp. The Yankees killed them with an axe and buried them in a shallow grave.[1]

But the Federal officers' days in Camp Sorghum were numbered. The status quo was as unendurable to South Carolina state officials as it was to the prisoners. The governor obtained permission to move the Yankees to the Lunatic Asylum in Columbia. The Board of Regents for the institution acquiesced because they desired to protect "defenseless women and children" from the number of escaped prisoners "going at large." The Federals marched to their new prison on December 12. Two hundred of the prisoners found shelter inside the building of the asylum, but 1,000 were turned out onto the grounds that were surrounded by a high wall. The Yankees managed to construct four makeshift buildings, but hundreds of the officers spent December and January with nothing but blankets for shelter. Recaptured fugitives continued to arrive at Camp Asylum through the end of December, some of whom had traveled for over a month before being caught. But they brought the good news that Sherman had captured Savannah. An adjutant from the Fifth

Iowa, S. H. M. Byers, who walked the prison grounds at night to keep warm, wanted to celebrate the campaign that brought new hope to the prisoners. He wondered how to describe a war feat that was not an epic battle, but rather a march. And then he thought the phrase "a march to the sea." Byers wrote a poem with those words as the title and chorus. A New York lieutenant set the poem to music and debuted the song at a performance of the prison glee club. The prisoners cheered until they were hoarse; encore followed encore. Every prisoner learned the song and every day the Yankees sang it.[2]

When Sherman captured Savannah, the Confederacy finally had both the U.S. officers and the enlisted men in South Carolina enclosed in stockades. The 11,424 Yankees at Florence lived in twenty-three and a half acres, but one-third of that, according to Confederate officials, was "morass." An inspector noted that "prisoners seem to be emaciated and in bad health . . . have shelter only as they have constructed for themselves." The onset of winter, unusually wet weather, starvation, and sickness from exposure at Florence and the confinement of officers in the Lunatic Asylum hampered breakout attempts in the state. The number of escapes declined drastically in January, when only eighteen prisoners managed to do so.[3]

But once again Sherman's movements interfered with the operation of Confederate military prisons. In September, his capture of Atlanta had precipitated the evacuation of Federal prisoners at Macon and Andersonville. In December, his "march to the sea" and capture of Savannah threatened to bring Union armies within range of the prisoners once again. At the end of the month, Confederate officials debated whether or not to remove the Federals held in South Carolina. Brigadier General John Winder, the recently appointed commissary general of prisoners, who was in Columbia, pointed out, "It will be difficult to feed the prisoners and the army now that the lines of communication are interrupted." General Beauregard ordered the evacuation of Florence on December 27, but Winder had no place to put the prisoners. Winder wrote a private letter to Samuel Cooper, the adjutant and inspector general, with a suggestion he feared would be misunderstood. "There is no place that can be considered as safe from the operations of the enemy," he said bluntly. The best solution would be to parole the Federal officers and enlisted men whose terms had expired in order to reduce the number of prisoners. Winder suggested the enlisted men could be sent over the lines in East Tennessee. Cooper suppressed this private letter, and sent other correspondence up the chain proffering Andersonville or points in Alabama as potential, though admittedly still unsafe, locations. On January 14, 1865, President Jefferson Davis advised Winder to wait for further developments before shifting the prison population again "unless the danger of being able to hereafter remove the prisoners or to feed them is imminent."[4]

At the time Davis penned these words, the danger was already imminent. On that date, a division of Sherman's Twentieth Corps went into camp near Hardeeville, South Carolina.[5] The collapse of Confederate military defense in the Carolinas during January and February 1865 was intertwined with the ultimate collapse of the Confederate prison system in the region. A gaping hole in the scholarly literature on the Civil War is a consideration of how the prisoner of war problem interacted with the conduct of military campaigns. Historians have provided no systematic analysis of how the process of capturing prisoners on the battlefield, transporting them behind the lines, and holding them in prisons located near active military operations was connected to military logistics and to the outcome of battles and campaigns. Considering the number of prisoners taken on both sides in 1864—more Federals were captured at the Battle of the Wilderness than were killed on the field, for example—this neglect is surprising.[6]

In the case of the Carolinas in early 1865, Sherman's invasion of South Carolina forced a chaotic evacuation of 7,672 prisoners of war to North Carolina. During this evacuation, more than 1,600 prisoners escaped or had to be abandoned. The Confederacy's attempt to deliver the remaining prisoners to Union military commanders during the Federal campaign against the coastal city of Wilmington interfered with and disrupted both Confederate and Union operations on that battlefield and had consequences for Sherman's invasion of North Carolina.[7]

Because the state government of South Carolina collapsed before the first of Sherman's troops arrived, and because Confederate-level operational control in the region was muddled, there was no effective military defense against the invasion. No one was in charge of stopping Sherman. General Beauregard, commander of the Military Division of the West, traveled to Augusta to plot a response, but he had no formal authority over Lieutenant General William J. Hardee and the troops Hardee commanded in the Department of South Carolina, Georgia, and Florida. Beauregard refused to learn from experience and operated in the realm of fantasy rather than reality. Back in November 1864, he had estimated that he could throw 29,000 men across Sherman's path in Georgia. "The forces I had been led to expect were not available," he later wrote in an understatement. On February 2, 1865, at a meeting to plan the defense of South Carolina, which took place two weeks after the Federals had already occupied several strong positions in the state, Beauregard somehow calculated that he could bring 33,450 troops to oppose the Yankees, and he decided to defend three potential paths: Augusta, Branchville, and Charleston. He thus scattered what turned out to be fewer than 20,000 "more or less demoralized" effectives, a number that included Junior and Senior Reserves, and provided Sherman with a relatively clear path to Columbia. The Federals' rapid and unhindered movements between the divided Rebel forces, despite incessant rains, then precluded the Confederates from concentrating to oppose the Yankees.[8]

Sherman's army soon approached the landscape that fugitive Federals had roamed over in November and December. By February 15, the Seventeenth Corps was camped just eight miles south of Columbia, the Fifteenth Corps was crossing a tributary of the Congaree River that escaped prisoners had canoed to find Union gunboats on the coast, and the Twentieth Corps was bivouacked twenty miles west of Columbia near Lexington, the first town Willard Worcester Glazier had passed through the night of his escape. The next morning, the entire Federal army united on the left bank of the Congaree River. The Yankees could see people walking the streets of the state capital. Sherman sent the Fifteenth Corps north to cross the Saluda River, the one that Charlie Mattocks had swum, and then to occupy Columbia. The soldiers marched past the Saluda Factory and the abandoned hovels and holes that were the remnants of Camp Sorghum.[9]

Before the Federals entered the city, Columbia degenerated into chaos. Because the state government and Confederate civilian authorities were not functional in South Carolina at this point, there was no one in charge. Confederate military commanders never told city officials that they did not intend to defend the capital. No one authorized, planned, or coordinated the evacuation of the city, which began spontaneously when the arrival of refugees from surrounding areas and the sound of cannon in the distance informed residents that Sherman's army was near. As a result, terrified civilians loaded with private baggage crowded into the train station—because of Sherman's movements, only the line to Charlotte, North Carolina, was open—and jammed into freight cars. When

Confederate and state officials, each man acting on his own impetus, arrived at the station with commissary, ordnance, or medical stores that needed to be saved, there was no transportation for them amid the pandemonium. The head of the Confederate Armory in Columbia later wrote to his superior in Richmond, "I am deeply mortified and chagrined to report that my entire establishment was lost."[10]

In this frenzied atmosphere, Confederate prison officials tried to evacuate the prisoners of war from Camp Asylum and the stockade at Florence. The same conflicting lines of authority and bureaucratic disorder between Richmond and officials in the field that marked the prisoners' arrival in South Carolina disrupted their departure. During the first few days of February, considering Sherman's movements, Commissary General Winder determined to move the prisoners at Columbia and Florence to some point in southwest Georgia. No one in Richmond had informed him that Confederate officials were about to conclude negotiations with the United States that set up the exchange of nearly all prisoners then resident in South Carolina. Public pressure stemming from publicity about conditions in Confederate prisons and Lieutenant General Ulysses S. Grant's confidence in the imminent success of Union arms caused the United States to agree in early February to a general exchange of prisoners. Winder died of a heart attack at Florence on February 6, 1865, and his subordinate Colonel Henry Forno continued his arrangements to transport the prisoners to Georgia. On February 12, Forno received a telegram informing him that he was not the commander over prisons in South Carolina, and then on the thirteenth another telegram informed him that he was in charge after all, and ordered him to remove all prisoners to North Carolina. Because the order neglected to mention that the prisoners were slated for exchange, Forno delayed the departure as he sought to convince authorities in Richmond that Georgia was a more suitable location. Federal disruption of the rail line into Georgia made the point moot, so Forno emptied the prisons in Columbia and Florence in two shifts on the fourteenth and fifteenth.[11]

The resulting fiasco destroyed the last semblance of Confederate control over the majority of its prisoners in South Carolina. The officer in charge of Camp Asylum's evacuation was Major Elias Griswold. He received half an hour's notice on the morning of February 14 that a train was ready to transport the first batch of prisoners. Griswold sent 500 prisoners to the station. A second message that afternoon informed him that a train would be ready for the rest of the prisoners at 6:00 P.M.

Griswold hurriedly assembled the remaining 700 captives and marched them to the station under a demoralized and undisciplined guard. He left a detail at the asylum charged with the task of finding any Federals who tried to stay behind. Sixty prisoners were in fact hiding in the roofs of the asylum's barracks and hospital, including S. H. M. Byers, author of "Sherman's March to the Sea." The detail searched the buildings but did not discover them. After dark, Byers and a lieutenant from Philadelphia emerged from their hiding place and tried to climb the wall, but saw a line of guards waiting on the other side for just such an attempt. When some of the guards set fire to one of the buildings to flush out the Yankees, they wrapped old blankets around their shoulders, which made them blend in with the Rebels around them; boldly walked up to the sentinel at the gate; and said they were under orders to get buckets to put out the fire. They walked through the streets and saw a light in a house window revealing an African American inhabitant. They knocked, and Edward Edwards, who lived adjacent to the headquarters of Brigadier General James Chesnut Jr., offered them the safety of his garret until Sherman arrived. The other fifty-eight Yankees, some of whom hid under the roof for three days, likewise successfully escaped. Some wandered the streets, and others found refuge with sympathetic Unionists in the city.[12]

Griswold and the rest of the prisoners marched to the depot through throngs of panicked people and a logjam of wagons and baggage. Rain fell in torrents, and it was so dark the paltry guards could not see prisoners who were more than three feet away. They arrived at the depot promptly at 6:00 P.M. After waiting an hour, the transportation quartermaster told Griswold that no train was available until the next morning because of a backlog of trains on the single line of railroad transporting people out of Columbia. During the delay, Griswold lost another fifty prisoners. "No guard, especially such as I had, could have prevented escapes on such occasion and in such darkness," he told his superiors later. The major took the prisoners back to Camp Asylum and refused to march them out again until the quartermaster personally escorted him to the train the next morning. On February 15 at 11:00 A.M., Griswold and the Federals boarded the train and started for Charlotte, North Carolina. An hour later, the train collided with a drove of government cattle that was wandering on the track. The hapless prison official waited with his captives until the next morning before a new track was built around the wreck. By the time he and the Federals boarded the train on February 16, another forty-four had escaped.[13]

When the Federal officers finally arrived at Charlotte, Griswold found no accommodation prepared for them. The officer in charge of the first batch of Yankees had turned them out into an open field located just over a mile from the town. The second batch joined them. "It was as futile an attempt at imprisonment as could be devised," Forno admitted in his report on the debacle. Two of the guards promptly deserted their post and took thirty prisoners with them. Federals left the field at will. Captain Daniel Meany, Thirteenth Pennsylvania Cavalry, dodged into a little wood, crawled some distance, and then took off running. When he looked back to see if Rebel guards pursued him, he saw instead a field "covered with blue jackets." The fugitives gathered in several groups of three to twenty men to discuss plans and to choose traveling companions. Most of the officers wanted to head south and link up with Sherman's army. But Meany thought with so many going in the same direction, it would increase the likelihood of recapture. He had heard from an African American that the Third North Carolina was on a raid in western North Carolina. He found five men who agreed with him. After an arduous journey that took them to the same "Rock House" that nearly defeated Drake, the Yankees arrived in Knoxville on March 17. Meany made the choice with the best odds. Fifty-one of the Federal officers who escaped from the open field in Charlotte successfully arrived in Union lines, and forty-four of them reported to Knoxville.[14]

Confederate officials had no control over the Federal prisoners in Charlotte. The Yankees who stayed in the open field, 992 of them, did so because they were too ill to travel or because they preferred to wait. Griswold had gone to every boxcar on the train and read the captives his orders to exchange them. Although prison officials had used this as a ruse in the past to keep prisoners from escaping during transport, the fact that Confederate officers made no effort to control the totally demoralized guards convinced the Yankees of its truth this time. "All is confusion," one prisoner observed. "The Confederacy is trembling to its very center."[15]

The loss in officers during the transit to Charlotte, amounting to 193, was nothing compared to the number of enlisted men who escaped or had to be abandoned on the journey between Florence and Wilmington, North Carolina: 1,410. On February 13, the commandant at Florence, Lieutenant Colonel John F. Iverson of the Fourth Georgia, wrote that 3,000 of his 7,000 Federals were sick. His prisoners had no clothes; he did not have enough rations to distribute. His guards amounted to two reliefs of reserves and seventy-five veterans. Two days later, under instruction from Forno, Iverson evacuated the prisoners deemed able to travel. A train took them to Cheraw, South Carolina, where the line terminated. The prisoners marched eighty-three miles from there to a station on the North Carolina Railroad, where cars took them to Goldsboro. Confederate military officials in that city had no idea what to do with the Yankees. In a succinct statement of the condition of the Confederate prison system in the region, one of them telegraphed Braxton Bragg, "Conflicting orders received about prisoners. No prison or sufficient guard here. Advise me what to do." The Yankees were once again turned out into an open field. "They told us to go where we pleased," one Federal recalled. "We thought sure we was to be exchanged so we did not try to run away." About 360 of the sick prisoners were put in a makeshift hospital on the fairgrounds outside of town. Confederate prison officials, no strangers to the suffering of Federal prisoners, reported that the "neglect, filth, and squalor" of this place was unequaled in their experience. It was a "state of affairs that I felt disgraced our character for humanity," admitted Forno.[16]

During the next few days, the collapse of Confederate military defense in the Carolinas trapped harried Confederate prison officials who had nowhere to confine or deliver their human cargo. They certainly could not return to South Carolina. The day after Griswold and the Federal officers reached Charlotte, Sherman entered the anarchic city of Columbia. Crowds of citizens plundered warehouses and the state commissary building. Retreating Confederate cavalry burned the railroad terminal to Charlotte; a pillager accidentally ignited some powder at the South Carolina Railroad depot, and the resulting explosion rocked the city. Burning cotton bales lined the streets. A strong northwest wind blew strands of cotton through the air and created the effect of a snowstorm. As Federal troops entered the capital, residents passed out liquor. Sherman rode to the town hall to meet with the mayor. Byers and a crowd of escaped Federal prisoners approached him. Byers handed his hero a paper with the lyrics to his song and asked the general to read it at his leisure. Sherman told the prisoners to report to Major General O. O. Howard, who would arrange for their transportation with the army. That night, as a drunken mob of soldiers and citizens rampaged and Columbia burned, Sherman read Byers's song and immediately appointed that officer to his staff. The escaped prisoners joined the crowds in the streets. Their activities after this are shrouded in obscurity. Some of them probably set fire to houses in Columbia out of revenge for their treatment at the hands of the Rebels. Some of them spent the evening protecting the families who had sheltered them from drunken Federal soldiers bent on pillage, harassment, and arson. All of them marched north out of Columbia two days later with Sherman's army and its vast train of 10,000 white and black refugees.[17]

On the coast of North Carolina, Federal offensives threatened to overrun the port city of Wilmington, the location Confederate prison officials believed was the delivery point for their prisoners. Forno had finally received clear orders from Richmond to exchange all of the enlisted men and officers there. This was a dangerous choice. On January 16, a Federal joint army-navy operation had captured Fort Fisher, situated on the tip of a peninsula where the Cape Fear River empties into the Atlantic Ocean. It was the last Confederate stronghold for blockade runners and the guardian of Wilmington, located twenty-eight miles up the river. When Fisher fell, the Confederacy lost its only remaining entry point for munitions and other supplies from the outside world. Admiral David Dixon Porter, commanding the Federal fleet that reduced the fort using the greatest concentration of firepower in military history to that point, summarized the significance of the victory with the comment, "Thus is sealed the door through which rebellion is fed."[18]

The goal of capturing Wilmington was a central part of the Federal grand strategy to conclude the war. The heavily fortified city was an important objective in itself. Its three railroad lines, sustained by ample repair facilities, served as the main supply route for Robert E. Lee and the Army of Northern Virginia besieged within Petersburg. Lee told officials in the Confederate War Department that if Wilmington fell, he could not maintain his army. They agreed and communicated to Jefferson Davis their supposition that the loss of Wilmington preordained the loss of Richmond. Wilmington also figured into Grant and Sherman's plans to envelop Lee between their two armies. It would serve as the base for reinforcements and supplies once Sherman entered North Carolina. Federal troops already occupied coastal New Bern, but its railroads were damaged and its rivers were shallow. Wilmington possessed those three vital railroad lines, and the Cape Fear River was navigable 100 miles northwest to the inland city of Fayetteville. With Wilmington in Yankee hands, Sherman could march to Goldsboro, the junction of two coastal railroads, via Fayetteville; receive additional troops and provisions; and be in prime position to advance into Virginia. During the last two weeks in January, the troops who captured Fisher, under the command of Major General Alfred H. Terry, and the Twenty-Third Corps under Major General John M. Schofield, recently transferred from Tennessee, prepared to advance. Once they captured Wilmington, they planned to unite with Sherman at Goldsboro.[19]

The Confederate defense of Wilmington quickly disintegrated due to the deadly combination of effective Union operations and inept Confederate leadership. General Braxton Bragg, head of the military department that encompassed North Carolina east of the Blue Ridge Mountains and in immediate command over the Confederate forces at Wilmington, was mired in controversy. His subordinates charged him with the loss of Fisher because he chose not to contest the landing of Federal troops on the peninsula and did not attack the rear of the Federals while they were busy assaulting the fort. His words and actions indicated that he never intended to make a serious defense of the city. In late January he had transferred important government and military property to Raleigh. On February 10, with Federal troops clearly preparing to advance toward the remaining defenses on the approach to Wilmington, Bragg left the field, going to Richmond for eleven days on purely bureaucratic business.[20]

The Federals launched an assault on the Confederate defensive line at Sugar Loaf, twenty-four miles south of Wilmington and located on the same peninsula as Fisher, the next day. When the frontal assault failed, the Yankees ferried troops from the peninsula across the Cape Fear River to the small village of Smithville on its west bank. From there, they marched on Fort Anderson, the last remaining earthwork defending the river-borne approach to Wilmington. Federal gunboats and monitors pounded the fort while the infantry entrenched in its front and effected a flanking maneuver that forced a hasty Confederate retreat on February 18. The Rebels then had to evacuate Sugar Loaf as well, since the loss of Anderson gave the Union navy control of the Cape Fear River. On February 19, Federal troops advanced overland on both sides of the river while the flotilla under Admiral Porter ascended the waterway in support.[21]

As the Yankees closed in on Wilmington from three directions, the military leaders conducting the campaign were unaware that 2,500 Federal prisoners of war from Goldsboro were on the way to the city. Neither Schofield nor Major General Robert F. Hoke, commanding in Bragg's absence, had been informed by their respective governments about the agreed-upon exchange. When the prisoners arrived, guards put the Federals in a field near the town. Curious townspeople came out to see the Yankees. The appalling condition of the naked and starving men touched them. The next morning a few hundred black and white men, women, and children returned with basketfuls of food, but the Rebel guards, under orders to prevent all communication between the prisoners and citizens, drove them off before they could deliver the eatables.[22]

Hoke was discombobulated when he learned that these were just the first of several thousand proposed deliveries. He was trying to move government property from the city in advance of evacuating his garrison. Under flag of truce, Hoke sent a message to Schofield proposing to deliver the prisoners immediately. Since Schofield was unaware of any exchange agreement and did not want anything to impede his advance, he asked the Confederate general for more information about the terms of delivery, and continued to press toward Wilmington with his troops. The beleaguered Hoke sent panicked dispatches to Confederate prison officials at Goldsboro and military officials along the railroad line, ordering them not to send any more prisoners to Wilmington. In his haste and busyness, he misrepresented Schofield's message to him. Hoke wrote that "the enemy declines having anything to do with the Yankee prisoners."[23]

The arrival of the Yankees altered Hoke's timeline. He would have to hold Wilmington longer than he anticipated. The general sent one of Bragg's staff officers to Major General Johnson Hagood, holding the Confederate line at Town Creek on the west bank of the Cape Fear River, to impress upon that commander the necessity of delaying the Federal advance. "Time was essential to get these prisoners off and out of reach" was the message. Hagood was unable to comply. The next day, the Federals flanked his position and he immediately abandoned the line. When Hagood's troops retreated to Wilmington on February 20, no Rebel forces were left to stop the Yankees on the west side of the river.[24]

The resulting shuffle of Federal prisoners of war hindered Confederate military operations in eastern North Carolina. Transporting the Federals out of Wilmington took up the train cars that were supposed to evacuate Confederate naval stores. Confederate prison officials and railroad managers had no idea where to put thousands of other prisoners that were on the way to Wilmington, who could not now be delivered, and ended up moving them back and forth between points on the railroad at Salisbury, Greensboro, Raleigh, and Goldsboro, consuming the transportation that was needed to move military supplies, which accumulated at Goldsboro. Manpower needed elsewhere was expended chasing down prisoners who escaped at each new movement of the trains. One lieutenant from the U.S. Colored Troops absconded and was recaptured three times along the route.[25]

When Braxton Bragg returned to Wilmington from Richmond on February 21, chaos greeted him. Looters carried off goods from stores and warehouses. Wagons clogged the streets. Terrified citizens crowded onto the platform of the Wilmington & Weldon Railroad and clamored for places on the trains that were slated to carry off more of the Federal prisoners of war. Residents could see Union troops across the river. "I find on arrival that our forces are driven from the west bank of Cape Fear," Bragg telegraphed Lee. "This compels me to cross the Northeast River or they will be in my rear tomorrow. Our small forces renders it impossible to make any serious stand. We are greatly embarrassed by prisoners." He wrote Cooper that Schofield "seems to avail himself of their presence to push his operations." Bragg hastened to complete the evacuation, but getting rid of the Yankee prisoners interfered with the process. Bragg ultimately removed the most important supplies from Wilmington before Schofield's troops took the city. "Some naval stores and a small lot of cotton and tobacco were destroyed by fire," he wrote. "These could have been saved but for the occupation of the trains in carrying prisoners."[26]

The last of the Confederate forces evacuated Wilmington early on the morning of February 22 and withdrew across the Northeast Cape Fear River, abandoning 270 Federal prisoners who had escaped and hidden in the swamps and woods around Wilmington. Former Florence inmate George Weiser was one of these. The day before, he and a friend walked away from the field outside Wilmington when they heard some of their guards say "it was time now to stop the war." They passed the house of an elderly African American woman and asked for shelter. She already had three other Yankees hidden away, but she found a friend who took them into a swamp and hid them in a hole. At sunset, two Confederate soldiers discovered them but did not disturb them. The Yankees spent the evening eating with two young black men who were also hiding in the swamp. They swapped tales and listened to the sounds of soldiers and citizens fleeing Wilmington. The next morning, one of the black men went to Wilmington to reconnoiter. He returned and reported that the Stars and Stripes were flying over the city. The advance units of the

Federal army, including the Third New Hampshire and the Seventh Connecticut, encountered Weiser and the other hundreds of escaped prisoners as they emerged from their hiding places in swamps, barns, and houses. Troops found others dead along the road.[27]

Unloading the Federal prisoners of war who were clogging the railways was a priority for the retreating Confederates. General Hoke, from his position across the river, contacted Schofield again and urged him "in the name of humanity" to accept delivery of the prisoners waiting at Goldsboro and other points. "They have been subjected to great suffering and considerable mortality by the delay," he pointed out. On February 23, firmly in command of Wilmington, Schofield agreed to halt active operations and to receive 2,000 prisoners a day, beginning three days later.[28]

Between February 26 and March 4, Confederate officials delivered 8,684 prisoners of war to the exchange point at a railroad crossing on the Northeast Cape Fear River. The prisoners arrived in boxcars that stopped right at the point where guard outposts marked the extent of the Federal lines outside of Wilmington. "I did not believe we would be paroled until within an hour of the time we were," one Yankee wrote. "We had been deceived so many times I had no faith in regard to it, even after we signed. What made me believe at last was seeing a colored soldier on picket by the side of the railroad, with Uncle Sam's uniform on." As the prisoners exited the trains, a Confederate and a Union agent counted them, placing a hand on each man's shoulder and yelling out the number. The healthier prisoners walked to the camps of Federal regiments stationed at the river, who had made banners wreathed in evergreens that read "We Welcome You Home Our Brothers," and had cooked rations and coffee to feed the liberated captives before they marched on to Wilmington. Ambulances and steamers picked up the sick, about 600 a day, and transported them to the city.[29]

For the returned prisoners and those who witnessed the moment they walked across the Federal lines, it was a scene that combined unspeakable joy with unspeakable horror, and that foreshadowed the long personal recovery that former prisoners of war would endure in the decades ahead. When the healthier prisoners saw the U.S. flag, the Federal guards presenting arms, and the welcome banner prepared for them, tumult erupted. Men leapt in the air "like ballet dancers," shouted, fell down on the side of the road and "wept like children," waved hats and caps, hugged and cried. "In a word," recalled one prisoner, "we surrendered to *bliss*." Another recorded, "After passing the officers I felt so happy that I ran and jumped the best I could, and tried to shout, but no sound would come, I was so overjoyed. That is what I call joy unspeakable." But witnesses also described a different homecoming, one that they found difficult to depict in words. "Ghastly faces! Human ghosts! Skeletons of human outline," was the attempt of one observer. "They were black as tar; alive with vermin; a majority of them helpless; many verging on insanity; others, who had been wounded, were actually rotten," wrote another. One Federal soldier who saw the returned prisoners wrote simply in his diary that night, "I think but few of them will ever make the same robust men they once were."[30]

Union medical officials scrambled to appropriately address the returned prisoners' medical needs. Regiments stationed at the Northeast Cape Fear River, on order from Schofield, had prepared a feast with plenty of strong coffee for the famished and starving prisoners, who mobbed the cooking kettles and devoured as much food as they could get their hands on. When the prisoners arrived at Wilmington, Federal soldiers stationed in the city also fed them, and initially the Federal Commissary distributed sugar, meat, onions, soft bread, and hardtack. "We drank the army coffee until we were filled, and still its delicious fragrance filled the air and intoxicated our senses," wrote one former prisoner. "I drank so much of it that I was positively and helplessly drunk." Others became desperately ill as their famished and debilitated stomachs rejected the food. Too late for many prisoners, who suffered for weeks the consequences of their orgy of eating, army physicians intervened. They placed watches over the prisoners to keep them from overeating and ordered the commissary to issue limited rations four times a day to keep the returned prisoners from eating their food all at once, a temptation that proved impossible to resist.[31]

Receiving and caring for the prisoners of war interrupted the Wilmington campaign and subsequent Federal movements related to Sherman's invasion of North Carolina. The exchange temporarily halted the pursuit of Bragg's army, and the arrival of more than 8,000 captives exhausted local resources and military supply lines. One goal of the campaign was to open a supply base for Sherman's army. On March 8, the entire right wing of that force crossed the state line into North Carolina, and two days later, its advance units arrived in Fayetteville. Sherman sent a dispatch to Wilmington proclaiming his presence, ordering Schofield to meet him near Goldsboro and requesting shoes and clothing for his depleted soldiers. A boat brought reply from Major General Terry. "Everything we had here has been expended for the paroled prisoners which we have received," he wrote. Terry had sent to Beaufort for more supplies and promised to send them "should they arrive in time." Two days later, Terry was able to fulfill Sherman's request, but ultimately, caring for returned prisoners of war delayed the advance of the Union army out of the city for its intended rendezvous with Sherman.[32]

Because the exchanged prisoners threatened the health of the entire community, they destabilized the Federal army's occupation of Wilmington. Brigadier General Joseph R. Hawley and Brevet Brigadier General Joseph C. Abbott, commanding the District of Wilmington and the Post of Wilmington, respectively, scrambled to address the sanitary crisis. Within a few days, they forwarded the majority of the prisoners by steamer to Camp Parole in Annapolis, Maryland, but 2,475 were too sick to be moved for several weeks, and several hundred of them died during that time. Deaths averaged seventeen a day. Medical care was improvised and ad hoc. Warehouses were converted to hospitals; citizens took men into their homes. Hawley levied a tax of shirts, socks, and bedding on Wilmington inhabitants in order to provide for the sick prisoners. The emergency was not alleviated until March 19, when the U.S. Sanitary Commission arrived to take charge of the prisoners. Its doctors brought on a steamer from New York City enough food (including 3,300 pounds of chocolate), clothing, and medical supplies to adequately care for the sick.[33]

The timing was perfect; two days later 6,000 of the refugees that had been following Sherman's army from Columbia arrived in Wilmington, escorted by a guard of 200 men that included S. H. M. Byers and other escaped prisoners. Sherman had sent them away when his army briefly paused at Fayetteville. Now the harried Hawley and Abbott had the burden of providing for 15,000 occupation troops, nearly 2,500 sick prisoners of war, Sherman's refugees, and thousands of needy residents of Wilmington. As infectious fevers rampaged through the city, they had neither time nor resources to combat the organized companies of Rebel deserters who terrorized the counties surrounding the city. Hawley asked Federal naval forces to patrol the Cape Fear River and to keep everyone away from the city except "deserters from the rebels, escaped Federal prisoners, and absolutely destitute, starving citizens."[34]

As the Federals struggled to house, feed, and clothe the swelling population of Wilmington, Confederates gathered their remaining resources to confront Sherman, but signs of collapse marked the preparations. Special Order 3 on February 22 assigned General Joseph E. Johnston command of "the two military departments known as the Department of Tennessee and Georgia, and the Department of South Carolina, Georgia and Florida, and the troops therein." His task was to concentrate "all available forces" and "to thwart the designs of the enemy operating in those departments." This special order starkly displayed the confusion in Richmond as the Confederacy buckled under the pressure of multiple Federal invasions. The order neglected to put Johnston in charge of the Department of North Carolina, where the Union armies under Schofield and Terry were already operating and where Sherman's army was clearly heading. This was rectified two weeks later. When Johnston wrote to Richmond about organizing his forces, the recently appointed secretary of war, John C. Breckinridge, responded, "I am not stating the case too strongly when I say that the War Department in all its branches is almost wholly paralyzed for want of means." The adjutant general for the state of North Carolina, following in the footsteps of South Carolina's governor two months before, wrote to officers in the Home Guard, "You must be aware that the condition of things demand that everyone should assist in the defense of his own home."[35]

Despite the collapse in other arenas, Johnston gathered a force whose determination and morale remained intact. The general commanded the troops that had evacuated Charleston, Columbia, and Wilmington. He also possessed a portion of the Army of Tennessee, which had been defeated at the Battle of Nashville in December and retreated to Tupelo, Mississippi. In January, Beauregard ordered half of the soldiers from this army to South Carolina to oppose Sherman. These "diehard Rebels" journeyed hundreds of miles in February and March to continue their fight for independence. They took trains to Augusta and then walked through the destruction Sherman had left behind in South Carolina to join Johnston and their depleted regiments in North Carolina. The Georgia and South Carolina militias decided not to cross state borders this time, however. On February 21, the commander of the South Carolina militia had informed Beauregard that the old men and young boys who constituted his troops were "completely exhausted" and "unable to continue the march" into North Carolina. Five days later, Georgia militia units abandoned their stations at the Confederate lines near Augusta. The governor of Georgia explained that these men were needed on the farms and that for the first time in ten months Federal forces did not threaten the interior of Georgia. Erased lines were redrawn in the wake of complete Confederate military collapse in those two states.[36]

Confederate forces gave battle to the Union armies invading eastern North Carolina after the fall of Wilmington but did not thwart the designs of the enemy. Bragg engaged one corps of Federals at Wise Forks on March 8 as the Yankees pressed westward from their coastal base at New Bern with the objective of securing Goldsboro for Sherman. The Rebels routed a portion of the Federal corps and captured 800 prisoners, but the Yankees entrenched and repelled further assaults as reinforcements arrived. Bragg fell back to Goldsboro. Johnston attacked the left wing of Sherman's army at Bentonville on March 19 in what proved to be the next-to-last full-scale Confederate tactical offensive of the Civil War. The Federal wing staved off defeat, and the rest of Sherman's army arrived on the battlefield the next day. After two days of severe and continuous skirmishing, Johnston withdrew. Although Sherman allowed Johnston's army to escape, the battle opened the road to Goldsboro. The Rebels did not prevent the planned rendezvous of two Union armies at Goldsboro on March 23–24 or their resupply from the coast by rail the next day. The Federal objectives in the Carolinas were met. Sherman was poised to complete his part of the Federal grand strategy to end the war. Lee's position in Virginia was no longer tenable.[37]

Yankee military invasions completed the ongoing "spatial contraction" of Confederate North Carolina as well. Irregular warfare and pressure from Unionists and other dissidents had already destabilized more than one-third of the state. When Federals applied external pressure in the form of Sherman's and Schofield's armies, there was not enough manpower to fight guerrillas and deserters at the county level and funnel sufficient troops to the front. The combination of extensive local chaos and full-scale invasion demolished the vestiges of Confederate command and control in the state.[38]

While the Confederate military defense of the Carolinas collapsed, from November 1864 to March 1865, former Federal prisoners of war released from the region's prisons made their way home. Although the experience of fugitive Federals diverged sharply from the experience of exchanged prisoners during the journey from a Confederate prison to Union lines, their experiences merged once they reached God's Country. All former prisoners marked the same phases in the transition from prisoner to free man.

Successful fugitives and exchanged prisoners alike counted themselves free when they glimpsed the U.S. flag; seeing the Stars and Stripes was the moment of release. Whether they wrote in diaries at the time or remembered the event years later, they lingered over that moment and drew on lines of poetry to capture their emotions. The flag made tangible the protection of the U.S. government and the personal freedom it provided. Seeing that symbol after long months of captivity was overwhelming. One escaped prisoner ran up to the flagstaff and embraced it, then sank at its base in tears. Others "bowed with reverence" as they "felt its protecting power." Exchanged prisoners at Wilmington fell silent when they approached the flag and stepped out of line to kiss "the sacred emblem of freedom." J. Madison Drake "breathed a fervent prayer that mine eyes had again been permitted to behold its glory. Months had elapsed since I had witnessed such a sight—I felt like a free man." When he published his reworked diary in 1866, he quoted the last stanza of Joseph Rodman Drake's "The American Flag," a poem published in the second decade of the nineteenth century and rendered into song during the first year of the Civil War:

Flag of the free heart's hope and home
By angel hands to valor given;
Thy stars have lit the welkin dome,
And all thy hues were born in heaven.
Forever float that standard sheet!
Where breathes the foe but falls before us,
With Freedom's soil beneath our feet,
And Freedom's banner streaming o'er us?[39]

Once the prisoners were released, the next stage in their transition was to do something that made them feel like their old selves again. This step was practical and focused on the outer man. Drake and Lewis visited a barber shop on the first night of their arrival in Knoxville. The owner of the establishment saturated their lice-covered prison clothing with camphene and burned it. He cut their hair and gave them baths. They put on clean uniforms and fastened their officers' bars to their collars. "We emerged in the open air different from what we had been an hour ago," Drake said. "Now we were soldiers indeed, not the ragged, filthy fellows we had been for months." The Union army provided this process free of charge for the exchanged prisoners from Wilmington when they reached Camp Parole in Annapolis. The former prisoners were lined up, issued a complete suit of clothes, and marched en masse to the bath house. Inside was an assembly line for cleanliness that was so efficient it took ten minutes per person. The returned prisoners stripped naked. Two "strong" soldiers worked each station: shaving heads to remove lice, scrubbing bodies in the bath, and wiping them dry with coarse towels. The exchanged prisoners then passed to the final room, where they put on their new clothes and "came out full-fledged Yankees." "We began to feel that we were really men once more," one wrote in his diary after his cleansing. The renewed Yankees then filled out paperwork and received twenty-five cents a day for every day spent in prison; the pay was for rations they did not receive from the Union army during their incarceration.[40]

The stage in the transition that prisoners most desired was to go home. They credited thoughts of family with keeping them alive. To be with wives, children, parents, and siblings again would finally terminate their status as prisoners of war. But the arduous journey home revealed that they still carried the effects of prison life inside. With excitement and adrenaline behind them, their bodies completely broke down as they traveled through unexpected obstacles and the maze of army bureaucracy that stood between them and their goal. In the case of escaped prisoners who arrived in Knoxville during November and December, Confederate military operations in central Tennessee had destroyed the railroad line below Nashville. John V. Hadley joined a party of sixty discharged soldiers, citizen refugees, and escaped prisoners who marched 190 miles north through the Cumberland Gap to catch a train at Nicholasville, Kentucky. It took them ten days. Major Charles G. Davis traveled by train from Knoxville to Chattanooga with twenty-five other escapees. The party had to wait there several days before another train was available. Then they endured an eleven-hour ride to Stevenson, Alabama, where they remained several more days, waiting for a train to take them to Nashville. Escaped prisoners who reached Hilton Head or Savannah and exchanged prisoners at Wilmington had to navigate a trip that involved steamer transportation and its consequent discomforts. Willard Worcester Glazier transferred steamers three times on his way from Savannah to New York City. One of them, the *Ashland*, hit a terrible gale off Cape Hatteras. Benjamin Booth, an exchanged prisoner, took the steamship *Sunshine* from Wilmington to Camp Parole. As the ship tossed on the open sea, "all at once I felt as though a one hundred pound shell had exploded in my stomach." When he saw every man in sight "paying penalty for having indulged too freely in Uncle Sam's hospitality in Wilmington . . . I vomited until I was as empty as a Salisbury Prison meal sack."[41]

The onerous and lengthy trip broke the returned prisoners. Just when the end seemed to be in sight, their bodies collapsed under the accumulated weight of their prison sufferings. Escaped prisoners had traveled on adrenaline. "The raging fever of *excitement* nourished our strength, and wonderfully increased our power of endurance," Glazier explained. "But with this strain upon our natures removed, a weakening and almost painful relaxation ensued." This reality hit Drake with full force when he reached Chattanooga and was incapacitated by stomach cramps. "I had never felt so bad before. I looked upon my end as near," Drake recalled. "The cramps continued to torture me for several days—it being impossible for me to describe the sensations which almost drove the breath out of my body." He and Lewis rode in the caboose of a freight train from Chattanooga to Nashville. At this point, Drake was too weak to continue his diary. He was in such a stupor that he did not know how he became separated from Lewis or how he was put on a train to Louisville, where he fainted in the depot waiting room. Two officers from Pennsylvania looked through his pockets and found the form from the provost marshal in Knoxville that identified him as an escaped prisoner and directed him to report to the adjutant general in Washington, D.C. They put him on the right train and traveled with him part of the way. Other sympathetic passengers helped. "I suffered continually and almost beyond endurance," Drake remembered.[42]

The organ that failed them all on the journey home was the stomach. Trains took exchanged prisoner Benjamin Booth on an eight-day expedition from Camp Parole through Baltimore, Columbus, and Indianapolis to Benton Barracks in Saint Louis. The trip was difficult because of Booth's extreme physical weakness. His digestive system was a wreck. "To me, everything eatable is loathsome, yet I am hungry all the time," he wrote of the common symptom that lasted for months after the war. His desire to get home obsessed his mind and turned minutes into weeks. "I can almost see my home and loved ones there," he wrote from St. Louis. "When I sleep I dream of home only to awake with aching head and burning fever, my stomach rolling as the waves of the ocean, my limbs aching with the excruciating pain of that terrible North Carolina fever." He hid his condition from the doctor so he would not have to go to the hospital. When Booth reached Iowa City, he had not eaten for two days and could hardly walk. The government did not provide transportation for the final twenty-five miles of his journey from the train station to his home. He and a comrade hired a ride and stopped at a farmhouse for dinner ten miles from his destination. There Booth collapsed, "powerless to move." The kind lady of the house offered her bed, but Booth refused on the grounds that he still had vermin crawling on him, despite his cleansing in Annapolis. He lay on the ground and writhed in pain. The next morning his wife and brother-in-law arrived to convey him home in a wagon. For the next three weeks, Booth was delirious and unconscious, unable to recognize the wife who nursed him day and night. Although he reached home in March, Booth was not able to record his homecoming in his diary until December 20, 1865.[43]

Drake was "half dead" when he reached Washington. Navigating army bureaucracy so that he could get home to his wife nearly finished him. At the office of the adjutant general, he waited for half an hour. He leaned against the wall for support, and when a clerk noticed his physical condition and brought a chair, Drake fell down while trying to sit. When he finally received his papers, he was shocked and angered to read that the assistant adjutant general ordered him to return to his regiment within fifteen days! "That's all. There was *gratitude* for you, with a vengeance," he later wrote. "He had seen me—he knew I was in no condition to go back to the army." The order neglected to provide transportation home, and Drake did not have enough money on him to purchase a ticket to New Jersey. He did not know anyone in the city. "I felt happier while wading through the swamps of South Carolina, for there we were sure of assistance, and from the poorest of God's creatures—the *slaves*," he ranted. "The Adjutant General could have given me an 'order for transportation,' or he could have asked me if I needed *help* in order to reach home, but he forgot all these little things." Drake's experience was typical. Escaped prisoner Chauncey Aldrich spent seven days in the capital trying to obtain his paperwork. He visited the adjutant general's office, spent two full days sitting in the Quartermaster's Department, and finished with an examination by auditors who finally issued the necessary certificates for him to visit the paymaster. His terse diary entry summarized his feelings: "Got very much vexed."[44]

The paymaster general eventually issued Drake $1,000 to get home. He walked from the depot in Trenton to the house his wife had adorned with the Stars and Stripes. He rang the doorbell several times, but no one answered. A neighbor recognized him and shouted greetings. Doors opened up and down the block, including the one across the street, where his mother-in-law lived. His wife and boy were out of town visiting his parents, but a telegraph message brought them all to him by that evening. "The joy of again embracing them will live in my memory as long as I have an existence," he said. He dated his deliverance from that moment. Being at home with his family seemed "like a resurrection, in which I stood with a crown on my head and shining pathways, leading heavenward, stretching away in reaches of splendor before my weary feet." Drake spent two weeks flat on his back while local doctors treated those weary feet. The skin peeled off both of them. When the doctors threatened amputation, the women of the neighborhood assisted his wife in applying salves and saved him that fate.[45]

Drake's story remained intertwined with the story of the Confederacy's collapse. Although an examining surgeon extended Drake's leave temporarily, he returned to his regiment in January 1865, wearing slippers because shoes were too painful for his wasted feet. He could not perform his duties, but he was with the Ninth New Jersey when it marched into Goldsboro, North Carolina, on March 21 and raised its flag over the courthouse as the first Federal regiment to enter the city. Drake's life as a soldier ended two weeks before Johnston surrendered his army to Sherman at Bennett Place. Drake's colonel wrote his discharge papers on April 11. "His feet are frosted, and he is otherwise generally used up," the colonel stated bluntly. "Lieutenant Drake is a most valuable officer, and I regret to lose his services, but I do not think he will be fit for field-service for many months to come."[46]

The Confederacy was generally used up, too. In the months to come, as the rebellion completed its final death throes, Drake and other escaped prisoners endured a long physical recovery or succumbed to the diseases that wracked their bodies. Those who lived pondered the meaning of their flight, the lives of the southerners they had met, and what they had witnessed within the South. They had a story to tell about suffering and sacrifice for a greater cause. And the heroes of that story were the slaves and the white Unionists who had saved their lives and helped to end the life of the Confederate States of America.

Epilogue

Terrible Times in the Past

The death of the Confederate prison system, like the death of the Confederacy itself, was an uneven process across space and time. After the exchange at the Northeast Cape Fear River, the Confederacy acquired new Federal prisoners of war during the subsequent military campaigns of Schofield and Sherman. Recaptured prisoners from the great escapes of late February still populated county jails. One thousand prisoners returned to Andersonville in early April. A few days before Robert E. Lee surrendered the Army of Northern Virginia to Ulysses S. Grant, Colonel Henry Forno, the Confederate prison bureaucrat still in charge of the system in the Carolinas, wrote the new commissary general of prisoners, Brigadier General Daniel Ruggles, about building a new prison on a site eighteen miles from Columbia on the Charlotte & South Carolina Railroad line. "I am receiving small lots of prisoners and have no place to keep them but open fields," Forno informed his superior. He estimated it would take him ten days to erect a stockade.[1]

Ruggles was busy in April reforming his department under the scrutiny of the adjutant and inspector general's office. One of the last acts of the Confederate government was to investigate how it lost so many Federal prisoners and why so many of them died during the transfer from South Carolina to North Carolina. Forno and Major Elias Griswold, in charge of the evacuation of officers from Camp Asylum, submitted detailed reports. The inspector in charge of the investigation submitted these with his summary findings. "My observation leads me to state that confusion and want of management have characterized the removal of prisoners on this occasion, but also the management of prisons during the war," he wrote. "The fact that 14,000 prisoners of war died at Andersonville alone, startling and shocking as it is, leads one to hope that, as a mere matter of policy, the Government will hereafter insist upon and enforce more system in the management of the prisons, a better care of the prisoners, and a stricter accountability from those in charge of them." Samuel Cooper endorsed the report with the terse comment that his office had repeatedly reported abuses in the prison system but prison officials had not adopted measures to "remove the reproach resting upon us in their treatment." His office recommended that the "totally inefficient and negligent" Griswold be dropped from the rolls.[2]

The surrender of Joseph E. Johnston's army in North Carolina, along with all the troops in the Department of South Carolina, Georgia and Florida, to William Tecumseh Sherman on April 26 ended plans to build more Confederate prisons in the region. The rebellion and its prisons continued to collapse unevenly. In the wake of a Federal cavalry raid into western North Carolina, Thomas's Legion surrendered on May 7. Confederate forces in Alabama, Mississippi, Louisiana, Arkansas, and Texas capitulated the same month. During April and May, Confederate authorities delivered Federal prisoners held in Georgia and Alabama to official exchange points such as Vicksburg, Mississippi, but in some remote locations, Confederate camp guards disappeared without telling prisoners the war was over. It took the Union cavalry until the end of May to find the minor Confederate camps, to liberate the prisoners inside, or to round up former prisoners running at large in the vicinity of abandoned prisons such as Andersonville.[3]

The United States did not recover all of its prisoners of war until 1866, and Federal soldiers liberated themselves throughout 1865. Between May and December, 257 Federal prisoners escaped from locations where they were still being held in the states of the former Confederacy. The bulk of these, 240, bolted in May. But former Yankee prisoners of war continued to trickle home in the following months. Ten arrived in June. A soldier who had been captured at Greenleaf Prairie, Oklahoma, reported back to the army in August. Four more arrived in September. In October, three sailors of the Union navy escaped from the vicinity of Camp Ford, Texas. The last recorded Federal prisoner of war to escape did so in January 1866, when Corporal Henry Scott of the Forty-Fourth U.S. Colored Troops showed up at the camp of the First Iowa Cavalry stationed in Sherman, Texas. He was the last of thirty-two soldiers from his regiment to escape captivity. Their colonel had surrendered his entire garrison at Dalton, Georgia, in October 1864, and Confederates returned many of the enlisted men to slavery. From January to December 1865, thirty-one of them fled from locations in Mississippi, Georgia, and North Carolina. Henry Scott's escape from slavery in Texas, several months after "Juneteenth," actually marked the end of the Confederate prison system.[4]

The patchwork and extended ending of the war for Federal prisoners of war reflected the bumpy and protracted end to the Confederacy. The collapse of borders, slavery, the state, and the home front continued forward across time and spread across space in the months after conventional military resistance ended. Scholars have rightfully studied the development of Confederate nationalism during the war, its function in maintaining support for the war through setbacks and hardships, and its metamorphosis into southern nationalism in the decades after the war.[5] But the question of nationalism has been largely divorced from the question of when and where there ceased to be a functioning Confederate state. Regardless of whether most southerners identified with the Confederate nation and developed a transcendent loyalty to it, their sentiments could not save it. At some point in 1864–65, the collapse of that nation manifested itself to citizens and changed their relationship to it. They had to improvise in order to survive. Carolinians who experienced the escaped prisoner debacle as the herald of the Confederacy's last months lived through the collapse of the state at different paces in different places.

In Spartanburg District, South Carolina, where escaped Yankees hid in David and Elizabeth Golightly Harris's gin house in December 1864, the home front never became a battle zone as it did in some of the coastal counties or in western North Carolina and East Tennessee, but movement across collapsed borders disrupted ordinary life, the state disintegrated, and slavery mutated into tenant farming. The Harris family felt the effects of this protracted process. David returned home on March 14, 1865, during his cavalry unit's retreat from the coast of South Carolina into North Carolina. "I made use of this opportunity to come home after another horse," he wrote in his diary. "I walked about 300 miles to flank the enemy, which was between me and my home." That month other returning soldiers raided the village grocer's storehouse because he started refusing Confederate money. Refugees and defeated soldiers walking home from Virginia and North Carolina moved through the district in astounding numbers and consumed the scarce provisions. Although the Harris slaves remained "troublesome" throughout March and April, they continued to plow, ditch, and plant. On May 1, Federal cavalry troops looking for the fleeing Jefferson Davis arrived in Spartanburg.[6]

During the rest of the month, Harris noted signs that the state was gone. Raiders and thieves robbed and terrorized unchecked. Citizens formed self-defense societies and patrolled the roads themselves. Because no one would take Confederate currency, all trade was barter, but travelers had taken the provisions people needed for exchange. "I have read of the time that Tried men's souls, I think that this is the time that tries mens souls, pockets and his bowels at the same time," Harris gloomily joked. On June 5, Harris rode to the village and heard that the Federal occupiers of South Carolina were going to enforce emancipation. His slave York disappeared the next day, although others remained at work. On August 15, Harris told his slaves they were all free. One left immediately, but the others decided to remain until Christmas. During the fall, Harris arranged to rent his land to a combination of black and white tenants, each of whom promised to build two houses, clear a field, work five hands, and give Harris half of the crop. On December 25, 1865, the remaining slaves left to find a new home. "Everything is quiet, though no one knows what to do," Harris admitted. As late as 1868, the governor of South Carolina wrote that there "was practically no government" in the western counties of the state.[7]

The dearth of Federal occupying forces in the aftermath of the war preserved what one scholar has termed the "nearly stateless" condition of portions of the former Confederacy well into 1868–69. The United States demobilized quickly, and its scattered troops in the South were unable to restore order. One recent study of Reconstruction described North Carolina during the period as "pockets of control surrounded by chaos." In other parts of the South, the condition was "legally and practically anarchy."[8] As the story of fugitive Federals demonstrates, this state of affairs was rooted in the Confederacy's "general crisis," a spectrum of political, social, economic, and military failures that culminated in its disintegration during 1864–65. Because of the wholesale nature of Confederate defeat in the Carolinas, Reconstruction required rebuilding on every one of these fronts.

The lives of former prisoners of war required rebuilding as well. Escaped and exchanged Federals spent the first few years after the war recovering from the physical and emotional infirmities they carried home from their imprisonment. They suffered from unquenchable hunger. "I may as well state here that hunger to the recently paroled prisoner was like the thirst subscribed to the drunkard, absolutely insatiable," one told his comrades in a veterans' organization. "It was not till months afterwards that the unnatural craving for food wore off. When I reached home my appetite was at a high water mark, and I became the great wonder of the neighborhood." Austin Carr ate incessantly and his stomach was filled with "wind and pain." His mother, concerned that she could not stop him from eating, gave him medicine to "work off" the food. His uncle washed him down regularly but could not remove all the dirt from his skin.[9]

Sharp, clear, unwanted memories of life in prison were deeply embedded in their minds. Biochemical reactions produced during the trauma caused persistent, detailed, and intrusive memories of the event. One former prisoner of war wrote that his experience "did not leave a misty impression upon the mind, but is eaten into the imagination as if by an acid—etched indelibly upon the memory." Another admitted, "When I become deeply absorbed in a recollection of the scenes still fresh and vivid before my mind, I sometimes forget that I am again surrounded by friends and humanity, and become despondent and depressed." Yet some men were unable to share these memories with loved ones. One Andersonville inmate recalled that his mother tried to get him to talk about it, but he could not. "It seemed such a stupendous undertaking," he wrote when he finally started telling his story at the turn of the century.[10]

Willard Worcester Glazier, J. Madison Drake, and John V. Hadley were among the former prisoners who told their stories as soon as they could to anyone who would listen. The need to share stories and grief with the public was a characteristic of some war survivors that was necessary for their healing. Ex-prisoners of war used narratives to make sense of their tenacious memories of prison life. Glazier kept a journal during his entire imprisonment and escape. He wrote on his knee with a lead pencil that he sharpened with his finger nails. A friend who was exchanged during the Federal officers' brief stay in Camp Sorghum smuggled out the first part of Glazier's diary in the crown of his hat. Glazier managed to conceal the rest during his subsequent escape, recapture, and second escape. When he arrived home in Albany, he read the diary aloud to his friends. He then worked it into a narrative and inserted chapters that contained previously published accounts by those incarcerated in different Confederate prisons than he was. An Albany publisher released *The Capture, the Prison Pen, and the Escape* in 1865. A New York firm with resources to advertise the "thrilling, authentic, and popular" book nationwide issued subsequent editions that sold over 150,000 copies by 1869. Drake, with ambitions to become a newspaper publisher himself, told his story to reporters in Knoxville and granted interviews as soon as he arrived in Elizabeth, New Jersey. *Harper's Weekly* printed an account of his escape and journey through the Confederacy in January 1865, and other stories appeared in the *Philadelphia Times*, the *Newark*

Advertiser, and the *Albany Press*. Drake self-published a narrative based on his diary in 1866 entitled simply *Narrative of the Capture, Imprisonment and Escape of J. Madison Drake, Captain Ninth New Jersey Volunteers.* Hadley, who did not keep a diary, published a narrative relying on his memory with an Indianapolis firm in 1868. These were three of the sixty-four books and articles on Confederate prison life issued between 1862 and 1871.[11]

The escape narratives published in the years immediately after the war for the most part shared a common message. The writers wanted the world to know that Federal prisoners of war had been victims of a savage Rebel government that deserved ignoble defeat. Glazier unleashed bitter sarcasm throughout his narrative whenever he had opportunity to highlight the Confederacy's "inhumane" and "barbaric" treatment of prisoners of war that he believed was an outgrowth of the "foulest and most unwarrantable rebellion . . . ever known within the annals of time." His diary entry written in Libby Prison on November 26, 1863, Thanksgiving Day, waxed eloquent on this theme. He tried to imagine what Rebels had to be thankful for and came up with a few ideas. "Thankful that their armies were occasionally successful in their strife against the best and freest and most liberal government on earth," he suggested. "Thankful that the chains were tightening on the limbs of the bondman. Thankful that a fierce and cruel aristocracy were triumphing over the equal rights of the people."[12]

Glazier's belief that the Confederate leadership and its minions deliberately and systematically abused Federal prisoners was pervasive in the North and played a critical role in wartime and postwar politics. The U.S. government used this accusation to justify retaliatory acts against Confederate prisoners of war and to proclaim to the international community the righteousness of the Union cause. The northern public was saturated with stories of atrocities and starvation that appeared regularly in the press and in congressional reports, and the resulting bitterness and sense of moral outrage was one important reason that northerners accepted their government's hard war against southern citizens who supported the rebellion. Andersonville in particular, and Federal prisoners of war in general, became the overarching symbol used in the North to represent the barbarity of the rebellion. Congressmen debating plans for Reconstruction in 1866 referred to reports about Confederate prisons to justify their proposed programs; the Republican Party's 1868 election campaign continually referenced Andersonville and images of

Confederate stockades. The initiation ritual for the Grand Army of the Republic, the politically powerful veterans' organization, involved dressing the initiate as a prisoner of war and marching him past a coffin labeled with the name and regiment of a soldier who died at Andersonville. The House of Representatives investigated the treatment of Federal prisoners of war again in 1869 and concluded that atrocities were the "inevitable results" of slavery, treason, and rebellion. Bitterness over this issue obstructed reconciliation between northerners and southerners through the decade of the 1870s. The historian for one of the Union regiments that witnessed the exchange at the Northeast Cape Fear River encapsulated in 1885 the lingering anger. Even though northern and southern soldiers now meet in fraternal friendship, he wrote, the deliberate abuse of prisoners "is a crime never to be forgotten nor forgiven."[13]

If the Confederate leadership were the villains of the escaped prisoners' story, its heroes were the slaves and white southerners who risked their lives to aid fugitive Federals. Escape narratives portrayed African Americans as racially inferior and generally amusing creatures, but nonetheless true friends of the Union whose freedom must be preserved in the reunited republic. The writers were overt in their goal. "Should these pages serve to throw any light upon the question 'What shall we do with the Negro?,'" Allen O. Abbott wrote in the preface to his 1865 *Prison Life in the South*, "I shall feel that my labor has not been in vain." He guided his readers to the conclusion that freed slaves were loyal to the United States and deserved its protection. John V. Hadley wrote *Seven Months a Prisoner* to publicly acknowledge his appreciation to blacks in South Carolina and whites in North Carolina. "Liberty we attained, life we now enjoy, merit for escape should all be ascribed to the unrequited kindness of these friends," he recognized. "Without their aid we would have been as powerless as the blind man." Publishing his book in 1868, in the context of widespread terrorist violence in the South targeting blacks and whites who supported Republican Reconstruction governments, Hadley hoped his narrative "will succeed in increasing the sympathy and action of the North in behalf of the loyal people of the South, who remained true and steadfast in all the trials of the war."[14]

Although Civil War veterans who escaped from Confederate prisons enjoyed unique access to the lives and thoughts of slaves in the South, their views on the fruits of Union victory for African Americans were not broadly different from their comrades who were never incarcerated. Black men fought and died in uniform for the United States, and most white veterans never forgot it. The Grand Army of the Republic was an interracial organization that celebrated and proclaimed the "Won Cause": preservation of the Union and freedom for the slaves. Although veterans in most cases were eventually willing to welcome back former Confederate soldiers as fellow citizens, they fought southerners' Lost Cause narrative to their dying day. They believed to the end that slavery caused the war, that secession was unjustified treason, and that freedom for the slave was worth the sacrifices of their generation. They insisted that reconciliation with southerners was conditional on remembering that the Union cause was righteous and the Confederate cause was wicked.[15]

Former fugitives incorporated a third element into their message about villains and saviors. The greatest heroes of the War of the Rebellion were the white southern women who remained loyal to the Union through unparalleled suffering and sacrifice. Their patriotism manifested itself in daily acts of courage that saved their men and defied the oppressive Confederacy. Escaped prisoners wanted the humble and unknown women who protected them to be heaped with credit and accolades. Yet in the first few years after the war, they often could not name their benefactors, who still lived in "nearly stateless" conditions and in constant physical danger from the vengeance of their Rebel neighbors. Hadley gave the Holinsworth sisters assumed names and contented himself with lecturing the ladies of Indiana. He asked how many of them would walk alone in freezing weather through robber-infested country, risk jail to conceal four men who were complete strangers, plow and harvest and carry wheat five miles to the miller, or bake bread and walk miles after dark to feed men hiding out in caves. "Yet the loyal North Carolina women, created in the same likeness and strength, during the war did all these things, and more, without a murmur."[16]

Two fugitives rewarded their heroine with all the honor and fame they could give her. The most celebrated escaped Federal prisoners were Albert D. Richardson and Junius Henri Browne, two *New York Tribune* reporters captured in May 1863 on the Mississippi River while trying to run the Confederate defenses at Vicksburg in order to follow Grant's campaign against the city. They were famous Republican polemicists with a string of articles behind them. Topics included the manipulations of oligarchical secession leaders who duped poor people into treason, the uncivilized and backward society of the South, and the evils consequent to cruel and brutal slavery. Deeply offended Confederate officials rejoiced to have such men in their hands and refused to exchange them, despite the paroles given to the reporters by the commander at Vicksburg. After stints in Libby and Castle Thunder prisons in Richmond, the duo ended up in Salisbury, North Carolina, where they escaped on December 18, 1864. On their successful journey to Knoxville they fortuitously met famous scout Daniel Ellis and joined the party of seventy recruits, refugees, and other escaped prisoners he was leading through the battle zones of East Tennessee.[17]

Fortune smiled on the two wordsmiths with a penchant for romantic expression when Rebel guerrillas closed in on the expedition near Kelly's Gap in Greene County, Tennessee. Ellis enlisted the services of a sixteen-year-old girl who was an expert horsewoman to pilot his party out of the neighborhood. At midnight, the beautiful and graceful teenager guided the desperate men around the guerrillas' camps, the farmhouses of those who helped them, and the pickets they had posted on the road. After seven miles of stealthy movement, the young lady left the men in the woods while she rode alone over a long bridge that spanned the Nolichucky River to see if guerrillas guarded the structure and to reconnoiter the situation on the other side. She reported that the coast was clear, rode past the long line of men, and headed home alone. When Richardson reached God's Country three days later, he immediately sent a widely publicized telegram to the *New York Tribune*: "Out of the jaws of Death; out of the mouth of Hell."[18]

The scenario was common for fugitive Federals, but Richardson and Browne were uncommon fugitives. They were already famous and well-connected writers whose narratives of their adventures would immediately reach a wide northern audience. Each journalist spent the spring of 1865 preparing his manuscript and publicizing parts of his story in newspaper articles. Richardson christened the pretty young pilot "The Nameless Heroine" because he did not want to risk her safety. It was an apropos name for one of the unknown number of unnamed women who saved fugitive Federals. She was the icon for the commonplace loyal woman of the South who deserved a prominent place in the pantheon of American heroes but who would remain anonymous. She represented every aspect of such women that fugitives highlighted in the stories they told about them. "Custom and order were reversed. Strong, self-reliant men who had passed two years in the field, who had often looked death in the face . . . were protected by, and leaned on, women and children," Browne wrote. "They could do for us what our own sex could not, and they did it with a silent and unconscious heroism that made it

Tennessee teenager Melvina Stevens became the symbol of the "Nameless Heroines" who aided escaped prisoners. This illustration of her daring feat appeared in *The Secret Service, the Field, the Dungeon, and the Escape* (1865).

all the more beautiful." He ascribed to her pure, uncomplicated motives. She acted "on the stage of our great National Drama without the least self-consciousness, or any other inducement than her attachment to the cause." Her generosity and courage elevated her above a setting that fugitives otherwise found poor and backward, and the extraordinary circumstances of danger and war transformed her into a romantic ideal. "Benisons on her dear head forever!" Richardson exclaimed. The phrase became the subtitle to popular writer Benjamin Russell Hanby's song "Nameless Heroine," published in March 1865, before Richardson's narrative was in print. The lyrics captured the spirit, tone, and language of all fugitives' tributes:

> Out of the jaws of death,
> Out of the mouth of hell,
> Weary and hungry and fainting and sore,
> Fiends on the track of them,
> Fiends at the back of them,
> Fiends all around but an angel before.
>
> Out by the mountain path,
> Down through the darksome glen,
> Heedless of foes, nor at danger dismayed,

Sharing their doubtful fate,
Daring the tyrant's hate,
Heart of a lion, though form of a maid;

"Nameless," for foes may hear,
But by our love for thee,
Soon our bright sabres shall blush with their gore,
Then shall our banners free
Wave maiden over thee,
Then noble girl thou'llt be nameless no more.

Hail to the angel who goes on before,
Blessings be thine loyal maid evermore.

Richardson was so anxious for the "noble girl" to be "nameless no more" that he inserted a footnote into the text of his narrative when it was published in the summer of 1865 proclaiming that the "substantial closing of the war, while these pages are in press, renders it safe to give her name—Miss Melvina Stevens." Most fugitives more wisely withheld the names of their benefactresses until well into the 1880s.[19]

Time did not alter the main themes of published escape narratives, but it did alter some of the details that fugitives included in the stories. Drake rewrote his adventures in 1880 and published them in a "handsome" new edition entitled *Fast and Loose in Dixie*. He obtained testimonials from comrades to verify elements of the story and comments on the book from Jared E. Lewis and Albert Grant. Drake sent the manuscript to Ulysses S. Grant, who wrote back that he would soon read what promised to be a "thrilling account," and Drake disingenuously quoted Grant on the cover as if the renowned general had used those words after actually reading the book. In the new edition, Drake named those he had kept anonymous in 1866 and corrected minor details, such as identifying two of the women who helped him as Mary Estes's sisters rather than cousins. He embellished portions of the narrative with more flowery language and with sweeping historical references. The men who resisted conscription in Caldwell County, North Carolina, were likened to the "brave defenders of Tyrol" and the "hardy Waldenses, fighting and dying among the hills for dear Liberty's sake." He presented Mary Estes as a courtly, queen-like romantic ideal in keeping with the image of the "Nameless Heroine" promulgated by

Richardson and Browne. The women he encountered were prettier and were pretty more often than they were when he wrote in 1866.[20]

Fast and Loose in Dixie propelled Drake into national prominence. He was elected historian of the Medal of Honor Legion. Newspapers around the country covered his controversial career and his divisive exploits in what continued to be an adventurous life. Drake published the *Elizabeth Daily Leader* and successfully fought off five indictments for criminal libel. The New Jersey National Guard court-martialed him for exclaiming, "Hurrah! Three cheers for President Arthur!" when someone told him of President Garfield's assassination. Drake claimed he was joking because he did not believe the news. His post of the Grand Army of the Republic publicly quarreled with other posts in Elizabeth over who would serve as Guard of Honor for the Washington Centennial celebration. New York veterans called for his head when he presented a badge to the governor of Georgia upon that dignitary's visit to New Jersey in 1889. He made headlines again in 1892 when he spent the day with James J. Corbett the month after "Gentleman Jim" knocked out John L. Sullivan to win the World Heavyweight Championship. New Jersey veterans held an "indignation meeting" against him in 1910 when he substituted wax for natural flowers on veterans' graves on Decoration Day. "It may be that the whole country will adopt wax flowers instead of the natural article," Drake said in self-defense. "They can be as readily planted and will look like the real thing for a long time." When Drake died in 1913 after an illness lasting several months, newspapers called him "a widely known civil war veteran."[21]

John V. Hadley published the second edition of his narrative in 1898 with the New York firm Charles Scribner's Sons. At that time he was an elected judge and former three-term state senator. In this version he named his guardian angels, misspelling their last name Hollingsworth. He retracted the implication in his 1868 version that he had visited the cave of the outlaws who guided his party before abandoning them, and corrected the names he gave for the Vance brothers. He updated readers on the fate of Henry K. Davis, who agreed to pilot the party to Knoxville on the promise they would protect him from the Union army. Davis stayed with Hadley's brother in Indiana until September 1865, when he returned to North Carolina for a visit. While out riding with his father, he ran into a Rebel neighbor who had pretended to be a deserter in order to expose those hiding out in the woods. Davis immediately pulled a revolver and fired, but missed. A criminal court sentenced him to three months for assault and battery with intent to kill, but the governor pardoned him. Davis returned to Indiana, married, and settled. The year after *Seven Months a Prisoner* was re-released, Hadley become a justice on the Indiana Supreme Court, a position he held for twelve years. He helped plan Indiana's part in the fiftieth anniversary of the Battle of Gettysburg and edited a volume of local history. He died in 1915.[22]

Former fugitives who told their stories publicly for the first time after 1880 had the same essential message as those who wrote immediately after the war and emphasized the same general categories of experience. The corpus of stories handed down about escape from previously published accounts became mingled with and indistinguishable from their own memories of the distant events, although many of them accurately remembered the names of people they met. Recognizing the parallels between their escape and the flight of slaves on the antebellum Underground Railroad, they also drew on the conventions of slave narratives when they wrote their own accounts. In contrast to the terse statements fugitives dictated to clerks in the provost marshal's office in Hilton Head immediately after they arrived within Union lines, postwar writers elaborated on familiar themes from the sentimental northern literature on slavery: fleeing from bondage, being hunted and tracked, following signs in the night sky, and traveling stealthily with the aid of heroes who risked their lives for the freedom of others. They frequently employed the metaphor of slavery to depict both their prison experience and subsequent escape. S. H. M. Byers wrote of the slave who offered his garret in Columbia as a hiding place that "a fellow bondman would loose our chains."[23]

Aging escaped prisoners produced an abundance of memoirs, articles in local newspapers, and speeches before veterans' organizations that highlighted the loyal friendship and generous hospitality of African Americans. They emphasized dogs and bloodhounds in order to depict the atrocious crimes of a rebellious slaveholding society that would turn these animals against white men. They uttered paeans to their heroines in North Carolina. And sometimes their memories distorted their lived experience. They remembered slaves sharing a cornucopia of food with them rather than meager rations. Often they succumbed to the demands of literary convention rather than the evidence they heard on the road in their decisions about how to portray black southern speech. They converted the Confederacy into a strong police state with troops patrolling every road. Other fugitives reminisced more accurately about the details of their journey. They remembered citizens, not state forces, hunting them down. Blacks and whites spoke in the same pronunciation, whether it was presented in the text as plain English or incomprehensible dialect.[24]

As men wrote their accounts of flight through the Confederacy, or their time in Confederate prisons beforehand, they reflected on the meaning of the experience. They knew confinement had separated them from other veterans as well as from civilians because they could never fully explain what they had been through and how it affected them. They were sometimes impatient with those who tried to congratulate them. After an acquaintance told Austin Carr he was covered with glory, Carr wrote, "If he had seen me at Andersonville, he would have seen me covered with something else. He is welcome to all the glory. I done what I thought was my duty, and that is all that I want to know."[25]

As the decades progressed, ex-prisoners of war articulated a coherent set of claims about the personal and national meaning of the suffering they endured. Some found significance in the suffering itself. Most nineteenth-century Americans, until well after the Civil War, believed that suffering was redemptive and inspirational. A man who bore physical and emotional pain with fortitude proved both his character and the righteousness of his cause. John Harrold was a shoemaker who escaped from Florence, became desperately ill on the journey, and survived because an elderly couple hid him and nursed him for weeks until Sherman's army arrived. After the war, Harrold was a physical "wreck" whose pain disrupted his work. "I am content to bear my afflictions, since they were acquired in the path of duty," Harrold wrote in a widely echoed sentiment that cultural historians interpret as sincere. "To have been an humble actor in the stirring scenes which put down rebellion and banished treason from the land, is a proud—a glorious—record; one that soothes the acute pain and adapts my wants to my means. I would scarcely exchange it for health, wealth, and luxury." Ex-prisoners of war believed the sacrifice of their health was an offering to their country equal in worth to a battle-wound.[26]

Escapees found additional meaning in having lived through a personal adventure as thrilling as any recorded in history or fiction. Their narratives emphasize the awestruck reaction of others to the story of their flight. Former fugitives savored the descriptions others gave to the epoch that elevated their lives above the ordinary. Drake quoted from these liberally, as a marketing ploy for his book but also because he repeatedly insisted that the comments accurately encapsulated the significance of his individual story. His escape was "one of the most remarkable on record" and surpassed "anything I ever read in novels." Drake was more of an unabashed self-promoter than most other fugitives, but all of them betrayed some level of satisfaction at what their feats revealed: they were manly heroes. They basked in the fact that others recognized their inspirational example. "If our boys could read such books as this," one gentleman who endorsed Drake's book wrote, "dime novel fiction would cease, and the country would grow more heroes and fewer Indian-story vagabonds."[27]

Former fugitives remembered that their own heroism was bound to the heroism of others. They found a profound beauty and a deep bond in the brief but intense relationships they established with those they met at the crisis point of their lives. Eventually the lure of reconnecting with their black and white friends drew escaped prisoners back to the South. Benjamin Hasson of the Twenty-Second Pennsylvania Cavalry could not forget Ben Foster, a slave who carried him from hiding place to hiding place when Hasson was too weak to walk. Years after the war, at great personal expense, Hasson traveled south and searched out the freedman. Foster did not recognize the Yankee when he approached, but then his expression changed to surprise and happiness, and the two men had a joyful reunion.[28]

Other Yankees were in a position to offer more tangible rewards for the friendship they received during the desperate flight out of the Confederacy. Daniel Langworthy and ten other fugitives sent money to Robert Hamilton, the North Carolina sheriff who hid them and procured a guide. In July 1865, Hannibal Johnson's battalion occupied Anderson, South Carolina, where he had traveled as a fugitive seven months before. In his role as the assistant adjutant general, Johnson wrote the labor agreements that replaced slavery, and he was proud that the planters hated his contracts because they provided so many benefits for the freedmen. "It was the only known means at my disposal by which I could reach the entire number of negroes who had been my only friends when they were most needed, and return a small portion of the great debt and obligation I was under to the loyal black men and women," he explained.[29]

Fugitives' southern heroes likewise yearned to know the end of the story they had helped to write. Jack Loftis contacted Harvard law student Charles Porter Mattocks in March 1866. Mattocks had been exchanged in February 1865 and rejoined his regiment in time for the Appomattox Campaign. Congress later awarded him the Medal of Honor for his actions at the Battle of Sayler's Creek on April 6. Loftis inquired what happened after Mattocks's escape party left him. "If you hav forgot me and my name remember the house you came to in the nite and got the Brandey out of the Barrell in the ground," he wrote. Mattocks apparently replied with a catalog of his misfortunes and with queries about the names and well-being of people he encountered. "The old darkey that gav you the tobacco has gon to House keping for hur self and is well," Loftis reported. The grandchild named after Julius Litchfield was thriving. Loftis told the future representative to the Maine legislature and brigadier general in the Spanish American War that Rebel scouts had dragged the Yankees' hapless guide Gilbert Semple in irons through three counties, shot him in the head, and left his body lying in a public road. The Loftis family was still bitter against their Rebel neighbors. "I was truley sorry to heare of your Suffering so from hungrey. My wife sais that She would be glad to hav this Brut that you speak of Joe Gunter to deal with a while upon a hungry Stumick," he confided sympathetically. "She thinks she could make him remember the starved Yankes that he carried off to prison."[30]

J. Madison Drake searched for the postwar address of Mary and Bill Estes until he achieved success in 1880. He wrote and asked if he could come visit them. Mary responded, "Absent Friend—I have often wondered what became of you. I very well remember the Sabbath morning I brought you your breakfast and the feather beds we brought you to sleep upon, but I hope I can give you a good bed to sleep on *in the house* when you come down. The ring you gave me I have yet, and will keep it as long as I live, as a memento of you." She sent a courier with Drake's letter to her son Joseph, who lived on a farm in Mitchell County twenty miles from his parents. He wrote Drake that there was "no man I want to see more than you." He informed the Yankee that his family was "about to recover at last" from the war. John V. Hadley visited the Holinsworth sisters in 1897 and was gratified to find them "all alive—all married and happy in their mountain homes, with large families about them."[31]

The interaction between fugitive Federals and the southerners who helped them was larger-than-life. The setting was the history-changing collapse of the Confederacy. It was simultaneously intensely personal. Wartime memories bound J. Madison Drake to Mary Estes for their lifetimes. When he located her after his sixteen-year search, he sent her his photograph. She found that his face was inextricably linked in her mind with the maelstrom of war. "It resembles you much," she wrote, "and reminds me of terrible times in the past."[32]

Note on Sources

At the heart of this book is a database I created with the assistance of Ms. Erin Hope that contains the names of 3,010 individuals who escaped from Confederate prison camps and successfully reached the lines of the U.S. Army. It includes the following information, if available: rank and regiment, when and where captured, when and where escaped, and when and where the person reported to Union lines. The database is a compilation of records found in the National Archives. Two important documents are the "Record of Escaped Prisoners of War, USA" and "Memorandum of Prisoners Escaped from the Hands of the Rebels as Reported to the Office of the Commissary General of Prisoners." These two documents are found in "Register of Federal Prisoners of War Who Escaped from Confederate Authorities," RG 249, entry 31, no. 45, and "Memorandum of Escaped Prisoners from the Hands of the Rebels," RG 249, entry 32, box 1. The "Register" also includes information from the "List of Federal Prisoners of War Who Escaped from Confederate Authorities," RG 249, entry 109. The database incorporates a list entitled "Escaped Union Prisoners of War from Rebeldom," which can be found in the National Archives under the designation "Union Prisoners of War—Escaped from Confederate Authorities," RG 393, part 1, entry 4318. Additional names and other information were included in the database from the following sources: "Rolls and Reports of Federal Prisoners of War Who Escaped from Confederate Prisons," RG 249, entry 32, box 1 (compiled by the provost marshal general in Knoxville, Tennessee); "Statements of Escaped Union Prisoners, Refugees, and Rebel Deserters," RG 393, part 1, entries 4294 and 4295 (record book of the Office of the Provost Marshal General, Hilton Head, South Carolina); "Lists of Escaped Prisoners, Deserters, and Refugees," RG 249, entry 107, box 11, roll 979; "Letters Received Relating to Union Naval POWs: Reports from Officers and Seamen of the U.S. Navy Who Were Prisoners of War in the South," RG 45, entry 56.

The count of escaped prisoners from locations in the Carolinas is derived from a combination of the database, official Confederate prison records, and diaries of imprisoned U.S. soldiers and sailors. Estimates of the number of escaped enlisted men from Florence in September ranged as high as 700, the figure provided on November 5, 1864, to the provost marshal on Morris Island, South Carolina, by a group of escaped prisoners. Brigadier General William M. Gardner reported on November 2, 1864, to Adjutant and Inspector General Samuel Cooper "400 to 600," and the *Darlington Southerner* claimed the figure to be 500. I chose to use the conservative number of 400. The tally of 500 Union officers who escaped between October and December 1864 combines the report of Brigadier General John H. Winder to Cooper on December 6, 1864, that 373 officers escaped from Columbia with prisoner diaries and database records that indicate at least another 127 escaped in Charleston and on the trains carrying prisoners from Charleston to Columbia. Some Federals keeping diaries in Camp Sorghum estimated escapes from that location at the end of November as totaling 400 to 550, but again I chose to use the most conservative calculation. The database indicates that sixty-five Federals successfully escaped from various locations in North and South Carolina in January 1865. Confederate prison officials reported on March 31, 1865, that 1,703 prisoners escaped during the February transfer of prisoners from Columbia, Florence, and Salisbury. The database tags another 158 Federal prisoners who escaped from other locations in North and South Carolina during February and March. This totals 2,826 escapes.

The database provided the heart of this story; the diaries and narratives of fugitive Federals provided its soul. The basic details of a fugitive's story were verified before they appeared in this book. I used a variety of sources to find the southerners that fugitives named, including Federal census records, state tax records, state marriage and death records, and state militia records. Fugitive accounts that were based on diary entries and that provided exact dates and locations were cross-referenced with each other because multiple escape parties encountered each other along the way. I used the provost marshal general's interviews with escaped prisoners who arrived at Hilton Head, which were generally conducted on the date fugitives arrived inside U.S. Army lines, along with manuscript diaries kept by fugitives, as important baselines to compare with narratives and memoirs published after 1865. The interviewees generally did not publish narratives, and they described what they encountered when events were still fresh in their minds. The interviews are a collective testimony to the hardships of the journey, to the friendship escaped prisoners received from slaves and deserters, and to the collapse of the Confederacy.

Appendix: Maps

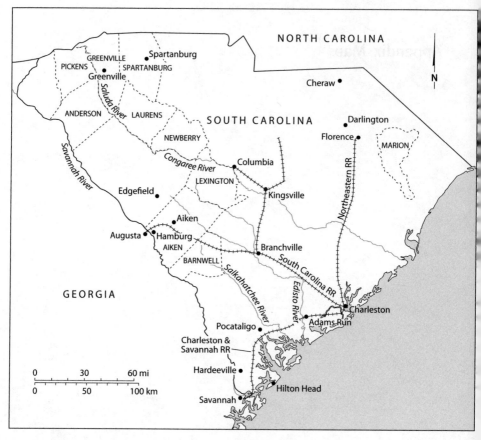

Map 1. South Carolina, September–October 1864

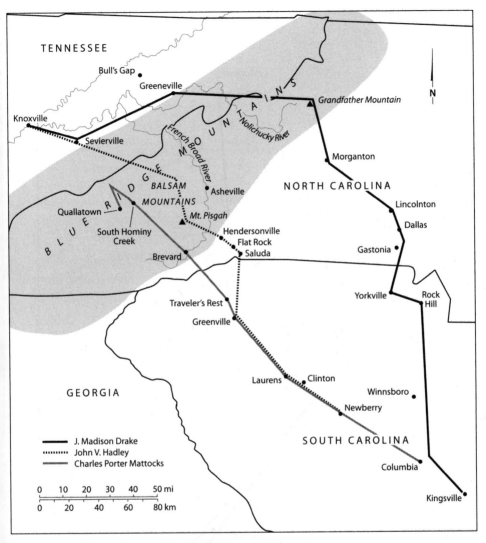

Map 2. Escape Routes of Drake, Hadley, and Mattocks

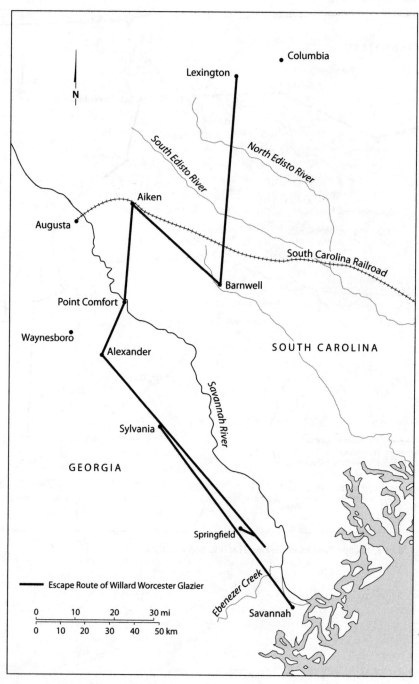

Map 3. Escape Route of Glazier

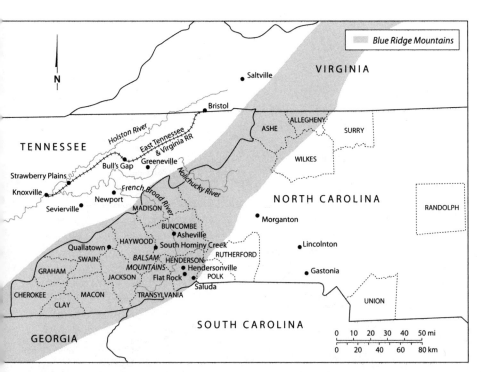

Map 4. Western North Carolina, East Tennessee, and Southwest Virginia

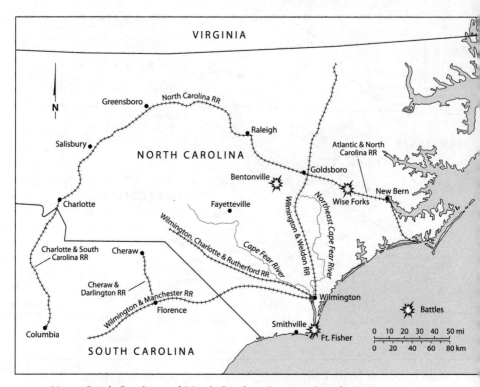

Map 5. South Carolina and North Carolina, January–March 1865

Notes

Introduction

1. *Daily Watchman* (Salisbury), October 14, November 11, and December 13, 1864; *Daily Conservative* (Raleigh), October 26, 1864; *Daily Southern Guardian*, November 4 and December 17, 1864; *Daily Confederate* (Raleigh), December 13, 1864; *Carolina Watchman* (Salisbury), October 10, 1864; *Charleston Daily Courier*, December 21, 1864; "Account of Captain Conley," 10, LC.

2. *Edgefield Advertiser*, November 30, 1864.

3. Foote, "Fugitive Federals Database." See "Note on Sources" for information on this database.

4. The count of escaped prisoners is derived from a combination of official Confederate prison records, a database I compiled using official Union records, and diaries of imprisoned Federals. See "Note on Sources" for an explanation of the numbers.

5. *Daily Southern Guardian*, December 17, 1864; *Daily Conservative* (Raleigh), October 26, 1864; *Carolina Watchman* (Salisbury), October 10, 1864; *Edgefield Advertiser*, December 14, 1864; Glazier, *Capture and Escape*, 205; Richardson, *Secret Service, Dungeon, and Escape*, 473–74; Langworthy, *Reminiscences of a Prisoner of War*, 55; Abbott, *Prison Life in the South*, 230–31; Benson, "Prison Life and Escape," 8; Hasson, *Escape from the Confederacy*, 56; Johnson, "Sword of Honor," 22–23.

6. Historians have examined how structural and bureaucratic problems in a declining Confederacy contributed to high death rates in Confederate prisons, but they failed to consider how the Confederacy's emergency transfer of nearly 14,000 prisoners of war from sites in Georgia to South Carolina fit into the story of the Confederacy's collapse in the region in the last winter of the Civil War. See Sanders Jr., *While in the Hands of the Enemy*; Pickenpaugh, *Captives in Blue*; Marvel, *Andersonville*; Hesseltine, *Civil War Prisons*. A nonscholarly work that considers prison escapes from individual prisons and misses National Archive evidence that point to the scale of escapes at the end of the war is Casstevens, *"Out of the Mouth of Hell."* For an essay discussing the various studies of individual prisons, see Gillispie, "Prisons," in Sheehan-Dean, *Companion to the U.S. Civil War*, vol. 1, 456–75. A few scholars have studied escaped prisoners of war without recognizing the scale of escapes, as examples of personal narratives or as windows into northern views of Appalachian culture. Inscoe, "'Moving through Deserter Country,'" in Noe and Wilson, *Civil War in Appalachia*, 158–86; Sarris, *Separate Civil War*; Fabian, *Unvarnished Truth*.

7. Barton A. Myers estimates that the Confederate government controlled less than 60 percent of North Carolina by 1864. See *Rebels against the Confederacy*, 13,

124; Grimsley and Simpson, *Collapse of the Confederacy*, 1–5, 11; Robinson, *Bitter Fruits of Bondage*, 3–11. Robinson borrows models from historians who study European wars to examine whether a "general crisis" explains the collapse of the Confederacy. He argues that slavery began to unravel in the opening days of the war and that efforts of slaveholders to protect the institution sparked internal social conflicts that undermined the Confederacy. My book does not argue that class conflict between slaveholders and non-slaveholders brought down the Confederacy, but it did benefit from Robinson's thoughtful consideration of what constitutes a "general crisis" for a society at war. There is only one scholarly monograph that covers South Carolina during the war years in depth. See Cauthen, *South Carolina Goes to War*. An important recent study of Sherman's march through the Carolinas argues that his actions served to reinvigorate Confederate nationalism and the desire for independence among southern women. Campbell, *When Sherman Marched North from the Sea*. My book begins with a different premise than works such as Campbell's that study what Confederates *said* and how individual women reacted when faced with Union armies at the end of the war. This book looks at whether institutions still functioned and what capabilities the Confederate and state governments possessed.

Chapter 1

1. This overview of the situation in 1864 was based upon the author's reading of the books provided in the bibliography. Particularly useful general overviews are McPherson and Hogue, *Ordeal by Fire*; Burton, *Age of Lincoln*; Stoker, *Grand Design*; Davis, *Look Away*.

2. Sanders Jr., *While in the Hands of the Enemy*, 3–4.

3. Gillispie, "Prisons," in Sheehan-Dean, *Companion to the U.S. Civil War*; Sanders Jr., *While in the Hands of the Enemy*, 51–52; Marvel, *Andersonville*; Hesseltine, *Civil War Prisons*.

4. Cooper to Winder, September 5, 1864, *OR*, ser. 2, vol. 7: 773.

5. Jones to Seddon, September 7, 1864, *OR*, ser. 2, vol. 7: 782; McLaws to Stringfellow, September 8, 1864, *OR*, ser. 2, vol. 7: 788; Pickenpaugh, *Captives in Blue*, 196–97.

6. Seddon to Jones, September 9, 1864, *OR*, ser. 2, vol. 7: 795.

7. Cooper to Jones, September 5, 1864, *OR*, ser. 2, vol. 7: 773; Jones to Seddon, September 5, 1864, *OR*, ser. 2, vol. 7: 773; Jones endorsement on McLaws to Stringfellow, September 8, 1864, *OR*, ser. 2, vol. 7: 789; Chesnut Jr. to Cooper, August 31, 1864, Military Letterbook, SCDAH; Chesnut Jr. to Jones, September 9 and 10, 1864, Military Letterbook, SCDAH.

8. Jones to Seddon, September 12, 1864, *OR*, ser. 2, vol. 7: 817; Jones to Cooper, September 23, 1864, *OR*, ser. 2, vol. 7: 866; Lay to Ripley, September 18, 1864, *OR*, ser. 2, vol. 7: 841; Feilden to Trapier, September 17, 1864, *OR*, ser. 2, vol. 7: 837; Gardner to Cooper, November 2, 1864, *OR*, ser. 2, vol. 7: 1086; Feilden to Ripley, September 30, 1864, *OR*, ser. 2, vol. 7: 900; Dufur, *Over the Dead Line*, 142–61. Dufur kept the memorandum book he made while a prisoner and a fugitive and used that to write his narrative.

9. Jones to Seddon, September 12, 1864, *OR*, ser. 2, vol. 7: 817; Jones to Cooper, September 23, 1864, *OR*, ser. 2, vol. 7: 866; Lay to Ripley, September 18, 1864, *OR*, ser. 2, vol. 7: 841; Feilden to Trapier, September 17, 1864, *OR*, ser. 2, vol. 7: 837; Feilden to Ripley, September 30, 1864, *OR*, ser. 2, vol. 7: 900; *Edgefield Advertiser*, October 12, 1864 (the *Advertiser* reprinted the article from the Darlington paper); Foote, "Fugitive Federals Database."

10. Gardner to Cooper, November 2, 1864, *OR*, ser. 2, vol. 7: 1086. Cooper launched an inquiry into the outbreak from Florence, and Gardner's missive was his report on the incident. Telegraph from Harrison to Stringfellow, November 27, 1864, Papers of Maj. Gen. Sam Jones, 1864–65, RG 109, entry 124, NA. One Federal prisoner observed that in the open field the camp guard performed their duty improperly. "Two sentinels would pace their beat facing each other until just in time to avoid a collision, when they would halt, about face, and march back. Old soldiers would have known better. The proper way would have been for all the sentries on the line to march one way, and then turn at the same time and march back. In that way no portion of the line is left unguarded." When he escaped Florence, he and his comrade headed in a northeast direction, trying to strike New Berne, North Carolina, "the nearest point we knew of in possession of Union troops." Williams, "From Spotsylvania to Wilmington, N.C.," 15–17.

11. "Statement of Cpt. Telford, N.D.," RBPMG, Hilton Head, S.C., RG 393, entry 4295, NA; Foote, "Fugitive Federals Database."

12. Duncan McKercher Pocket Diary, October 9, 1864, Duncan McKercher Papers, MssHM 48562–48568, HL; "Account of Captain Conley," 2, LC; Trautman, *Twenty Months in Captivity*, 105; Foote, "Fugitive Federals Database"; Drake, *Narrative of Capture and Escape*, 12–13.

13. Drake, *Narrative of Capture and Escape*, 14–15, 93; Drake, *Fast and Loose in Dixie*, 304. These books contain signed testimonials of the witnesses.

14. Moore, *Columbia and Richland County*, 182–96; Edgar, *South Carolina*, 369.

15. Edward E. Dickerson Account, October 23, 1864, Edward E. Dickerson Papers, LC; "Statement of 23 Officers," December 23, 1864, RBPMG, Hilton Head, S.C., RG 393, entry 4295, NA; "Statement of Cpt. S.A. Clarke," December 22, 1864, RBPMG, Hilton Head, S.C., RG 393, entry 4295, NA; Childs to Lee, October 8, 1864, Huston Lee Papers, SCHS; Christianson, "Community Study," 51.

16. Winder to Cooper, December 6, 1864, *OR*, ser. 2, vol. 7: 1196; Jones to Cooper, September 29, 1864, *OR*, ser. 2, vol. 7: 894; Hardee to Bonham, October 7, 1864, *OR*, ser. 2, vol. 7: 930; Christianson, "Community Study," 42–43, 73–74; Sanders Jr., *While in the Hands of the Enemy*, 228–29, 251; Urquhart to Cooper and endorsements, October 26, 1864, *OR*, ser. 2, vol. 7: 1046. On November 4, Seddon ordered that the prison at Columbia be placed under the authority of Gardner.

17. Gardner to Bonham, October 12, 1864, *OR*, ser. 2, vol. 7: 975; Bonham to Davis, October 29, 1864, *OR*, ser. 2, vol. 7: 1062; Gardner to Davis, October 30, 1864, *OR*, ser. 2, vol. 7: 1063; Martin to Andrews, October 31, 1864, *OR*, ser. 2, vol. 7: 1076; Davis to Chesnut Jr., October 31, 1864, *OR*, ser. 2, vol. 7: 1077; Chesnut Jr. to Bonham, November 15, 1864, and Chesnut Jr. to Davis, November 17, 1864, Military Letterbook, SCDAH; Special Order 275, November 19, 1864, *OR*, ser. 2, vol. 7:

1145; Seddon to Bonham, November 21, 1864, *OR*, ser. 2, vol. 7: 1151; telegraph from Means to Nance, November 21, 1864, Papers of Maj. Gen. Sam Jones, 1864–1865, RG 109, entry 124, NA; Gardner to Andrews, December 4, 1864, *OR*, ser. 2, vol. 7: 1188; Winder to Cooper, December 6, 1864, *OR*, ser. 2, vol. 7: 1196; Sanders Jr., *While in the Hands of the Enemy*, 255; Foote, "Fugitive Federals Database."

18. Chesnut Jr. to Hardee, October 23, 1864, Military Letterbook, SCDAH. When the second batch of prisoners arrived on October 6, local officials temporarily mobilized two professors and all the cadets at the Arsenal Academy to help guard the prisoners. John B. Patrick Diary, October 6, 1864, SCL; "Statement of J. L. Paston," November 14, 1864, RBPMG, Hilton Head, S.C., RG 393, entry 4295, NA; "Statement of James Morgan," November 21, 1864, RBPMG, Hilton Head, S.C., RG 393, entry 4295, NA; Christiansen, "Community Study," 47. Reports of disloyal and incompetent guards are ubiquitous in fugitive diaries and narratives. Several prisoners inside the camp were shot by prison guards. Ferguson, *Life-Struggles in Rebel Prisons*, 146; McKercher Papers, Pocket Diary, December 1, 1864, HL; Christiansen, "Community Study," 33.

19. They had planned to escape, but the moment they chose to do so was based on spontaneity. Racine, *"Unspoiled Heart,"* 229; Hunt, "Our Escape," 89.

20. Racine, *"Unspoiled Heart,"* xiv–xxi, 65–66, 100–124.

21. Ibid., 172–73.

22. Hunt, "Our Escape," 90–94; Racine, *"Unspoiled Heart,"* 228.

23. Robertson Jr., "An Indiana Soldier in Love and War," 282; Hadley, *Seven Months a Prisoner* (1868), 29, 57, 59–60, 75–76.

24. Hadley, *Seven Months a Prisoner* (1868), 85.

25. Ibid., 80–81.

26. Foote, "Fugitive Federals Database." Of the 241 fugitives who successfully escaped from Columbia, 114 reported to Knoxville.

27. Billings Memoir, 96–99, LC; Foote, "Fugitive Federals Database."

28. Steele to Hall, December 7, 1864, "Statement of Cpt. James F. Morgan," November 21, 1864, "Statement of Bledsoe," n.d., RBPMG, Hilton Head, S.C., RG 393, entry 4295, NA; Foote, "Fugitive Federals Database."

29. Glazier, *Capture and Escape*, 185–95.

Chapter 2

1. Glazier, *Capture and Escape*, 202, 246; Fahs, *Imagined Civil War*, 13–14, 279–80. According to Fahs, popular literature of the Civil War era relied heavily on the imagery of minstrelsy and authors used a well-established convention of assigning black characters a "virtually unintelligible dialect." Thomas H. Howe, a fugitive from Andersonville who traveled in Georgia, wrote that "many of the whites talked very similar to the negroes." Howe, *Adventures of an Escaped Union Soldier*, 22. One prisoner commented that white southerners in Danville, Virginia, "talk a great deal like the darkies, that is, the tone of their voice and the manner of uttering their words." Carr, *Three Years Cruise*, entry for July 4, 1864.

2. Langworthy, *Reminiscences of a Prisoner of War*, 43–45; Foote, "Fugitive Federals Database." The escape party of Chauncey S. Aldrich and four other officers from Columbia twice mistook white people for African Americans. C. S. Aldrich Civil War Diary, SM1, folder 1, Chauncey S. Aldrich Collection, PMM.

3. Schwalm, *Hard Fight for We*, 4–5, 79–80, 113–14; Weiner, *Mistresses and Slaves*, 170–79; Moore, *Columbia and Richland County*, 174–82.

4. Drake, *Narrative of Capture and Escape*, 19–20.

5. Russell, "Reminiscences of Prison Life and Escape," 47–48. Russell escaped twice from Camp Sorghum, the first in early November, but was recaptured in Anderson District. The second successful escape was from the asylum prison on December 17. This time Russell tried to find Sherman's army and was successful. The database has him report to Hilton Head. His memoirs vaguely state that he found Sherman's lines, visited Sherman's headquarters, and received an escort to Washington, D.C. Foote, "Fugitive Federals Database."

6. Racine, *"Unspoiled Heart,"* 231–33; Hunt, "Our Escape," 96.

7. Hadley, *Seven Months a Prisoner* (1868), 82–84. Reid Mitchell, in his study of Civil War soldiers, argues that many Union soldiers held blacks responsible for the war. *Civil War Soldiers*, 123.

8. Edward E. Dickerson Account, 9–10, Edward E. Dickerson Papers, LC.

9. Hadley, *Seven Months a Prisoner* (1868), 86–91.

10. Ibid., 82–83. Fugitives were commonly surprised about black knowledge of Lincoln and the Emancipation Proclamation. Fugitives make of a point of mentioning in their diaries and later narratives how slaves did not believe the stories their masters told and how impressed they were with slaves' knowledge of geography and the vast amount of information they possessed about their neighborhoods. Two other good examples, among many, are Edward E. Dickerson Account, 10, Edward E. Dickerson Papers, LC (Dickerson escaped from Sorghum on October 28); "In Search of Liberty," an anonymous account written in January 1865 of a party that escaped from Sorghum on November 28 in Abbott, *Prison Life in the South*, 223–25, 233.

11. Hadley, *Seven Months a Prisoner* (1868), 91–94. One escape party took the slaves' advice to separate and take different paths. Hasson, *Escape from the Confederacy*, 22.

12. Scholar Alice Fahs discusses the coexisting and multilayered stereotypes northerners developed of slaves during the Civil War based on black characters in popular literature. At the start of the war, black characters were generally buffoonish, but this gave way to celebrations of black manhood and heroism around the time of emancipation. Popular northern literature during the Civil War also contained slave characters who laughed at their masters and outwitted them. Northern audiences enjoyed reading about slaveholders getting a comeuppance. But ambivalence and mixed messages about blacks never completely disappeared. Fahs, *Imagined Civil War*, 13, 151–78. Theater and minstrel shows also portrayed slaves in a variety of ways: tricksters, rebels against authority, foolish imbeciles, and innocent helpless victims. Slaves were unhappy but resigned

to their fate. Lawson, "Imagining Slavery," 28–42. Scholars of Union soldiers agree that exposure to southern blacks generally led to hatred for slavery and respect for blacks' dedication to freedom and support for Union armies but that ambivalence and racial boundaries remained. Mitchell, *Civil War Soldiers*, 117–26; Glatthaar, *March to the Sea and Beyond*, 52–65; Manning, *What This Cruel War Was Over*, 191–92.

13. Walt Wolfram and Guy Bailey are at the forefront of linguists whose research suggests that black and white southern vernacular English was partially aligned in the mid-nineteenth century, was distinct to its region, and grew farther apart after World War I. Southern vernaculars are complex and vary from one region to another, from one social group to another, and from one generation to another. A historian who studied All Saints Parish, South Carolina, with its Gullah creole language, notes that antebellum English travelers to the region commented that whites learned to talk like their slaves and that planters' pronunciation, accent, and tone were the same as their slaves'. Montgomery and Bailey, *Language Variety in the South*, 2, 27–28; Wolfram and Thomas, *Development of African American English*, 184–205; Lanehart, *Sociocultural and Historical Contexts of African American English*, 53–57, 78–94; Joyner, *Down by the Riverside*, 208–9, 216. Stephanie M. H. Camp has adapted the term "rival geography" to describe slaves' alternative ways of using plantation space that defied masters' demands. Camp, *Closer to Freedom*, 6–7, 36, 49. Anthony Kaye argues that slaves created neighborhoods that served as the locus for their lives. They forged enduring bonds across plantations that weakened masters' power over them. Kaye argues that there was no monolithic "slave community" but rather "many neighborhoods." Kaye, *Joining Places*, 4–10, 120–24.

14. "Statement of James Morgan, November 21, 1864" and "Statement of J. L. Paston, November 14, 1864," RBPMG, Hilton Head, S.C., RG 393, entry 4295, NA.

15. Sylvanus Crossly Diary, February 20, 1865, LC; "Statement of W. H. Bledsoe," n.d., RBPMG, Hilton Head, S.C., RG 393, entry 4294, NA; Abbott, *Prison Life in the South*, 216–17; "Account of Captain Conley," 15, LC; Long, *Twelve Months in Andersonville*, 116–20. Drake and his party likewise denied a request to accompany them, but in this case the age and crippled condition of the slave was a factor as well. Drake, *Narrative of Capture and Escape*, 22.

16. Glenn David Brasher points out that slaves could not be sure at the start of the war which side offered better prospects and which side would win. The majority of slaves waited to see how the situation developed. In the Virginia Peninsula, slaves who tested the waters learned that the Union welcomed runaways and that most interactions with the Union army were positive. This helped dispel the lies—such as South Carolina slaves heard—about what Yankees would do to slaves. As this news spread, blacks ran to Union lines in increasing numbers. Union advances and Confederate retreat made going to the Yankees seem to be a safer decision. Brasher, *Peninsula Campaign and the Necessity of Emancipation*, 46–47, 135–45. Anthony Kaye's study of the Natchez District likewise finds that slaves assessed the balance of power, saw signs of their masters' increasing powerlessness, and acted when the time was ripe. Kaye, *Joining Places*, 189–93.

17. Sabre, *Nineteen Months a Prisoner of War*, 157–58. This book provides the diary of Lieutenant J. N. Whitney, Second Rhode Island Cavalry, during his escape from Columbia on October 20, 1864, until his recapture on November 28. His escape party headed toward Augusta.

18. Abbott, *Prison Life in the South*, 207; Sabre, *Nineteenth Months a Prisoner of War*, 148–52. According to one study of slave folk life in All Saints Parish, South Carolina, spirituals in the region were heavily imbued with themes that slavery was temporary, that God would wreak vengeance on oppressors, that God works miracles to bring about immediate change, and that God would deliver his people from bondage. Joyner, *Down by the Riverside*, 164–65. Good studies of slave religion include Raboteau, *Slave Religion*, and Fountain, *Slavery, Civil War, and Salvation*.

19. Berlin, *Destruction of Slavery*, 811–12, 817.

20. Dufur, *Over the Dead Line*, 176. When Dufur published his account in later years, he reworked the language of the prayer into the typecast vernacular northern audiences expected. I have presented the prayer in plain English.

21. Glazier, *Capture and Escape*, 211; Judges, chapter 7, New International Version. Again I have presented this prayer without the vernacular Glazier used. Glazier kept a diary during his travel and published his account in November 1865. R. A. Ragan, a Unionist in East Tennessee who served as a scout and guide taking Unionists, deserters, and escaped prisoners to Union lines in Tennessee and Kentucky, published an account of his life in 1910 that also records the prayer of an African American over an escape party. The first part of the prayer asks for God to bring Egyptian darkness over the eyes of the Rebels. The second part of the prayer plagiarizes Glazier's account. However, the fact that Ragan included a prayer meeting in his account, even if the text was lifted from others, provides more evidence that such meetings were common among fugitives of all types who were helped by blacks in the South. Ragan, *Escape from East Tennessee*, 50–51.

22. Schwalm, *Hard Fight for We*, 79; "Statement of Ephraim Russell, July 22, 1864," RBPMG, Hilton Head, S.C., RG 393, entry 4295, NA; "Statement of Capt. B. C. G. Reed and Lieut. T. B. Stevenson, forwarded by Lt. Col. and Provost Marshal General James F. Hall," *OR*, ser. 1, vol. 35, pt. 2: 220–21.

23. Racine, *"Unspoiled Heart,"* 231–35; Hunt, "Our Escape," 98–106; "Account of Captain Conley," 8, LC.

24. For good examples, see "Account of Captain Conley," 7, LC, and Hasson, *Escape from the Confederacy*, 21–22; Camp, *Closer to Freedom*, 46–59, 119; Joyner, *Down by the Riverside*, 76.

25. Johnson, "Sword of Honor," 28–34; Cochran, "Reminiscences of Life in Rebel Prisons," 51–53.

26. Abbott, *Prison Life in the South*, 230–31; Chesnut Jr. to Magrath, December 21, 1864, Magrath Order Book, 1864–65, SCDAH; Magrath to Green, December 21, 1864, Magrath Order Book, 1864–65, SCDAH; Magrath to Frederick, December 21, 1864, Magrath Order Book, 1864–65, SCDAH; Gayle to Magrath, December 30, 1864, Magrath Letters Received, SCDAH; Schwalm, *Hard Fight for We*, 107; McCurry, *Confederate Reckoning*, 256–61. There were reported slave uprisings

in Anderson, Chesterfield, Darlington, Sumter, and Lancaster Districts. Edgar, *South Carolina: A History*, 367.

27. Racine, *Piedmont Farmer*, 319–32; Racine, *Living a Big War in a Small Place*, 1–9, 44.

28. Racine, *Piedmont Farmer*, 346–51.

29. Ibid., 355–57.

30. Hadden, *Slave Patrols*, 42–43, 57, 67–74, 166–83.

31. Berlin, *Destruction of Slavery*, 806–7; Walsh to Bonham, November 14, 1864, Bonham Official Correspondence, 1862–1864, SCDAH; Petition from Laurens District, January 3, 1865, Gayle to Magrath, December 30, 1864, Rogers to Magrath, December 30, 1864, Memorial from Citizens, January 3, 1864, Letters Received and Sent, December 19, 1864–April 25, 1865, Gov. Andrew Gordon Magrath Papers, SCDAH.

32. Parker to Magrath, December 24, 1864, Magrath Letters Received, SCDAH.

33. Berlin, *Destruction of Slavery*, 816–17.

34. Billings Memoir, 94–97, LC.

35. "Statement of James Morgan, November 21, 1864," and "Statement of J. L. Paston, November 14, 1864," RBPMG, Hilton Head, S.C., RG 393, entry 4295, NA; Abbott, *Prison Life in the South*, 124–31; Ferguson, *Life-Struggles in Rebel Prisons*, 140, 147; Glazier, *Capture and Escape*, 188; *Palmetto Herald*, November 17, 1864; Byers, *What I Saw in Dixie*, 63; Campbell, "Seminoles, the 'Bloodhound War,' and Abolitionism, 1796–1865," 273, 284–88.

36. Wilson, *Sufferings Endured for a Free Government*, 227; Smith, "From Andersonville to Freedom," 49–51; Murray, "From Macon, Georgia, to the Gulf," 93–95; Langworthy, *Reminiscences of a Prisoner of War*, 40; Geer, *Beyond the Lines*, 127–28; Billings Memoir, 99, LC.

37. "Account of Captain Conley," 11, LC; Edward E. Dickerson Account, 15, Edward E. Dickerson Papers, LC; Newlin, *Account of the Escape of Six Federal Soldiers*, 48–49.

38. Drake, *Narrative of Capture and Escape*, 23; Billings Memoir, 91, LC.

39. Jaime Amanda Martinez, in *Confederate Slave Impressment in the Upper South*, argues that the Confederacy developed an effective federalized impressment system with slaveholder cooperation in Virginia and North Carolina. Other scholars argue that when masters and slaves colluded to resist impressment, they undermined both slavery and the Confederate government. These include McCurry, *Confederate Reckoning*; Robinson, *Bitter Fruits of Bondage*; Mohr, *On the Threshold of Freedom*.

40. An Act to Organize and Supply Negro Labor for Coast Defense, December 18, 1862, No. 4614; An Act to Amend an Act Entitled An Act to Organize and Supply Negro Labor, February 6, 1863, No. 4615; An Act to Amend an Act Entitled An Act to Amend an Act Entitled An Act to Organize and Supply Negro Labor, April 10, 1863, No. 4616; An Act to Amend an Act Entitled An Act to Amend an Act to Organize and Supply Negro Labor for Coast Defense, September 30, 1863, No. 4665; An Act to Amend the Act in Relation to the Supply of Labor

Passed in September 1863, December 16, 1863, No. 4673. All of the above are found in *Published Laws of South Carolina*, SCDAH.

41. Jones to Bonham, June 29, 1864, *OR*, ser. 1, vol. 35, pt. 2: 542–43; Magrath to Barnwell, December 30, 1864, Andrew Gordon Magrath Papers, SCL; Stringfellow to Ransom, December 1, 1864, *OR*, ser. 1, vol. 44: 918; Cauthen, *South Carolina Goes to War*, 147–48, 178–82; Moore, *Columbia and Richland County*, 199.

42. Racine, *Piedmont Farmer*, 317, 329, 345; Chesnut Jr. to Seddon, October 6, 1864, Military Letterbook, SCDAH; Hayes to Fox, October 28, 1864, John Fox Papers, RL. The impressment agent obtained slaves from Hayes on the promise that he would not have to provide any more.

43. Preston to Seddon, December 29, 1864, and January 15, 1865, *OR*, ser. 4, vol. 3: 979, 1019; An Act to Repeal All Acts and Parts of Acts heretofore Passed by the Legislature of this State on the Subject of Furnishing Slave Labor, December 23, 1864, No. 4702, *Published Laws of South Carolina*, SCDAH. Preston believed South Carolina's law was an assertion of state sovereignty because its provisions conflicted with the instructions of the War Department. "This legislation is an explicit declaration that this State does not intend to contribute another soldier or slave to the public defense, except on such terms as may be dictated by her authorities," he wrote the secretary of war. Historian Stephanie McCurry argues that South Carolina's planters ultimately sacrificed Confederate independence in a futile effort to save their property. McCurry, *Confederate Reckoning*, 285.

44. Johnson to Magrath, January 10, 1865, *OR*, ser. 4, vol. 3: 1022; Cauthen, *South Carolina Goes to War*, 182–84; Barrett, *Sherman's March through the Carolinas*, 44.

Chapter 3

1. Racine, *"Unspoiled Heart,"* 232–33.
2. Ibid.; Hunt, "Our Escape," 99–101. The glut of prisoners on the roads at this time is explained by Major Charles G. Davis, who estimated that 105 men escaped Sorghum on November 3 and another 200 to 300 the next day, when he and five others absconded. They picked up another officer on the road, ran into another party of five officers a few days later, and added a second officer to the original party after they ran into the man three times in three days. "Prison Experiences of Major Charles G. Davis," SCTN.
3. *Edgefield Advertiser*, October 19, November 30, and December 7, 1864; Russell, "Reminiscences of Prison Life and Escape," 54–59; Robbins, "Life in Rebel Prisons," 7–8.
4. *Edgefield Advertiser*, December 7 and 14, 1864.
5. *Edgefield Advertiser*, November 30, December 14, and December 28, 1864. In Aiken, located twenty-two miles southeast of Edgefield, men in the community enrolled in a company for local defense on November 28 when rumors reached them that Sherman was moving toward Augusta and would thus threaten their district. Henry W. Ravenel Private Journal, November 28, 1864, SCL.

6. Abstract of Return of Department of South Carolina, Georgia, and Florida for October 31, 1864, *OR*, ser. 1, vol. 35, pt. 2: 643; Report of Bureau of Conscription, Preston to Seddon, December 31, 1863, *OR*, ser. 4, vol. 2: 1071.

7. B. F. Perry Journal, May 17, 1863, ser. 2, vol. 2, SHC; Huff Jr., *Greenville*, 112–15, 128–43; McLeod, "An Account of Greenville," 1–5; Cauthen, *South Carolina Goes to War*, 4–12, 27–28, 150. In Anderson District, during July 1863, the Soldier's Board of Relief distributed funds to 610 families. Anderson District, July 9, 1863, Report of Soldiers' Board of Relief, Green Files, SCDAH.

8. Ashmore to Melton, August 7, 16, and 17, 1863, *OR*, ser. 4, vol. 2: 771–74; Bonham to Vance, August 22, 1863, *OR*, ser. 4, vol. 2: 741; Melton to Preston, August 25, 1863, *OR*, ser. 4, vol. 2: 769–70; "An Act to Prevent Desertion from Confederate or State Military Service, and Evasion of Conscription," September 30, 1863, No. 4666, *Published Laws of South Carolina*, SCDAH.

9. Palmer to Ashmore, February 5, 1864, *OR*, ser. 1, vol. 35, pt. 1: 575; Westmoreland to Beauregard, February 7, 1864, *OR*, ser. 1, vol. 35, pt. 1: 574–75; Maxwell to Ashmore, February 7, 1864, *OR*, ser. 1, vol. 35, pt. 1: 576; Norton to Grisham, February 7, 1864, *OR*, ser. 1, vol. 35, pt. 1: 581; Ashmore to Beauregard, February 7 and 8, 1864, *OR*, ser. 1, vol. 35, pt. 1: 576–77, 580.

10. Ashmore to Jordan, March 26, 1864, *OR*, ser. 1, vol. 35, pt. 2: 376; Simkins to Boylston, May 7, 1864, *OR*, ser. 1, vol. 35, pt. 2: 478; Feilden to Ashmore, June 4, 1864, *OR*, ser. 1, vol. 35, pt. 2: 521.

11. Special Order 101, April 30, 1864, *OR*, ser. 1, vol. 35, pt. 2: 456; Jones to Cooper, July 29, 1864, *OR*, ser. 1, vol. 35, pt. 2: 596; Chesnut Jr. to Perryman, August 24, 1864, to Cooper, August 31, 1864, to Jones, August 31, 1864, to Bonham, September 1, 1864, Military Letterbook, SCDAH; Hayne to Harrison, September 8, 1864, Military Letterbook, SCDAH. Chesnut wrote Jones on August 31 that a tour of northwest South Carolina convinced him that section was peaceful and the citizens secure, but this statement was illusory.

12. Chesnut Jr. to Cooper, September 6, 1864, Military Letterbook, SCDAH.

13. Chesnut Jr. to Cooper, September 6 and October 5, 1864, to Jones, September 10, 1864, to Hardee, September 23, 1864, to Perryman, October 7, 1864, Military Letterbook, SCDAH.

14. Racine, *Living a Big War in a Small Place*, 13–14, 47, 55, 81.

15. "Account of Captain Conley," 15–18, LC. Historian Stephanie M. H. Camp argues that whites entered slaves' "rival geography" in significant numbers for the first time during the Civil War, and she notes that Confederate deserters and Union soldiers joined with southern whites who had traded illegally with slaves before the war. Camp, *Closer to Freedom*, 135–36. Victoria E. Bynum also found increasing cross-racial communication between blacks and disaffected southern whites. Bynum, *Long Shadow of the Civil War*, 3.

16. Browning, *Shifting Loyalties*, 4; King-Owen, "Conditional Confederates," 349–79; Sheehan-Dean, *Why Confederates Fought*, 10; Doyle, "Understanding the Desertion of South Carolina Soldiers," 657–79; Marrs, "Desertion and Loyalty in the South Carolina Infantry," 47–65. Doyle argues that desertion of South Carolina

soldiers had an ideological component, and my evidence supports his conclusion. Aid from deserters is ubiquitous in fugitive diaries and narratives.

17. Edgar, *South Carolina*, 358, 375; Poole, *South Carolina's Civil War*, 52, 59; Bonham to Seddon, June 2, 1864, *OR*, ser. 1, vol. 35, pt. 2: 519–20.

18. "Statement of Number of Persons in South Carolina, exempted from Conscription under provisions of Act of Congress, February 17, 1864," Green Files, SCDAH; Bonham to Seddon, June 2, 1864, *OR*, ser. 1, vol. 35, pt. 2: 519–20.

19. "Act for the Better Organization of the Militia, and for Other Purposes," February 6, 1863, No. 4613, *Published Laws of South Carolina*, SCDAH.

20. M. L. Bonham Proclamation, August 23 (?), 1863, Adj. Gen. Scrapbook, Clippings of General Orders, SCDAH.

21. "Act to Provide Volunteer Companies of Mounted Infantry, and for Other Purposes," September 30, 1863, No. 4663, *Published Laws of South Carolina*, SCDAH; Chesnut Jr. to Cooper, September 6, 1864, Military Letterbook, SCDAH.

22. Circular, August 3, 1864, Adj. Gen. Order and Letter Book, SCDAH.

23. Garlington to Causey (?), November 9, 1864, Adj. Gen. Order and Letter Book, SCDAH; Garlington to Bonham, November 25, 1864, Adj. Gen. Order and Letter Book, SCDAH; Special Order 23, November 28, 1864, Adj. Gen. Order and Letter Book, SCDAH; Garlington to Desaussure, December 1, 1864, Adj. Gen. Order and Letter Book, SCDAH; McMicken to Jones, December 2, 1864, *OR*, ser. 1, vol. 44: 923.

24. Special Orders 23 (November 28, 1864), 36 (December 3, 1864), 42 (December 7, 1864), 44 (December 8, 1864), Adj. Gen. Order and Letter Book, SCDAH; Garlington to Godbold, December 8, 1864, Adj. Gen. Order and Letter Book, SCDAH; Henry W. Ravenel Private Journal, September 12 and November 25, 1864, SCL; John B. Patrick Diary, November 22, 1864, SCL; Louis W. Haskell to Sophy, November 29, 1864, Haskell Family Correspondence, SCHS.

25. Walsh to Bonham, November 14, 1864, Bonham Official Correspondence, 1862–64, SCDAH; *Daily South Carolinian*, December 9, 1864.

26. Steele to Hall, December 7, 1864, RBPMG, Hilton Head, S.C., RG 393, entry 4295, NA; "Statement of Cpt. James F. Morgan," November 21, 1864, RBPMG, Hilton Head, S.C., RG 393, entry 4295, NA; "Statement of J. L. Paston," November 14, 1864, RBPMG, Hilton Head, S.C., RG 393, entry 4295, NA; "Statement of Bledsoe," n.d., RBPMG, Hilton Head, S.C., RG 393, entry 4295, NA. Paston's statement was signed by seven other Union officers.

27. Drake, *Narrative of Capture and Escape*, 18–20.

28. Racine, *"Unspoiled Heart,"* 234–36; Hunt, "Our Escape," 103–6; Elias Montgomery Entry, Greenville District, Tax Record Book, 1865, SCDAH.

29. Hadley, *Seven Months a Prisoner* (1868), 105–6. Isaiah Conley's party encountered an equally ineffective cavalryman on the outskirts of Spartanburg. "Account of Captain Conley," 12, LC.

30. Foote, "Fugitive Federals Database." Although 144 successfully escaped Camp Sorghum, as stated in note 26 of chapter 1, a total of 241 fugitives escaped

from the city of Columbia, from Camp Asylum, the Richland County Jail, or other locations.

31. Billings Memoir, 102, LC; "Statement of James Morgan, November 21, 1864," RBPMG, Hilton Head, S.C., RG 393, entry 4295, NA; Russell, "Reminiscences of Prison Life and Escape," 50–58. Fugitives encountered more frequently organized state and Confederate security in North Carolina and Georgia, where the governors and state legislatures had defied Confederate authority to preserve their state militias and home guards to a greater extent than South Carolina.

32. Cochran, "Reminiscences of Life in Rebel Prisons," 56–57.

33. Abbott, *Prison Life in the South*, 247–48.

34. Glazier, *Capture and Escape*, 205–8; Langworthy, *Reminiscences of a Prisoner of War*, 44–46.

35. Seddon to Davis, November 8, 1864, *OR*, ser. 4, vol. 3: 802–16; Davis to Senate and House of Representatives, November 9, 1864, *OR*, ser. 4, vol. 3: 819–20; Davis to Senate and House of Representatives, February 3, 1864, *OR*, ser. 4, vol. 3: 67–70; General Order 31, March 10, 1864, *OR*, ser. 4, vol. 3: 203.

36. Drake, *Narrative of Capture and Escape*, 19–20. Russell, "Reminiscences of Prison Life and Escape," describes a similar incident (57).

37. Glazier, *Capture and Escape*, 215–20.

38. Abstract from Return of the Department of SC, GA, and FL for November 20, 1864, *OR*, ser. 1, vol. 44: 874; SO 249, October 12, 1864, *OR*, ser. 1, vol. 35, pt. 2: 637; Hardee to Seddon, November 29, 1864, *OR*, ser. 1, vol. 44: 905; Roy to Smith, November 29, 1864, *OR*, ser. 1, vol. 44: 906; Roy to Jones, and Smith to Jones, November 30, 1864, *OR*, ser. 1, vol. 44: 911–14. The Georgia militia were under the command of Major General Gustavas Smith. See also Poole, *South Carolina's Civil War*, 140–41.

39. Glazier, *Capture and Escape*, 222–25.

40. Hartride to Elliot, December 1, 1864, *OR*, ser. 1, vol. 44: 917; Bragg to Wheeler, December 2, 1864, *OR*, ser. 1, vol. 44: 921; McMicken to Jones, December 2, 1864, *OR*, ser. 1, vol. 44: 923; Hardee telegram to DeSaussure, December 8, 1864, CSA Manuscripts, CLS; Garlington to Desaussure, December 3 and 7, 1864, Adj. Gen. Order and Letterbook, SCDAH.

41. Glazier, *Capture and Escape*, 224–26.

42. Milledge Bonham Proclamation, December 5, 1864, SCDAH.

43. Beauregard to Cooper, December 8, 1864, *OR*, ser. 1, vol. 44: 940; Grimsley, "Learning to Say Enough," in Grimsley and Simpson, *Collapse of the Confederacy*, 40–41; "Map of the Military Division of the West, 1864, Hd. Qrs. Engr's Officer," Library of Congress, http://www.loc.gov/item/2009579249 (accessed July 4, 2014).

44. Beauregard to Cooper, December 12, 1864, *OR*, ser. 1, vol. 44: 951; Beauregard to Hardee, December 8, 1864, *OR*, ser. 1, vol. 44: 940; Hardee to Davis, December 21, 1864, *OR*, ser. 1, vol. 44: 974; "Statement of George Colcock Jones, December 21, 1864," Letterbook of the Chief of Artillery, Military District Georgia & 3rd Military District South Carolina, August–December 1864, M-2031, George Colcock Jones Papers, RL; Beauregard to Cooper, December 15, 1864,

OR, ser. 1, vol. 44: 959; Special Field Order 17, December 22, 1864, OR, ser. 1, vol. 44: 974–75. It is difficult to assess the numerical contributions of Wheeler's cavalry, as Confederate authorities had no accurate returns at this time. Beauregard estimated that the force numbered 3,000, but what the effective numbers were is impossible to tell. Widespread reports in official sources and letters and diaries from Georgia and South Carolina indicate that a large portion of his command straggled across the countryside and was not effectively with Wheeler. Citizens in Georgia and South Carolina complained that his forces engaged in widespread pillaging and horse stealing. Wheeler claimed that bushwhackers and thieves claiming to be part of his command were responsible. Wheeler issued general orders to stop any abuses committed by his troops, but placed most of the responsibility on the citizens of South Carolina. He informed them that if their horses were stolen or trespass made on their property, they had to follow the culprit until they got help arresting him or traced him back to Wheeler's camp. Wheeler to Bragg, December 28, 1864, OR, ser. 1, vol. 44: 998–99; GO 7, December 29, 1864, OR, ser. 1, vol. 44: 1002–3. It is important to note the state and Confederate commanders called the modern-day Salkehatchie River the Combahee River.

45. Petition of South Carolina Citizens to Seddon, December—, 1864, OR, ser. 1, vol. 44: 1011; Magrath to Davis, December 25, 1864, Magrath Papers, SCL.

46. SO 50, December 28, 1864, Adj. Gen. Order and Letter Book, SCDAH; Chesnut Jr. to Horton and McCray, December 27, 1864, Military Letterbook, SCDAH; Estimate of State Forces as Called for by Rolls and Returns, February 17, 1865, Green Files, SCDAH; Magrath to Barnwell, December 30, 1864, Magrath Papers, SCL; Charleston Daily Courier, December 30, 1864.

47. Daily South Carolinian, November 2, 1864; Magrath Proclamation, ND, Magrath Letters Received, SCDAH.

48. Smith to Hardee, November 30, 1864, OR, ser. 1, vol. 44: 911; Field Returns of Effective Troops between Grahamville and Combahee River, December 28, 1864, OR, ser. 1, vol. 44: 999–1000; Barrett, Sherman's March, 44. The troops were stationed at Grahamville, Coosawahatchie, and Pocotaligo.

49. Campbell, When Sherman Marched North from the Sea; Grimsley, "Learning to Say Enough," in Grimsley and Simpson, Collapse of the Confederacy, 71–72.

Chapter 4

1. Drake, Narrative of Capture and Escape, 41–43.
2. Ibid., 44–46; Staley and Hawkins, 1860 Census of Caldwell County, 3.
3. Ibid., 46.
4. Racine, "Unspoiled Heart," 236; Hadley, Seven Months a Prisoner (1868), 106.
5. Vance to Secretary of War Seddon, July 25, 1863, OR, ser. 4, vol. 2: 674; Lay to Preston, September 2, 1863, OR, ser. 4, vol. 2: 783–86; Inscoe and McKinney, Heart of Confederate Appalachia, 8–24, 75–84, 114–15, 126–28, 145, 167–75; Inscoe, Mountain Masters, 223–28. Inscoe and McKinney claim that the coercive power of the Confederate and state government remained strong throughout the war in western North Carolina because deserters and Unionists never assumed military

control of any significant segment and were subject to repression. This chapter argues that the Confederate and state governments never suppressed such activity and thus did not maintain effective control either.

6. The account of the initiation ceremony comes from a fugitive Federal who was initiated during his journey through western North Carolina. His account is similar to accounts from a Confederate detective in Alabama. Benson, "Prison Life and Escape," 8, and Walter to Bragg, May 8, 1864, *OR*, ser. 4, vol. 3: 393–96.

7. Seddon to Davis with enclosures of reports from detectives investigating the secret societies, November 8, 1864, *OR*, ser. 4, vol. 3: 802–13.

8. Davis to Senate and House of Representatives of the Confederate States, February 3, 1864, *OR*, ser. 4, vol. 3: 67–70. State records for the Guard for Home Defense include courts-martial of officers who aid and abet deserters. The state tried to crack down in February and March. A sample of charges indicate that officers removed deserters from jail, disobeyed orders to arrest deserters, and associated with "tories and deserters." Many of the officers were charged with being "notoriously disloyal." See, for example, SO 22, February 11, 1864, GO 3, February 8, 1864, GO 4, February 17, 1864, GO 6, March 29, 1864, Military Board. Executive Department. General and Special Orders, August 18, 1863–April 11, 1865, AG 35, NCSA.

9. Myers, *Rebels against the Confederacy*, 4–13, 124, 137, 244–45. Myers argues that thirty-two counties, or one-third of the state, were embroiled in irregular warfare. He lists the following counties in the mountains: Alexander, Burke, Caldwell, Cherokee, Henderson, Iredell, Madison, Watauga, Wilkes. My research agrees with the larger point Myers makes in his study: "The Confederacy as a functioning government had collapsed in many [North Carolina] counties months before the surrender of major Confederate armies at Bennett Place and Appomattox Court House" (127). Inscoe and McKinney, *Heart of Confederate Appalachia*, 83–93, make the point about the extent of Unionism in western North Carolina.

10. Ash, *When the Yankees Came*, developed the concept of the no-man's land as it applied to the Civil War. Mackey, *Uncivil War*, identified three typologies of irregular warfare in the upper south. Myers, *Executing Daniel Bright*, categorized four types of combatants that can be termed irregulars, and in *Rebels against the Confederacy* described three types of irregular warfare in North Carolina and the countermeasures employed by Confederate officials and state troops.

11. Although historians have written about the characteristics of guerrilla warfare during the Civil War and have asserted that women's resistance activities marked a second front of the war, scholars have not overtly explained how to recognize places within the Confederacy where the home front merged into battle fronts. "Survival lying" was the term coined by historian Michael Fellman to describe how individuals in Missouri coped with the guerrilla warfare and terror that overwhelmed the state during the Civil War. He wrote that the safest course for people trying to live through the violence was "prevarication." Fellman, *Inside War*, 48–49. Barton A. Myers, in *Rebels against the Confederacy*, argues that

widespread guerrilla warfare and Confederate counter-guerrilla measures in North Carolina counties collapsed "any neat distinction between a peaceful home-front and the conventional battlefield" (137).

12. Drake, *Narrative of Capture and Escape*, 25–26; Act Related to Militia and Guard for Home Defense, July 7, 1863, Public Acts of North Carolina, NCSA; Gatlin to Vance, November 19, 1864, AG 55, NCSA.

13. Hadley, *Seven Months a Prisoner* (1868), 107–9.

14. Ibid., 110–19. Reuben gave the surname of the captain at Saluda as Pace. The 1860 Federal census shows several Paces living in the vicinity. In 1861 Ransom W. Pace and John C. Pace were second lieutenants in the Green River Company of the 106th Regiment of North Carolina Militia, Henderson County. Bradley Jr., *North Carolina Confederate Militia Officers*, 282–83.

15. David Brown and Patrick J. Doyle, in a comparison of guerrilla violence in the South Carolina and North Carolina piedmont, argue that guerrilla violence was less widespread in South Carolina because the majority in South Carolina supported the Confederacy and accepted its attempts to suppress internal resis-tance. By contrast, North Carolinians were divided over the legitimacy of the Confederacy and thus the state's attempt to suppress violence only served to exac-erbate it. See "Violence and Loyalty in the Carolina Piedmont," in Beilein Jr. and Hulbert, *Civil War Guerrilla*.

16. Act Related to Militia and Guard for Home Defense, July 7, 1863, and December 14, 1863, Public Acts of North Carolina, NCSA; SO 67, August 4, 1864, and SO 78, August 20, 1864, Military Board, Executive Department. Gen-eral and Special Orders, August 18, 1863–April 11, 1865, AG 35, NCSA; Gatlin to Vance, October 14, 1864, and Report to Governor, November 19, 1864, and to Mal-lett, December 2, 1864, and to Baker, November 18, 1864, Adj. Gen. Dept. Letter Book, May 2, 1864–April 8, 1865, AG 55, NCSA; Gatlin to MacMillan, November 12, 1864, and to Mastin, October 27, 1864, and to Cooper, December 10, 1864, and to Scales, December 6, 1864, and to McElroy, December 3, 1864, and to Hargrave, August 24, 1864, and to Harbin, August 26, 1864, and to Vanney, Octo-ber 27, 1864, Adj. Gen. Home Guard Letter Book, August 20, 1863–March 10, 1865, AG 52, NCSA; *Weekly Conservative*, November 30, 1864; John F. Flintoff Diary, September 23, 1864, May 1, 1865, no. 1484, NCSA. At a public meeting on September 3, a large number of citizens in Wilkes County passed resolutions asking the governor to remove the "strong military force" in their district. They claimed reports of deserters' activity were slanderous and exaggerated, and that the county had enjoyed more quiet during the past month than it had for the past year. They feared the county would descend into famine if they had to feed so many troops and promised to put down the deserters "without help from the outside." The troops were not removed. *Weekly Conservative*, September 14, 1864. Wilkes was the region's strongest bastion of Unionism. Other "concentrated pockets" of Unionist strength included the county seat of Madison, the Ed-neyville area of Henderson, and portions of Caldwell and Yadkin. Inscoe and McKinney, *Heart of Confederate Appalachia*, 68, 93–94, 124–26.

17. Gatlin Report to Governor, November 19, 1864; *Daily Watchman* (Salisbury), November 25, 1864; Act for Local Defense, December 23, 1864, *Public Laws of North Carolina*, NCSA.

18. Drake, *Narrative of Capture and Escape*, 25–27. Fugitive Federals did not always have such an easy time convincing a Unionist of their identity. The region where Yankees had the most difficulty was in southwest Virginia. In the spring of 1864, there were a spate of escapes from the Confederate prison at Danville and from trains ferrying the Yankees from Richmond to Georgia. W. H. Newlin and his companions, who escaped from Danville, were given the name of a Unionist family and boldly identified themselves as Yankees. The family refused to help, proclaimed their support for the Confederacy, and could not imagine why their names had been given to the Yankees. It turned out that Confederate officials in the region dressed detectives in ragged clothes who pretended to be escaped Federal prisoners of war and arrested those who helped the "bogus Yankees." Although Newlin and his companions were eventually able to obtain help from that family because they could describe in detail two bona fide escaped prisoners who had moved through the region a few weeks before, there were other families they could not convince of their real identity. Newlin, *Account of the Escape of Six Federal Prisoners*, 87–101.

19. Drake, *Narrative of Capture and Escape*, 30–31.

20. Hadley, *Seven Months a Prisoner* (1868), 130–32.

21. Ibid., 133–40. In the 1868 edition of his narrative, Hadley does not provide a surname for the sisters and identifies his particular benefactors as Florence and Juan. It was common for fugitives who published diaries and accounts before 1870 to hide the names of Unionists they believed might still be in danger from neighbors. In an edition published in 1898, a year after his return to North Carolina to visit the family, he names the family as Hollingsworth and the sisters as Martha and Alice. Hadley, *Seven Months a Prisoner* (1898), 182–86. Various local records confirm the existence and some details about the family, although these records indicate the name was spelled Holinsworth. Christopher G. Memminger's account book records payment in 1857 to J. Holinsworth. Christopher G. Memminger Account Book, box 1, folder 9, SHC 502, SHC. The 1850 census lists laborer Josiah Holinsworth, age forty-four, and his household, including Delitha, age eleven; Elizabeth, ten; Martha, seven; Isaac, six; and Allise, three. The daughters have the right names and approximate ages as those given by Hadley. There were problems with the census in Henderson County in 1850, but none that affect identification of the Holinsworth family. Dorsey, *United States Census 1850 Henderson County*, 38, 106; Cowart, *Cowart's 1850 Census Henderson Co.*, 271A. Marriage records also confirm names used by this author. *Henderson County, North Carolina Marriage Records*, 104. John Inscoe misidentifies the family as Hollinger. Inscoe and McKinney discuss the rarity of divided families and the importance of kinship solidarity in determining allegiance. Inscoe and McKinney, *Heart of Confederate Appalachia*, 95–97; see also Inscoe, *Race, War, and Remembrance*, 125–40.

22. Langworthy, *Reminiscences of a Prisoner of War*, 57–58. Fugitive Junius Henri Browne wrote that the children they met "were unnaturally developed;

their senses acute; their secretiveness perfect." Browne, *Four Years in Seces-sia*, 379.

23. Categorizing women's activities during the Civil War is difficult, despite the ease with which some scholars now assert that women were combatants. As of 2015, international laws of war still did not clearly define who is a civilian and who is a combatant, nor do they provide a list of behaviors that constitute "direct participation" in warfare. These concepts are endlessly debated because there are so many gray areas. The activity of most women in western North Carolina falls into the gray areas. Van Engeland, *Civilian or Combatant?*, 31–36, 42, 102–6; Proctor, *Civilians in a World at War*, 11.

24. LeeAnn Whites, Alecia P. Long, and Kristen Streater are among the forefront of scholars who point out that women were the supply line for Confederate guerrillas operating against Union armies. Whites and Long argue that such women were combatants and that Federal officials recognized and treated them as such. While this assertion accurately describes women's direct participation in guerrilla warfare, it does not accurately reflect the thinking of the Union military, the civilian leadership, or soldiers. Whites and Long take the position that guerrillas were combatants, but neither General Order 100, the code that governed the Union armies, nor the repeated statements of commanders and soldiers in the field support the idea that Federals considered guerrillas to be combatants. Indeed, Article 82 of General Order 100 specifically states that guerrillas were "pirates" rather than combatants. Federals targeted women for their active support of guerrillas, knew that irregular warfare was impossible without women, and arrested women for their activities. But such thinking and such actions are not the equivalent of considering and treating women as "combatants" as understood in mid-nineteenth-century America. See Whites and Long, *Occupied Women*, 7, and Streater's essay in that volume entitled, "'She-Rebels' on the Supply Line: Gender Conventions in Civil War Kentucky," 88–100; Whites, "Forty Shirts and a Wagonload of Wheat," 56–78.

25. GO 31, March 10, 1864, *OR*, ser. 4, vol. 3: 203; An Act to Prevent Desertion from Confederate or State Military Service, and Evasion of Conscription, September 30, 1863, no. 4666, *Published Laws of South Carolina*, SCDAH; Cauthen, *South Carolina Goes to War*, 176; McCurry, *Confederate Reckoning*, 116–19. The official Union definition of a combatant, in order to exclude members of irregular companies officially sanctioned and commissioned by the Confederate government, claimed that combatants had to serve in units "who shared continuously in the war" without "intermitting returns to their homes." Article 82. Several recent works of scholarship emphasize the importance of "loyalty" and "disloyalty" to the targeting of noncombatants. John Fabian Witt argues that Lieber's Code, or General Order 100, simultaneously set humanitarian limits on the treatment of unarmed citizens and tore down the wall between soldiers and noncombatants. Citizens were enemies subjected to the hardships of war. During civil war, the code authorized military commanders to throw the burden of war on the "disloyal citizen." Witt recognized that Lieber defines a combatant in such a way as to exclude commissioned irregulars and guerrillas. Witt, *Lincoln's Code*, 191–94,

233–34. Helen M. Kinsella discusses how classifying citizens as "manifestly disloyal" came close to undermining their status as noncombatants because it acknowledged they gave positive aid and comfort to the enemy. Kinsella, *Image before the Weapon*, 86. William A. Blair, in *With Malice toward Some*, argues that "treason" was the central term Unionists used to understand the role of citizens in the war. Union officials used Swiss philosopher Vattel's definition of a civil war to claim that Rebels could simultaneously be enemy belligerents and remain citizens who could be punished for treason later. In the occupied South, the military handled women as potential enemies of the state and tied provisions and the ability to practice certain professions to loyalty.

26. Chesnut Jr. to Harrison, October 15, 1864, Military Letterbook, SCDAH; Settle to Vance, October 4, 1864, Thomas Settle Jr. Letters, NCSA. Stephanie McCurry argues that white southern women challenged the assumption that women were apolitical and outside war. Confederate officials remained reluctant to punish women as traitors, but increasingly targeted them as a key part of military strategy. The actions, as opposed to the official ideology, of the Confederate government acknowledged that women were enemies of the state whose actions were politically significant (McCurry, *Confederate Reckoning*, 86–99, 104, 126–31). Barton A. Myers also discusses the torture of Mrs. Owens in "Dissecting the Torture of Mrs. Owens: The Story of a Civil War Atrocity," in Berry, *Weirding the War*, 141–59.

27. But loyal Confederates, even as they terrorized them, did not consider disloyal women, armed and violent bands of deserters, or Unionist guerrillas to be legitimate combatants. They were all enemies who needed to be crushed on the way to military victory, but their activities were not legitimate acts of war. Confederates thought and spoke of such enemies using terms like "traitor," "ruffian," or "lawless person." They were outlaws in predatory bands, not irregulars. Union military authorities likewise termed guerrillas, and hence the women who supplied them, "brigands," "banditti," "highway robbers," and "pirates." When the Union army conquered and occupied a territory, any citizen, male or female, who rose up in arms was a "war-rebel" who could be executed, rather than a combatant entitled to prisoner-of-war status. Article 82 of General Order 100 for Union armies in the field proclaims that men who commit hostilities without "being part and portion" of an organized army and without "sharing continuously in the war" shall be "treated summarily as highway robbers or pirates." Article 85 defines war-rebels as "persons within an occupied territory who rise in arms. . . . If captured they may suffer death. . . . They are not prisoners of war." Article 102 establishes that the law of war, like criminal law, "makes no difference on account of the difference of sexes, concerning the spy, the war-traitor, or the war-rebel," http://avalon.law.yale.edu/19th_century/lieber.asp (accessed July 25, 2014). Scholars of Union occupation demonstrate how military officials came to categorize disloyal citizens as enemies who should be targeted while claiming that such persons were "unauthorized to wage war." Danielson, *War's Desolate Scourge*, 46–51. Also Ash, *When the Yankees Came*, 67. For examples of Confederate of-

ficial terminology, see Ashmore to Melton, August 16, 1863, *OR*, ser. 4, vol. 2: 773; Lay to Preston, September 2, 1863, *OR*, ser. 4, vol. 2: 784–85; Feilden to Ashmore, June 4, 1864, *OR*, ser. 1, vol. 35, pt. 2: 521; Bonham to Vance, August 22, 1863, *OR*, ser. 4, vol. 2: 741; Seddon to Davis, November 8, 1864, *OR*, ser. 4, vol. 3: 802–4.

28. The waterfall count comes from Ruscin, *Hendersonville and Flat Rock*, 101–3.

29. Inscoe, *Mountain Masters*, 9–10; Inscoe and McKinney, *Heart of Confederate Appalachia*, 209–11, 225–31; Inscoe, *Race, War, and Remembrance*, 83–96.

30. Hunt, "Our Escape," 108–10.

31. "Account of Captain Conley," 23, LC; Racine, *"Unspoiled Heart,"* 236–40; Hunt, "Our Escape," 110–13.

32. Racine, *"Unspoiled Heart,"* 236–40. The story of the shootout and the pickets comes from other fugitive Federals who stayed in the vicinity. "Account of Captain Conley," 23, LC; Fales, *Prison Life*, 57.

33. Racine, *"Unspoiled Heart,"* 240; Hunt, "Our Escape," 113.

34. Racine, *"Unspoiled Heart,"* 240–41; Hunt, "Our Escape," 113–14.

35. Governor's Office, Lists of Justices of the Peace, 1865, NCSA; "Robert Hamilton," in Turner and Philbeck, *Transylvania County North Carolina Will Abstracts*; "Account of Captain Conley," 21–23, LC. Captain Isaiah Conley, Captain. F. B. Dawson, and First Lieutenant W. C. Davidson, all of the 101st Pennsylvania, escaped from the train on October 5. When they arrived at Hamilton's house, five fugitives were hiding at the house: Captain Chauncey S. Aldrich, Captain Daniel Avery Langworthy, and First Lieutenant J. E. Twillinger, all of the Eighty-Fifth New York, First Lieutenant G. S. Hastings of the Second New York Independent Battery, and Captain G. H. Starr of the 104th New York, who had escaped from Camp Sorghum in early October. These eight men belonged to a Union garrison at Plymouth that was surrounded and surrendered en masse on April 20, 1864. They were in prison together until their escape and knew each other well. Two other officers from the Plymouth garrison, Captain Cady of the Twenty-Fourth New York and Lieutenant Masters of the Second North Carolina, who also escaped from the train, were hiding in "The Pennsylvania House." October 27–30, C. S. Aldrich Civil War Diary, SM1, folder 1, Chauncey S. Aldrich Collection, PMM.

36. Racine, *"Unspoiled Heart,"* 240–41; Hunt, "Our Escape," 114–15; Fales, *Prison Life*, 56–58. Hunt was so sure that the party would be in Knoxville within three days of leaving Loftis's house that he quit keeping a diary. His last entry was November 21.

37. Racine, *"Unspoiled Heart,"* 240–41.

38. Ibid., 241–42; Hunt, "Our Escape," 116.

39. Racine, *"Unspoiled Heart,"* 242. Mattocks was not the only fugitive to find mountain women sexually alluring. John Inscoe comments that they spared "no romantic cliché or florid Victorian flight of prose" to describe their feelings on this matter. See his essay " 'Moving through Deserter Country,' " in Noe and Wilson, *Civil War in Appalachia*, 172. Alice Fahs, in her study of sensational literature, found that women in the border states were portrayed with a sexuality that

was rare in domestic fiction. In one *Harper's Weekly* story, the author twice lingered on details of a Kentucky woman's bare feet and ankles (Fahs, *Imagined Civil War*, 234).

40. Drake, *Fast and Loose in Dixie*, 152.

41. Drake, *Narrative of Capture and Escape*, 39. John Inscoe developed these insights in his essay on fugitive views of Appalachia, "'Moving through Deserter Country,'" in Noe and Wilson, *Civil War in Appalachia*, 171–76. Reid Mitchell discusses Federal soldiers and "she-devils" in *The Vacant Chair*.

42. "Account of Captain Conley," 23, LC; Hunt, "Our Escape," 115; Racine, *"Unspoiled Heart,"* 240; Hadley, *Seven Months a Prisoner* (1868), 139.

43. Welch, "Escape from Prison," 36, SCL. Hadley distinguished between the Holinsworth sisters, who were illiterate but innately refined, and the female relatives of the outlaw Vances. Of the latter he wrote, "Though the women had been uniformly kind to us, yet there prevailed among them such a spirit of ruffianism, and such uncivilized manners, that our stay among them was anything but agreeable." Hadley, *Seven Months a Prisoner* (1868), 152.

44. Browne, *Four Years in Secessia*, 32, 113–15.

45. Ibid., 383–84; Browne, *Great Metropolis*, 150–51.

Chapter 5

1. Drake, *Narrative of Capture and Escape*, 52–57. Other fugitive accounts that mention the Rock House include Ferguson, *Life-Struggles in Rebel Prisons*, 191; "Account of Captain Conley," 20, LC.

2. Racine, *"Unspoiled Heart,"* 243–45; Fales, *Prison Life*, 59–62; Hunt, "Our Escape," 117–18.

3. Sternhell, *Routes of War*, 155.

4. Seddon to Davis, January 11, 1865, *OR*, ser. 4, vol. 3: 1015; Taylor, *Divided Family in Civil War America*, 93; Freehling, *South vs. the South*, argues the case for the significance of the southerners who fought in the Union army, both for what they contributed to Union manpower and for what they took away from Confederate manpower.

5. Racine, *"Unspoiled Heart,"* 246–47; Hunt, "Our Escape," 119–21; Fales, *Prison Life*, 62–63.

6. Brown and Coffey, *Thomas's Legion*, 2–7, 25–28; Crow, *Storm in the Mountains*, 1–4.

7. Thomas to the Governor and Council of South Carolina, February 28, 1864, *OR*, ser. 1, vol. 53: 313–14; Brown and Coffey, *Thomas's Legion*, 134–35, 226; Crow, *Storm in the Mountains*, 59, 99.

8. Woodworth, *Jefferson Davis and His Generals*, 23–24, 256, 293; McMurry, *Two Great Rebel Armies*, 58–66.

9. Eicher and Eicher, *Civil War High Commands*, 866–85; Brown and Coffey, *Thomas's Legion*, 144, 209.

10. Vance to Seddon, December 13, 1864, Davis endorsement December 26, 1864, Seddon endorsement December 30, 1864, *OR*, ser. 1, vol. 42, pt. 3: 1253–54; Report

of John B. Palmer, Commanding Mountain District, North Carolina, January 12, 1865, *OR*, ser. 1, vol. 45, pt. 1: 841–42; Brown and Coffey, *Thomas's Legion*, 214, 224–25, 231; Memminger to Davis, December 4, 1864, *OR*, ser. 1, vol. 42, pt. 3: 1252–54. Technically, Thomas reported to Robert E. Lee. Special Order 139 from the Confederate War Department required officers who exercised separate commands in Virginia and North Carolina to report to and receive orders from Lee. Davis consulted Lee about the situation in the District of Western North Carolina. Lee wanted the district separated from the Department of North Carolina and its commander Martin to answer directly to him. Martin subsequently divided the district in two, giving the southwestern counties to Thomas and the area around Asheville to Palmer. This, however, did not solve all the problems related to overlapping jurisdictions in the Appalachians. Thomas had permission from the War Department to fill his legion "from those counties where conscription cannot be enforced." Confederate conscription officers in North Carolina complained to Secretary of War Seddon that Thomas enrolled men who had already been conscripted to other units. Seddon ordered Thomas to desist from this practice, but Thomas does not seem to have complied. North Carolina Adjutant General to Martin, December 7, 1864, AG 55, NCSA; Crow, *Storm in the Mountains*, 114–15.

11. December 31, 1864, R. W. Roone, Haywood Co., NC, Register of Letters Sent by the Provost Marshal, District of East Tennessee, RG 393, pt. 2, entry 2758, NA; Ragan, *Escape from East Tennessee*, 4; Ellis, *Thrilling Adventures of Daniel Ellis*; Fisher, *War at Every Door*, 65–68; Current, *Lincoln's Loyalists*, 48–49, 71; Thomas Doak Edington Diary, MS. 1181, SCTN; McKenzie, *Lincolnites and Rebels*, 84, 122; Scott and Angel, *History of the Thirteenth Regiment Tennessee Volunteer Cavalry, U.S.A*, 136, 141, 394, 423–36; Sarris, *Separate Civil War*, 103–5; Myers, *Rebels against the Confederacy*, 105. Scott and Angel wrote of the recruits for the Thirteenth Tennessee from East Tennessee and western North Carolina that they were "separated only by an imaginary line (261)."

12. Myers, *Rebels against the Confederacy*, 128, 149; Killian, *History of the North Carolina Third Mounted Infantry*, 1–3, 150–52; Bumgarner, *Kirk's Raiders*, 15–18, 145; Crow, *Storm in the Mountains*, 105–6.

13. Johnson, "Sword of Honor," 37–47. Another great example of joining forces with deserters and recruits was the escape party of Captain Isaiah Conley, Captain F. B. Dawson, and First Lieutenant W. C. Davidson, all of the 101st Pennsylvania, and the group they met at Sheriff Hamilton's house in Transylvania County, Captain Chauncey S. Aldrich, Captain Daniel Avery Langworthy, and First Lieutenant J. E. Twillinger, all of the Eighty-Fifth New York, First Lieutenant G. S. Hastings of the Second New York Independent Battery, and Captain G. H. Starr of the 104th New York (see note 35 of chapter 4). The group ultimately included ten escaped officers, one African American, eighteen deserters and conscripts, and sixty recruits for the Third North Carolina. "Account of Captain Conley," 20–21, LC; C. S. Aldrich Civil War Diary, SM1, folder 1, Chauncey S. Aldrich Collection, PMM.

14. Drake, *Narrative of Capture and Escape*, 59–65. According to enlistment records, James Hartley enlisted in the Third North Carolina Mounted Infantry at

Knoxville on June 11, 1864, as a private in Company B and was promoted to Lieutenant of Company I on March 13, 1865. The thirty-four-year-old was from Watauga County, North Carolina. Killian, *History of the North Carolina Third Mounted Infantry*, 152. Drake's description of the soldiers in the Thirteenth Tennessee as "boys" was purposeful. The historians of the regiment note that 200 of its soldiers were under eighteen and some were well below sixteen. Scott and Angel, *History of the Thirteenth Tennessee*, 259. On occasion, large parties of escaped Yankees and recruits for the Union army joined with bushwhackers to skirmish against the Rebels. Fugitive James Ferguson and several other Yankees joined with fifty men he described as "bushwhackers" to "skirmish" after hearing about the brutal murder of a local Unionist. Their original plan was to assault a Rebel camp, but not enough men gathered at the Rock House rendezvous to do so. Ferguson safely reached Knoxville with a large, well-armed party of recruits. Ferguson, *Life-Struggles in Rebel Prisons*, 191–92. Isaiah Conley and his group of escaped prisoners and recruits for the Third North Carolina formed a skirmish line and fired on a company of the North Carolina Home Guard. "Account of Captain Conley," 24, LC.

15. Drake, *Narrative of Capture and Escape*, 66–68; Killian, *History of the North Carolina Third Mounted Infantry*, 1–3, 150; Bumgarner, *Kirk's Raiders*, 15–18, 145.

16. Drake, *Narrative of Capture and Escape*, 70–73; Fisher, *War at Every Door*, 130; McKenzie, *Lincolnites and Rebels*, 196–97; Bumgarner, *Kirk's Raiders*, 51–52; Brown and Coffey, *Thomas's Legion*, 208, 227. When Andrew Benson's escape party was stuck in Crab Orchard, Tennessee, because Breckinridge controlled the passes, they joined a raid into Johnson County with 100 other men. They captured horses, mules, and cattle. Benson, "Prison Life and Escape," 9.

17. Drake, *Narrative of Capture and Escape*, 73–75.

18. Samuel P. Carter Biographical Sketch, 1–7, MSS 16, 791, LC; Fisher, *War at Every Door*, 6–14, 19–41, 179; McKenzie, *Lincolnites and Rebels*, 16, 101. A study of Confederate officers from East Tennessee indicates that Confederate supporters were younger than their Union counterparts, lived near the major transportation routes that connected the region with other parts of the South, and were members of a rising commercial professional middle class who had clients in the Deep South and Virginia. Groce, *Mountain Rebels*, 49–59.

19. Fisher, *War at Every Door*, 132–45; Carter Biographical Sketch, 107, LC; Department of the Ohio, Register of Letters Sent by PMG, District of E. TN, RG 393, pt. 2, entry 2758, NA; Powell, January 31, 1865, Letters Sent, April 1864–March 1866, District of E. TN, RG 393, pt. 2, entry 2740, NA; Curtis, Register of Letters Sent by PMG, District of E. TN, RG 393, pt. 2, entry 2758, NA. A primary source collection with great insight into the arrest of women in East Tennessee by the provost marshal general's office is the Mary Jane Johnston Reynolds Letters, MS. 0246, SCTN. See, in particular, Mary Reynolds to Simeon Reynolds, April 18, May 1, June 5, and June 20, 1864.

20. An Act to Alter and Amend the Militia Laws of this State, December 6, 1864, no. 4705, *Published Laws of South Carolina*, SCDAH; Resolution of Thanks to Junior Reserve and Home Guard, December 17, 1864, *Public Laws of North*

Carolina, NCSA; Davis to Bragg, November 23, 1864, *OR*, ser. 1, vol. 42, pt. 3: 1226; Resolution of Meeting of Governors, October 17, 1864, *OR*, ser. 1, vol. 42, pt. 3: 1149; Harriet Middleton to Susan, December 25, 1863, Cheeves-Middleton Papers, Susan-Harriott Middleton Correspondence, SCHS; Mary Reynolds to Simeon Reynolds, May 13, 1864, Mary Jane Johnston Reynolds Letters, MS. 0246, SCTN; Steedman, Register of Letters Sent by Provost Marshal, District of E. TN, RG 393, pt. 2, entry 2758, NA; Fisher, *War at Every Door*, 83, 93–94; Brown and Coffey, *Thomas's Legion*, 208; Scott and Angel, *History of the Thirteenth Tennessee*, 151.

21. Seddon to Vance, November 30, 1864, *OR*, ser. 1, vol. 44: 915; Hardee to Cooper, November 30, 1864, and to Jones, November 30, 1864, *OR*, ser. 1, vol. 44: 911–13; Report of Effective Strength for Taliaferro's Command, December 26, 1864, *OR*, ser. 1, vol. 44: 992–93; Burton, *Siege of Charleston*, 307.

22. Glazier, *Capture and Escape*, 230–35.

23. Billings Memoir, 89–93, LC; Dufur, *Over the Dead Line*, 163; Geer, *Beyond the Lines*, 116–17; *Prison Life in Texas*, 42–44; Meier, *Nature's Civil War*, 18, 52–53; Brady, *War upon the Land*, 3–6, 15–23, 95, 121, 132–33; Campbell, *When Sherman Marched North from the Sea*, 39–41.

24. Glazier, *Capture and Escape*, 236–42; Bailey, *War and Ruin*, 85, 91.

25. Glazier, *Capture and Escape*, 243–52. Other fugitives who traveled through swamps in South Carolina and Georgia encountered contrabands, Confederate deserters, and Unionists moving through and living there. See, for example, Murray, "From Macon, Georgia, to the Gulf," 110–11. Union troops also reported the presence of men in the swamps. Norris Crossman Diary, February 11, 1865, SCHS.

26. Glazier, *Capture and Escape*, 253–63.

27. Billings Memoir, 95, LC; Dufur, *Over the Dead Line*, 196; Racine, "Unspoiled Heart," 247–61; Hunt, "Our Escape," 123–28; Fales, *Prison Life*, 65–66. Southern newspapers reprinted a report from the *Asheville News Weekly* that twenty Yankees (two majors, six captains, and twelve lieutenants) were captured by Thomas's men after escaping from Columbia. Thomas's "Ingins gobbled them up" was the punch line. *Weekly Conservative*, December 21, 1864. The lost guide, Gilbert Semple, a deserter from the Confederate army, faced a worse fate than the Yankee fugitives. When the party was captured, several of the officers exchanged clothes with him and tried to pass him off as an officer from Ohio. But Semple was recognized in Asheville. After the war, Jack Loftis wrote Mattocks that Rebel scouts had dragged Semple in irons through three counties, shot him in the head, and left his body lying in a public road. Racine, "Unspoiled Heart," 408; Hunt, "Our Escape," 123–27.

28. Glazier, *Capture and Escape*, 264–87. Other recaptured prisoners were accused of spying and given fair investigations. For example, see Byers, *What I Saw in Dixie*, 42–46; Robbins, "Life in Rebel Prisons," 8–9. Robbins was captured by the local militia and tried by citizens at a crossroads tavern. He was convicted, but a deacon intervened, took him to Augusta, and telegraphed to Columbia to confirm his identity. Fugitive narratives are replete with stories of prisoners of war who escaped multiple times. In Mattocks's party, Litchfield had previous escape

experience. Hadley escaped in Virginia when he was first captured in May 1864, and was recaptured, then escaped again in South Carolina.

29. Glazier, *Capture and Escape*, 288–311.

30. Hadley, *Seven Months a Prisoner* (1868), 140–50. In a later edition of his narrative, Hadley writes that the brothers who guided them were Jack and Lem Vance. Ibid. (1898), 201–4.

31. Ibid. (1868), 152–71. Henry K. Davis was the son of Asbury and Margaret Davis, who were landowners in Buncombe County. The sheriff of Buncombe had an arrest warrant for Davis on a charge of assault and battery, issued June 29, 1864. The sheriff noted that Davis could not be found. *Buncombe County Grantor Deed Index*, 928–929D, Buncombe County Criminal Action Papers, 1866, NCSA. Hadley, Chisman, Good, and Baker are among the twenty-two names listed as escaped prisoners of war who reported to the provost marshal general of East Tennessee and were forwarded to their commands. Brigadier General S. P. Carter to Brigadier General H. W. Wessels, December 21, 1864, RG 249, entry 32, box 1, NA. Carter issued the party clothing and ordered them to report to Brigadier General Lorenzo Thomas, adjutant general of the U.S. Army, in Washington, D.C. Carter to Ammen, December 10, 1864, Letters Sent by PMG, District of E. TN, RG 393, pt. 2, entry 2757, NA, and SO 79, December 10, 1864, Special Orders Issued by PMG, District of E. TN, RG 393, pt. 2, entry 2762, NA.

32. Report of Brigadier General Alvan C. Gillem, December 30, 1864, *OR*, ser. 1, vol. 45, pt. 1: 819; Vaughn to Breckinridge, December 1 and December 7, 1864, Stoneman to Thomas, December 6, 1864, Schofield to Stoneman, December 6, 1864, Martin to Johnston, December 14, Breckinridge to Johnston, December 15, Gillespie to Breckinridge, December 16, Bruch to Eckert, December 17, *OR*, ser. 1, vol. 45, pt. 2: 80, 244, 632, 664, 689, 695, 698; Scott and Angel, *History of the Thirteenth Tennessee*, 197, 224–25; Brown and Coffey, *Thomas's Legion*, 228.

33. Brown and Coffey, *Thomas's Legion*, 228–31.

34. Breckinridge to Johnston, December 15, 1864, Langhorne to Johnston, December 18 and December 19, 1864, Johnston to Taylor, December 19, 1864, Lee to Johnston, December 19, 1864, Johnston to Breckinridge, December 19, 1864, Stanton to Breckinridge, December 19, 1864, Stanton to Johnston, December 19, 1864 (five separate dispatches), Johnston to Breckinridge, December 20, 1864, *OR*, ser. 1, vol. 45, pt. 2: 695, 709, 711–16; Brown and Coffey, *Thomas's Legion*, 228.

35. Newlin, *Account of the Escape of Six Federal Soldiers*; "Prison Experience of Maj. Charles G. Davis," SCTN; Billings Memoir, 93–94, LC; Abbott, *Prison Life in the South*, 217–18; Harrold, *Libby, Andersonville, Florence*, 88–91; *Prison Life in Texas*, 49–53; Robbins, "Life in Rebel Prisons," 10; Dufur, *Over the Dead Line*, 162; Ferguson, *Life-Struggles in Rebel Prisons*, 192; Johnson, "Sword of Honor," 43–44; Meier, *Nature's Civil War*, 1–7.

36. Drake, *Narrative of Capture and Escape*, 73–77. In a later edition of his narrative, Drake identified this man as Bryan. Drake, *Fast and Loose in Dixie*, 249.

37. Drake, *Narrative of Capture and Escape*, 78–81.

38. Ibid., 81–82; Browne, *Four Years in Secessia*, 430; Carter to Hoffman, November 19, 1864, Letters Sent by PMG, District of E. TN, RG 393, pt. 2, entry 2757,

NA; SO 69, November 18, 1864, and SO 75, December 3, 1864, Special Orders Issued by PMG, District of E. TN., RG 393, pt. 2, entry 2762, NA; Grant, December 1, 1864, Register of Letters Received by the PMG, District of E. TN, RG 393, pt. 2, entry 2761, NA. Drake and Lewis were ordered to report to the adjutant general of the U.S. Army in Washington, D.C.

39. Hadley, *Seven Months a Prisoner* (1868), 174; Glazier, *Capture and Escape*, 311–12; Cavada, *Libby Life*.

40. Foote, "Fugitive Federals Database"; Drake, *Narrative of Capture and Escape*, 82–86. Drake does not name the hotel. The Bell House Hotel was adjacent to the headquarters of the Union general commanding the District of East Tennessee (McKenzie, *Lincolnites and Rebels*, 85).

41. Hadley, *Seven Months a Prisoner* (1868), 175; Dufur, *Over the Dead Line*, 145–51; Bowley, "Seven Months in Confederate Military Prisons," 12; Hasson, *Escape from the Confederacy*, 53; Welch, "Escape from Prison," 7, SCL.

42. Hadley, *Seven Months a Prisoner* (1898), 250.

43. Foote, "Fugitive Federals Database"; C. S. Aldrich Civil War Diary, November 13, 1864, SM1, folder 1, Chauncey S. Aldrich Collection, PMM; "Prison Experience of Maj. Charles G. Davis," December 5, 1864, SCTN; SO 66, November 13, 1864, Special Orders Issued by the PMG, District of E. TN, RG 393, pt. 2, entry 2762, NA; December 28, 1864, January 16, February 21 and 27, March 3, 13, 16, 28, 29, 31, April 4 and 10, 1865, and Mrs. Henry Caldwell, Register of Letters Sent by the PMG, District of E. TN, RG 393, pt. 2, entry 2758, NA; January 14, 1865, Register of Letters Received by the PMG, District of E. TN, RG 393, pt. 2, entry 2761, NA; November 15, 18, 19, 30, December 1, 2, 3, 5, 6, 7, 9, 10, 12, 14, 15, 21, 23, 26, 27, 28, 30, 1864, January 2, 3, 4, 12, 13, 14, 16, 1865, Letters Sent by PMG, District of E. TN, RG 393, pt. 2, entry 2757, NA; SO 77, December 5, 1864, Special Orders Issued by PMG, District of E. TN, RG 393, pt. 2, entry 2762, NA; Stoneman to Thomas, December 6, 1864, *OR*, ser. 1, vol. 45, pt. 2: 80; GO 3, January 20, 1865, *OR*, ser. 1, vol. 45, pt. 2: 620; Escaped Prisoner Form, Escape Rolls, Knoxville, RG 249, entry 32, box 1, NA.

Chapter 6

1. November 26, December 3, December 8, December 15, 1864, Duncan McKercher Papers, Pocket Diary, HM 48562, HL; Sabre, *Nineteen Months a Prisoner*, 140–41; Trautman, *Twenty Months in Captivity*, 111; Byers, *What I Saw in Dixie*, 70–71.

2. December 12 and 26, McKercher Diary; M. LaBorde, President Board of Regents Lunatic Asylum to Governor Bonham, December 2, 1864, *OR*, ser. 2, vol. 7: 1179; Sabre, *Nineteen Months a Prisoner*, 165; Abbott, *Prison Life in the South*, 150; Ferguson, *Life-Struggles in Rebel Prisons*, 154; Pickenpaugh, *Captives in Blue*, 183; Trautman, *Twenty Months*, 116; Mead, *Southern Military Prisons and Escapes*, 25; Byers, "Historic War Song," 396–97; Cochran, "Reminiscences of Life in Rebel Prisons," 61; Bowley, "Seven Months in Confederate Military Prisons," 9.

3. Foote, "Fugitive Federals Database"; Rutherford to Andrews, November 5, 1864, *OR*, ser. 2, vol. 7: 1097–98; Winder to Cooper, December 13, 1864, *OR*, ser. 2, vol. 7: 1220; Pickenpaugh, *Captives in Blue*, 205.

4. Winder to Cooper, December 22, 1864, Winder to Beauregard, December 24, 1864, Otey to Winder, December 27, 1864, Winder to Cooper, December 31, 1864, and Davis endorsement, January 14, 1865, *OR*, ser. 2, vol. 7: 1262, 1271, 1286, 1302, 1304.

5. Barrett, *Sherman's March through the Carolinas*, 44.

6. Grant's Overland Campaign in Virginia and Sherman's Campaign against Atlanta contributed thousands of prisoners to the Confederate prison system and caused serious logistical problems for Confederate military and prison officials. Prisoners from these campaigns constituted a significant portion of fugitive Federals. One hundred and nineteen of the successful escapees were captured at the Battle of the Wilderness, and 116 of them were captured at Atlanta. Four hundred and ten of the successful fugitive Federals were captured in Georgia during the months of Sherman's campaign. Yet military historians who write about these operations are generally silent on the issue of prisoners. Three commonly cited books that treat Sherman's campaign discuss the process of burying the dead but not the disposal of prisoners of war, the numbers involved, the troops committed to guarding and removing prisoners from the battlefield, and the locations where prisoners were sent. None of these books has the word "prisoners" in the index. Although data on casualties for the Atlanta campaign are imprecise and frustrating to obtain, and prisoners were probably not a significant factor in the Battle of Ezra Church considered by one of the authors, Confederate prison records and the accounts of Federal prisoners that describe in detail their experience in the immediate environs of the battlefield provide enough sources to integrate prisoners into campaign narratives. The standard tactical history of the Battle of the Wilderness does have prisoners of war in the index, but any mention of prisoners in the text serves merely the purpose of anecdote. Two important works on the Battle of the Wilderness completely ignore prisoners of war. One of them is a collection of essays rather than a narrative of the battle, but the absence of an essay about prisoners in a collection offering new interpretations is another example of the neglect of this issue. See Castel, *Decision in the West*; Hess, *Battle of Ezra Church*; McMurry, *Atlanta 1864*; Rhea, *Battle of the Wilderness*; McWhiney, *Battle in the Wilderness*; Gallagher, *Wilderness Campaign*.

7. Smith to Cooper, March 31, 1865, *OR*, ser. 2, vol. 8: 449–50. This is the report to the Confederate adjutant general's office regarding the mass escape of prisoners. See "Note on Sources" in this book.

8. Beauregard to Cooper, April 15, 1865, Papers of General P. G. T. Beauregard, 1864–1865, RG 109, entry 116, box 2, NA; Barrett, *Sherman's March through the Carolinas*, 49; Lucas, *Sherman and the Burning of Columbia*, 42–43; Grimsley, "Learning to Say 'Enough,'" in Grimsley and Simpson, *Collapse of the Confederacy*, 41–47, 71–72; Bradley, *This Astounding Close*, 5.

9. Barrett, *Sherman's March through the Carolinas*, 59–62.

10. Lucas, *Sherman and the Burning of Columbia*, 39–63; Barrett, *Sherman's March*, 67–68.

11. On February 14, the assistant secretary of war informed Beauregard that prisoners should be sent to North Carolina because they were slated for exchange. Campbell to Beauregard, February 12, 1865, Forno to Booth, February 13, 1865, Gardner to Johnson, February 13, 1865, Forno to Gardner, February 13, 1865, Beauregard to Cooper, February 14, 1865, Campbell to Beauregard, February 14, 1865, Forno to Assistant Adjutant General, March 10, 1865, OR, ser. 2, vol. 8: 210, 218, 224, 451–53; Pickenpaugh, *Captives in Blue*, 229.

12. Griswold to Forno, February 24, 1865, OR, ser. 2, vol. 8: 455; Byers, *What I Saw in Dixie*, 78–81; Mead, *Southern Military Prisons*, 29; Sabre, *Nineteen Months a Prisoner*, 169–70.

13. Griswold to Forno, February 24, 1865, Forno to Assistant Adjutant General, March 10, 1865, OR, ser. 2, vol. 8: 453–56. Forno reported to his superiors that 144 was the number unaccounted for between Columbia and Charlotte. Although Forno agreed that the guard was totally inefficient and the conditions unfavorable, he charged Griswold with not exercising "sufficient diligence."

14. Stewart to Forno, March 28, 1865, Griswold to Forno, February 24, 1865, OR, ser. 2, vol. 8: 443, 456; Ferguson, *Life-Struggles in Rebel Prisons*, 183–92. Meany wrote that the raid was on Morganton, which actually occurred in June 1864. However, in February 1865, Kirk's men were in western North Carolina, pillaging and partially burning the town of Waynesville. The state of North Carolina used its Home Guard to protect the citizens of Charlotte and its public stores from escaped prisoners rather than offering its Home Guard to serve as prison guards. North Carolina Adjutant General to Brem, February 15, 1865, AG 52, Home Guard Letter Book, NCSA.

15. Hoke to Johnson, February 15, 1865, Griswold to Forno, February 24, 1865, OR, ser. 2, vol. 8: 234, 456; Abbott, *Prison Life in the South*, 177–79; Ferguson, *Life-Struggles in Rebel Prisons*, 180–82; Pickenpaugh, *Captives in Blue*, 231–32.

16. A special exchange with the United States had removed the most ill prisoners from Florence at an earlier date, which accounts for the difference between the 11,424 prisoners present in November and the 7,000 in February. Iverson to Booth, February 13, 1865, Holmes to Bragg, February 19, 1865, Forno to Assistant Adjutant General, March 10, 1865, Smith to Cooper, March 31, 1865, OR, ser. 2, vol. 8: 218, 270, 378, 449–54; Weiser, *Nine Months in Rebel Prisons*, 48. The enlisted men who successfully escaped from Goldsboro generally traveled to the Union lines at coastal New Bern, North Carolina, sixty miles to the east. In his report, Forno claims that most of the losses in enlisted men prisoners occurred at Wilmington. Accounts of escapees and enlisted men make it clear that hundreds escaped en route. It is also worth noting that Confederate and Federal officials spelled the modern-day Goldsboro as Goldsborough.

17. Sherman, *Memoirs*, 759–62; Lucas, *Sherman and the Burning of Columbia*, 69–102, 151; Howard, *Autobiography*, vol. 2, 121–22; Royster, *Destructive War*, 18–20; Byers, *What I Saw in Dixie*, 82–88; Harrold, *Libby, Andersonville, Florence*, 106–13;

Mead, *Southern Military Prisons*, 30–31; Sabre, *Nineteen Months a Prisoner*, 172–73; Nichols, *Story of the Great March*, 166, 342; Barrett, *Sherman's March through the Carolinas*, 91–93, 312.

18. Fonvielle Jr., *Wilmington Campaign*, 34, 311, 436; Barrett, *Civil War in North Carolina*, 244–45, 279.

19. Fonvielle Jr., *Wilmington Campaign*, 15–17, 79, 193, 334; Barrett, *Civil War in North Carolina*, 293; Moore, *Moore's Historical Guide to the Wilmington Campaign*, 131.

20. Whiting to Lee, January 18 and February 19, 1865, Papers of Major General W. H. C. Whiting, RG 109, entry 137, NA; Fonvielle Jr., *Wilmington Campaign*, 218, 323–24, 340, 437; Barrett, *Civil War in North Carolina*, 279.

21. Fonvielle, *Wilmington Campaign*, 344–82; Barrett, *Civil War in North Carolina*, 281.

22. Hoke to Johnson, February 20, 1865, Parker to Jackson, February 18, 1865, *OR*, ser. 2, vol. 8: 276, 264; Weiser, *Nine Months in Rebel Prisons*, 48.

23. Hoke to Johnson, February 20, 1865, Hoke to Parker, February 20, 1865, and Schofield to Hoke, February 21, 1865, *OR*, ser. 2, vol. 8: 276, 286.

24. Fonvielle Jr., *Wilmington Campaign*, 386, 393, 413–14; Hagood, *Memoirs of the War of Secession*, 342–43.

25. Forno to Johnson, February 22, 1865, Baker to Johnson, February 22, 1865, Baker to Bragg, February 21, 1865, Forno to Assistant Adjutant General, March 10, 1865, *OR*, ser. 2, vol. 8: 288, 294, 378; Bowley, "Seven Months in Confederate Military Prisons," 10–11.

26. Bragg to Lee, February 21, 1865, Bragg to Cooper, February 21, 1865, *OR*, ser. 1, vol. 47, pt. 2: 1241–42; Bragg to Cooper, February 21, 1865, *OR*, ser. 2, vol. 8: 286; "Report of Gen. Braxton Bragg, C.S. Army of Operations Feb. 21–March 15," *OR*, ser. 1, vol. 47, pt. 1: 1077; Fonvielle Jr., *Wilmington Campaign*, 418–21.

27. Foote, "Fugitive Federals Database"; Weiser, *Nine Months in Rebel Prisons*, 49–51; Fonvielle Jr., *Wilmington Campaign*, 421; Eldredge, *Third New Hampshire*, 636–37; Walkley, *History of the Seventh Connecticut*, 196–99; Williams, "From Spotsylvania to Wilmington, N.C.," 43–45.

28. Hoke to Commanding General U.S. Forces, Wilmington, February 22, 1865, Grant to Mulford, February 26, 1865, Special Orders 12, Headquarters Department of North Carolina, Army of the Ohio, February 23, 1865, *OR*, ser. 2, vol. 8: 290, 310, 296. The Federal prisoners waiting to be exchanged included 5,149 from Salisbury Prison in North Carolina. On February 22, Confederate officials marched these prisoners out of the stockade. They had to march rather than take the trains because the road was needed for military supplies. They walked in the rain fifty miles over four days to Greensboro to catch trains. Guards allowed the Federals "to straggle over the county and town, to purchase liquor, and to annoy the citizens." As one Yankee wrote in his diary, "Much to our astonishment we were allowed to travel as we please, and even to visit houses along the road." One hundred of the prisoners escaped and twenty died on the road. Campbell to Lee, February 22, 1865, *OR*, ser. 1, vol. 47, pt. 2: 1246; Smith to Cooper, March 31, 1865, *OR*, ser. 2, vol. 8: 449–50; Booth, *Dark Days of the Rebellion*, 207.

29. Wherry to Terry, February 23, 1865, Bragg to Lee, February 24, 1865, Abbott to Campbell, March 5, 1865, Smith to Cooper, March 31, 1865, *OR*, ser. 2, vol. 8: 297, 304, 358, 449–50; Walkley, *History of the Seventh Connecticut*, 199–200; Little, *Seventh New Hampshire Volunteers*, 412–16; Booth, *Dark Days of the Rebellion*, 226; Basile, *Diary of Amos E. Stearns*, 113–14; Joseph R. Hawley to Hattie Foote Hawley, February 28, 1865, Joseph R. Hawley Papers, reel 6, LC.

30. Basile, *Diary of Amos Stearns*, 113–14; Trautman, *Twenty Months*, 121; Booth, *Dark Days of the Rebellion*, 226; Travis, *Story of the Twenty-Fifth Michigan*, 341; Thompson, *History of the 112th Regiment of Illinois Volunteer Infantry*, 309; Walkley, *History of the Seventh Connecticut*, 200–201; John Watkins to Sarah Probert, March 5, 1865, box 1, folder 11, John Watkins Papers, SCTN.

31. Wherry to Terry, February 23, 1865, *OR*, ser. 2, vol. 8: 297; Travis, *Story of the Twenty-Fifth Michigan*, 342; Walkley, *History of the Seventh Connecticut*, 201; Booth, *Dark Days of the Rebellion*, 227; Basile, *Diary of Amos Stearns*, 115.

32. Terry to Sherman, March 13, 1865, *OR*, ser. 1, vol. 47, pt. 2: 818–19; Barrett, *Civil War in North Carolina*, 299, 311.

33. Fonvielle Jr., *Wilmington Campaign*, 446–50; Hawley to Campbell, March 20, 1865, *OR*, ser. 1, vol. 47, pt. 2: 926–27; Murray and Bartlett Jr., "Letters of Stephen Chaulker Bartlett," 82; U.S. Sanitary Commission, No. 87, *Preliminary Report of the Operations of the U.S. Sanitary Commission in North Carolina, March, 1865*, 3–9, 17; Medical Director to Joseph R. Hawley, March 5, 1865, and Receipt, February 27, 1865, Joseph R. Hawley Papers, reel 6, LC.

34. Hawley to Terry, March 21, 1865, Hawley to Senior Naval Officer, March 21, Special Field Order 29, March 12, 1865, Hawley to Campbell, March 20, 1865, Special Field Order 32, March 13, 1865, Sherman to Slocum, March 6, 1865, Sherman to Grant, March 12, 1865, *OR*, ser. 1, vol. 47, pt. 2: 945–46, 926–27, 795, 807, 704, 794; Hawley to Campbell, March 26, 1865, *OR*, ser. 1, vol. 47, pt. 3: 30; Nichols, *Story of the Great March*, 210; Sherman, *Memoirs*, 777, 782; Howard, *Autobiography*, vol. 2, 127, 140; Harrold, *Capture, Imprisonment, and Escape*, 120; Barrett, *Civil War in North Carolina*, 312; Fonvielle Jr., *Wilmington Campaign*, 450–51.

35. Special Order 3, February 22, 1865, *OR*, ser. 1, vol. 47, pt. 2: 1248; North Carolina Adjutant General to Cooke, February 13, 1865, AG 52 Home Guard Letter Book, NCSA; "Important Appeal, Headquarters Division of the West," February 23, 1865, Breckinridge to Johnston, March 1, 1865, *OR*, ser. 1, vol. 47, pt. 2: 1265, 1297; Barrett, *Civil War in North Carolina*, 290–91. In December, North Carolina Governor Zebulon Vance had called on "every man physically able" to go to the defense of Wilmington and for those left behind to "mount themselves and patrol their counties, looking after the women and children and preserving order." Proclamation of Governor Vance, December 20, 1864, *OR*, ser. 1, vol. 42, pt. 3: 1284.

36. Beauregard to Lee, February 21, 1865, Beauregard to Hampton, February 21, 1865, Brown to Beauregard, February 24, 1865, Brent to Beauregard, March 4, 1865, *OR*, ser. 1, vol. 47, pt. 2: 1238, 1245, 1271, 1323; Barrett, *Sherman's March*, 112; Bradley, *This Astounding Close*, 10. Historian Jason Phillips analyzes a Confederate culture of invincibility that led some soldiers to believe they were

unconquerable. Despite the carnage and the setbacks, thousands of Confederate soldiers in early 1865 still expected to win. See Phillips, *Diehard Rebels*.

37. Fonvielle Jr., *Wilmington Campaign*, 435–36; Barrett, *Civil War in North Carolina*, 343–48; Bradley, *This Astounding Close*, 12, 24–25, 33. Bradley argues that in early April, once more of the troops from the Army of Tennessee arrived, Johnston had a numerically strong force that was well supplied and possessed high morale. Because Johnston kept his army eighty miles from Sherman's, he was in position to march into the Deep South and prolong the war. Sherman knew this and was motivated to give Johnston generous terms in order to obtain surrender. Johnston thus negotiated from a position of strength. When the men of his army heard rumors of the surrender negotiations, it was fatal to morale and the army disintegrated by April 18, 1865.

38. Myers, *Rebels against the Confederacy*, 14, 152.

39. Drake, *Narrative of Capture and Escape*, 81; Harrold, *Capture, the Imprisonment, the Escape*, 108; Abbott, *Prison Life in the South*, 189–91; *Prison Life in Texas*, 47; Swift, *My Experiences as a Prisoner of War*, 21; Shurtleff, "Year with the Rebels," 408; Smith, "From Andersonville to Freedom," 73–74; Hasson, *Escape from the Confederacy*, 56–57; Trautman, *Twenty Months in Captivity*, 122; Ferguson, *Life-Struggles in Rebel Prisons*, 203–4. In 1862, 1,400 soldiers who were exchanged published a book they wrote to entertain themselves during their time in Confederate prison. In their introduction, they wrote, "As prisoners of war, we were unable to fight for that glorious flag of our love, and naturally chose to call this collection of papers which should testify to our faithfulness to God, our country, and our manhood, by that name dearest to our hearts—'The Stars and Stripes.'" *Stars and Stripes in Rebeldom*, iii–iv, LC. Alice Fahs, in *Imagined Civil War*, 11–12, found that paeans to the flag were pervasive in 1861 but more episodic after that. Stuart McConnell argues that it was not until the 1890s that the flag acquired "semi-sacred trappings." See McConnell, *Glorious Contentment*, 228. The writings of former prisoners of war do not fit with those general conclusions.

40. Drake, *Narrative of Capture and Escape*, 83–84; Booth, *Dark Days of the Rebellion*, 233–43; Carr, *Three Years Cruise*, March 20–April 6, 1865; Roe, "Richmond, Annapolis, and Home," 29–30.

41. Hadley, *Seven Months a Prisoner* (1868), 177–78; "Prison Experiences of Major Charles G. Davis," December 7–9, 1864, SCTN; Edward E. Dickerson Account, 20–22, Edward E. Dickerson Papers, LC; Williams, "From Spotsylvania to Wilmington," 45; Booth, *Dark Days of the Rebellion*, 230–34; Glazier, *Capture and Escape*, 315–17.

42. Glazier, *Capture and Escape*, 310; Drake, *Narrative of Capture and Escape*, 86–89.

43. Booth, *Dark Days of the Rebellion*, 237–43. J. E. Wilkins, who escaped in June 1864, wrote in his diary, "Although what I have now would have made me very happy a month ago, now I cannot enjoy them: for I am sick. I am surrounded with every luxury but dare not taste." J. E. Wilkins, Civil War Diary, 1862–1864, HM 30474, HL.

44. Drake, *Narrative of Capture and Escape*, 89–90; C. S. Aldrich Civil War Diary, December 21, 1864, SM1, folder 1, Chauncey S. Aldrich Collection, PMM.

45. Drake, *Narrative of Capture and Escape*, 90–92.

46. Ibid., 92; Drake, *Fast and Loose in Dixie*, 293–95; Everts, *Complete and Comprehensive History of the Ninth Regiment New Jersey Vols.*, 165–66; Bradley, *This Astounding Close*, 39.

Epilogue

1. Forno to Ruggles, April 2, 1865, *OR*, ser. 2, vol. 8: 463; Marvel, *Andersonville*, 227–28, 234–40. Union captives in the Trans-Mississippi theater of war continued to arrive at Confederate prisons located there through March as well. Pickenpaugh, *Captives in Blue*, 236.

2. Smith to Cooper, March 31, 1865, Chilton to Breckinridge, April 1, 1865, *OR*, ser. 2, vol. 8: 449–51, 462. One subject of the investigation was the claim of Federal prisoners of war that Confederate prison officials stole the money and valuables they had in their possession when they were captured or that were sent to them while imprisoned. Ruggles admitted that there were no returns regarding the subject and that a "rigid system of accountability in this branch of the service" was necessary. On April 25, as the investigation continued with the Confederate government on the run, an assistant quartermaster reported on how he transported prisoners' valuables out of Richmond. Ruggles to Cooper, March 31, 1865, Morfit to Ruggles, April 25, 1865, *OR*, ser. 2, vol. 8: 457, 512.

3. Springer and Robins, *Transforming Civil War Prisons*, 23–24; *Proceedings of the Ohio Association of Union Ex-Prisoners of War*, 6; Brown and Coffey, *Thomas's Legion*, 246.

4. Foote, "Fugitive Federals Database"; http://www.nps.gov/civilwar/search -soldiers-detail.htm?soldierId=61B12FCE-DC7A-DF11-BF36-B8AC6F5D926A (accessed June 22, 2015). The colonel of the Forty-Fourth reported to superiors of the Union army that his men were abused, mistreated, and sold into slavery after his surrender. He asked for measures of retaliation to be implemented in order to relieve the suffering of his men held in captivity. http://usctchronicle .blogspot.com/2011/02/what-happened-to-private-pryor-and-44th.html (accessed June 22, 2015). It is my surmise that Scott escaped from slavery; Federal records do not indicate his escape location. It is a logical conclusion considering the history of the Forty-Fourth and the fact that other African American soldiers were listed as escaping from a "rebel plantation." The Camp Ford prison in Texas closed in May and the Tenth Illinois Cavalry burned the remnants of the compound in July 1865. Lawrence and Glover, *Camp Ford C.S.A.*, 76–79.

5. Thomas, *Confederate Nation*; Faust, *Creation of Confederate Nationalism*; Gallagher, *Confederate War*; Rubin, *Shattered Nation*; Quigley, *Shifting Grounds*.

6. Racine, *Piedmont Farmer*, 368, 372–73.

7. Ibid., 374–400; Downs, *After Appomattox*, 207. My thoughts on the elements of the extended process of collapse were also influenced by reading the numerous

letters of Charles F. A. Holst, a carriage maker in Chester, South Carolina, to Isabella Ann Woodruff. Although Holst was an eccentric with a tendency toward depression and exaggeration, his letters capture the disintegration of the society around him. Fugitive Federals traveled across the village in February and March after they escaped from trains during the transfer into North Carolina. Citizens there had already taken over security, but as the military defense collapsed in February, disgruntled elements began to wreak havoc, Confederate armies on the retreat into North Carolina consumed the area's resources, and by April there was a total breakdown in law and order. In May, soldiers returning home from Johnston's surrender mobbed the roads and took the dregs of the community's resources. By that point, some in the community actually longed for the victorious Union army to occupy Chester and restore order. See Isabella Ann (Roberts) Woodruff Papers, RL.

8. Downs, *Declarations of Dependence*, 17–18, 76–77, 82–89; Downs, *After Appomattox*, 32–33, 154.

9. Langworthy, *Reminiscences of a Prisoner of War*, 72–73; Roe, "Richmond, Annapolis, and Home," 29–30; Carr, *Three Years Cruise,* April 1865 entries.

10. Gannon, *Won Cause*, 10, 125; Hazelett, "Prison Life, East and West," 388; Sabre, *Nineteen Months a Prisoner of War*, 9; Lyon, *In and out of Andersonville Prison*.

11. Glazier, *Capture and Escape* (1865). The New York publisher R. H. Ferguson & Co. issued subsequent editions, including the 1870 version cited throughout this book, and advertised in western newspapers for agents to sell the book. An ad in the *Leavenworth Bulletin*, November 27, 1869, 1, is the source of the quote about the book and the sales numbers. In later editions, Glazier attached one appendix listing the names of officers confined in Richmond's infamous Libby Prison written by Captain Robert J. Fisher and another listing officers captured after Federal prisoners were removed from Richmond. Drake, *Narrative of Capture and Escape*. This 1866 rare edition is located at the Huntington Library, San Marino, Calif. In a January 12, 1880, letter to Colonel John P. Nicholson, placed inside the copy held at the Huntington, Drake wrote that his 1866 "hastily written narrative" was "written when I felt I could not long survive." Drake lists the various newspapers that published his story in the introduction to his 1880 book, *Fast and Loose in Dixie*, vi, 293. The full title of Hadley's work, not provided elsewhere, is worth noting: Hadley, *Seven Months a Prisoner; or Thirty-six Days in the Woods. Giving the Personal Experience of Prison Life in Gordonsville, Lynchburg, Danville, Macon, Savannah, Charleston, and Columbia, Together with a Description of How New Captures Are Received into Prison, or How They Act and What They Do, Etc., Etc., and Two Escapes, the Last Successful, from Columbia to Knoxville, over a Distance of Four Hundred Miles, Extending through Thirty-six Days and Fraught with Many Thrilling Adventures and Hair-breadth Escapes. Containing None but Entirely New Items. By an Indiana Soldier.* The book count comes from Hesseltine, *Civil War Prisons*, 247. The conclusions of war psychologists about the need for public sharing and healing is discussed in Jordan, *Marching Home*, 133.

12. Glazier, *Capture and Escape*, 183, 58.

13. "Joint Committee on the Conduct and Expenditures of the War. Report. Returned Prisoners. May 9, 1864," HL; *Narrative of Privations and Sufferings of United States Officers & Soldiers While Prisoners of War*, HL; Cloyd, *Haunted by Atrocity*, 24–45; McConnell, *Glorious Contentment*, 93–94; Thompson, *History of the 112th Regiment of Illinois Volunteer Infantry*, 310. Brian Matthew Jordan argues that at the end of the 1860s, the northern public was tired of the prisoner of war issue and that ex-prisoners of war no longer had a friendly audience for their tales. They became more bitter and vocal, and more unable to heal as the rest of society tried to move on. See Jordan, *Marching Home*, 130–34.

14. Abbott, *Prison Life in the South*, Preface; Hadley, *Seven Months a Prisoner* (1868), 179–80. I reached a different conclusion after my reading of escape and prison narratives than did Ann Fabian in *The Unvarnished Truth*. She included fugitive accounts in her study of nineteenth-century personal narratives and claims that escaped prisoners of war acknowledged help from slaves but told their stories in a way that undermined their gratitude. They portrayed themselves as the agents who made history and portrayed slaves as comic characters on a minstrel stage (119). Although fugitives filtered their experience through racial stereotypes, they repeatedly pointed out that slaves risked their lives, gave up the last crumb of food, and possessed key geographic and social knowledge. There is evidence that escaped prisoners spread this story verbally as well as in published narratives. One of William Tecumseh Sherman's staff officers wrote that "the universal testimony of our escaped soldiers" about the actions of slaves "impresses me with the weight of obligation and love for them that stir to the depth of my soul." Nichols, *Story of the Great March*, 101.

15. Gannon, *Won Cause*, 4–8, 140–41. Other historians who argue that most Union veterans preserved a righteous cause memory of the war that inhibited reconciliation include Neff, *Honoring the Civil War Dead*; Hunt, *Good Men Who Won the War*. Caroline E. Janney argues that even northerners willing to reconcile adamantly condemned slavery, believed it caused the war, and were proud the Union army liberated slaves. Reconciliation was conditional based on a firm belief in the righteousness of the cause. See Janney, *Remembering the Civil War*, 7–9, 104.

16. Hadley, *Seven Months a Prisoner* (1868), 136. Caroline Janney points out that Union veterans rarely publicly acknowledged the role of Union women in supporting the war effort. They believed women's support had been tangential to victory. See Janney, *Remembering the Civil War*, 235–36.

17. "Petition of Albert D. Richardson and Junius Henri Browne to James Seddon," January 21, 1864, Correspondence and Reports (1863–1864) Relating to Federal Citizens, Clerks and Sutlers Confined in Castle Thunder Prison, Richmond, Va., RG 249, entry 131, NA; Richardson, *Secret Service, Dungeon, and Escape*, 1–55, 61–94, 337–50, 400–431, 487; Browne, *Four Years in Secessia*, 91, 231, 250–61, 303–4, 313, 404, 411; January 16, 1865, Knoxville Escape Rolls, RG 249, entry 32, box 1, NA. The correspondence between the U.S. and Confederate agents of exchange regarding Richardson and Browne make clear the special animus the Confederate leadership held against the two reporters. See *Official Correspondence between the Agents of Exchange, Together with Mr. Ould's Report*, 68–70, HL. I had planned

to make Richardson and Browne central characters in this book until the publication of Carlson, *Junius and Albert's Adventures in the Confederacy*.

18. Richardson, *Secret Service, Dungeon, and Escape*, 501–2; Browne, *Four Years in Secessia*, 421–23.

19. Richardson, *Secret Service, Dungeon, and Escape*, 502, 510–12; Browne, *Four Years in Secessia*, 379, 423–26; "Nameless Heroine" by B. R. Hanby, http://www.loc.gov/item/ihas.200001311/ (accessed June 24, 2015).

20. Drake, *Fast and Loose in Dixie*, cover, title page, 93–94, 147–52, 166–78, 280–81, 297–305.

21. "A Much-Sued Editor," *New York Times*, November 15, 1889, 9; "Indictments Defective," *New York Times*, November 19, 1889, 9; "General Drake in the Soup," *Aberdeen Daily News*, May 24, 1889, 1; "Gotham Gossip," *Daily Picayune* (New Orleans), December 15, 1881, 10; *New York Times*, July 28, 1889, 1; *Times-Picayune* (New Orleans), April 15, 1891, 4; *Daily Evening Bulletin* (San Francisco), April 11, 1891, 4; *Times-Picayune* (New Orleans), October 4, 1892, 6; "Veterans Kick on Wax Flowers," *Salt Lake Telegram*, June 1, 1910, 3; "Widely Known Veteran Dies," *Albuquerque Morning Journal*, November 29, 1913, 3.

22. Hadley, *Seven Months a Prisoner* (1898), 207, 219, 257; Hadley, "Day with Escaping Prisoners," 278–79. "Justice John Vestal Hadley," http://www.in.gov/judiciary/citc/museum/hadley/ (accessed June 25, 2015). There is also an action against Davis in November 1865 for disturbing a congregation during worship by "laughing and talking in a loud manner, and uttering profane and unbecoming language, and attracting the attention of the congregation, by rude and improper actions, gestures, and behaviors." Buncombe County, Criminal Action Papers, 1866, North Carolina Department of Archives and History, Raleigh, N.C.

23. Byers, *What I Saw in Dixie*, 80. Ann Fabian, in *Unvarnished Truth*, discusses escaped prisoners' narratives and their use of the slavery metaphor. She believes that white prisoners depicted themselves "as worse off" than slaves (140). After a more extensive reading of prisoner accounts, I do not share that conclusion.

24. Fugitives who wrote narratives before 1870 and after 1880 varied in their decisions about writing black speech. Early accounts written by Glazier (1865) and Isaiah Conley (1868) use different speech patterns for different slaves they met on their journey, with some of the blacks speaking plain English with the common southern expression "you uns" and others assigned minstrel-like dialect. The 1865 accounts written by different fugitives in different chapters of Allen O. Abbott's compilation generally employ minstrel dialect. Freeman S. Bowley's 1890 paper quotes a white militia captain using the pronunciations that literary conventions typically gave to blacks. Daniel Langworthy, in his 1915 reminiscences, has blacks speak in plain English and use the expression "you uns."

25. Carr, *Three Years Cruise*, April 30, 1865, entry; Marten, *Sing Not War*, 28–30.

26. Harrold, *Libby, Andersonville, Florence*, 126–27; Clarke, *War Stories*, 19, 53–54; Fahs, *Imagined Civil War*, 94; Cloyd, *Haunted by Atrocity*, 61–65; Jordan, *Marching Home*, 146–48. Cloyd and Jordan argue that ex-prisoners of war made claims of heroism in the face of a public that preferred to ignore their sufferings because tales of Civil War prisons were too horrible for the public to process. They also

claim that ex-prisoners emphasized escape attempts in narratives produced later in the century because escape plots appeared more heroic and manly than passive imprisonment. I believe the number of escape stories simply reflects the large number of escapes.

27. Drake, *Fast and Loose in Dixie*, 297–301. Entrepreneurs and veterans joined forces to memorialize the war and make a profit in the emerging consumer economy of the Gilded Age. Publications and museums about prison life and tours of prison sites were just one aspect of the commodification of the war during the period. See Marten, *Sing Not War*, 126.

28. Hasson, *Escape from the Confederacy*, 27–28.

29. Langworthy, *Reminiscences of a Prisoner of War*, 74; Johnson, "Sword of Honor," 50–55.

30. Racine, *"Unspoiled Heart,"* 258–59, 274–89, 405–8. Mattocks died in 1910.

31. Drake, *Fast and Loose in Dixie*, 301–2; Hadley, *Seven Months a Prisoner* (1898), 258. Other examples of letters between former fugitives and the southerners who helped them include Newlin, *Account of the Escape of Six Federal Soldiers*, 7; Smith, "From Andersonville to Freedom," 69–71.

32. Drake, *Fast and Loose in Dixie*, 302.

Bibliography

Primary Sources

Manuscripts and Rare Books

Chapel Hill, N.C.
  Southern Historical Collection, Wilson Library, University of North
        Carolina (SHC)
    Collier, Elizabeth, Diary
    Gatlin, R. C., Papers
    Henderson, John S., Papers
    Inman, Myra, Diary
    Jones, Edmund Walter, Papers
    Magrath, A. G., Papers
    Marsh, John B., Sunday School Roll Book with Notes, 1856–77
    Memminger, Christopher G., Papers
    Mercer Family Papers
    Miles, William Porcher, Papers
    Perkins Family Papers
    Perry, B. F., Papers
    Porter, Nimrod, Papers
    Woodfin, Nicholas Washington, Papers
Charleston, S.C.
  Charleston Library Society (CLS)
    C.S.A. Manuscripts, 1861–65
  South Carolina Historical Society (SCHS)
    Cheeves-Middleton Papers, Susan-Harriott Middleton Correspondence
    Crossman, Norris, Diary, 1864–65
    Gilman, Caroline H., Papers
    Haskell Family Correspondence, Cheves Papers
    Lee, Huston, Papers
    McColl, James W., Letters
    McCord, Louisa Cheves, Letters, McCord Family Papers
    McLeod, John B., "An Account of Greenville During the War Between
      the States and Reconstruction." Presented to the Greenville Co.
      Historical Society, October 8, 1995.
Chicago, Ill.
  Pritzker Military Museum and Library (PMM)
    Aldrich, Chauncey S., Collection

Columbia, S.C.
    South Carolina Department of Archives and History (SCDAH)
        Adj. Gen. Abstracts of Letters Received and Replies, 1864–65
        Adj. Gen. Order and Letter Book, 1863, 1864, 1865
        Adj. Gen. Scrapbook, 1862–65
        Gov. Milledge L. Bonham Papers
            Letters Rcvd and Sent, December 22, 1862–November 24, 1864
            Proclamations, 1863–64
            Official Correspondence, 1862–64
        Comptroller General. Darlington District, Tax Record Book. 1865.
        Comptroller General. Greenville District, Tax Record Book. 1865.
        Comptroller General. Lexington District, Tax Record Book. 1865.
        General Assembly Papers. Committee Report. Committee on Military and
            Pensions, September 24, 1863.
        General Assembly Papers. Report of Comm. on Confederate State
            Relations on Resolution Relative to Parolling Yankee Prisoners not
            Commissioned Officers. December 15, 1864.
        Greenville Co. Clerk of Court, Writs of Habeas Corpus for Conscription
            Violations, 1864 Legislative (Green) Files. Military Affairs. 1864.
        Military Letterbook of James Chesnut Jr., 1864–65
        Published Laws of South Carolina
        Gov. Andrew Gordon Magrath Papers
            Letterbook, 1864–65
            Order Book, 1864–65
            Telegraph Book, 1864–65
            Letters Received and Sent, December 19, 1864–April 25, 1865
    South Caroliniana Library, University of South Carolina (SCL)
        Hammet Family Papers
        Magrath, Andrew Gordon, Papers
        Nance, James Drayton, Letters
        Neves Family Papers
        Patrick, John B., Diary, 1861–65
        Perry, Benjamin Franklin, Papers
        Ravenel, Henry W., Private Journal
        Smith, Elihu Penquite, Papers
        Taylor, Maria Baker, Diary
        Watts, Beaufort Taylor, Papers
        Welch, John Collins. "An Escape From Prison During the Civil War—
            1864," Typescript.
        Wingate Family Papers
Durham, N.C.
    David M. Rubenstein Library, Duke University (RL)
        Brown, Charles S., Papers
        De Saussure, Henry William, Papers

Fox, John, Papers
Gray, Mrs. Hiram, Papers
Grimball, John Berkeley, Papers
Henderson, Samuel, Papers
Jones, George Colcock, Papers
Williams, Benjamin S., Papers
Woodruff, Isabella Ann (Roberts), Papers
Knoxville, Tenn.
Special Collections, University of Tennessee-Knoxville (SCTN)
"Army Life and Prison Experiences of Major Charles G. Davis"
Boyd, Samuel B., Papers
Crozier, Elizabeth Baker, Journal
Edington, Thomas Doak, Diary
Hill, John Willard, Diary
Kingsley, Roswell, Papers
Maynard, Horace, Papers
McTeer, Will A., "Among the Loyal Mountaineers"
Ragan, Robert A., Letters
Ramsey Family Papers
Reynolds, Mary Jane Johnston, Letters
Sayler, James K. P., Papers
Temple, Oliver Perry, Papers
Vaughn, J. C., Notice
Watkins, John, Papers
Watkins, John, Transcriptions of Speeches and Letters, 1862–1865
Raleigh, N.C.
North Carolina State Archives (NCSA)
Adjutant General's Department Records
General Correspondence and Misc. Materials, 1771–1868 (AG 77)
Home Guard Letter Book, August 20, 1863–March 10, 1865 (AG 52)
Letter Book, 1863–66 (AG 53)
Letter Book, May 2, 1864–April 8, 1865 (AG 55)
Military Board, Executive Department, General and Special Orders,
August 18, 1863–April 11, 1865 (AG35)
Militia Letter Book, April 9, 1862–September 8, 1864 (AG 44)
Militia Letter Book, September 8, 1864–April 8, 1865 (AG 54)
Misc. Records, 1861–65 (AG 78)
Bacot, R. H., Letters
Buncombe County Criminal Action Papers, 1866
Buncombe County Minute Docket, Superior Court, 1857–69
Cathey, Joseph, Papers
Clark, David, Papers
Cowles, Calvin J., Papers
Flintoff, John F., Diary

Gash, Mary, and Family Papers

General Assembly, Session Records, November–December 1864, January–
    February 1865

Governor's Office, Lists of Justices of the Peace

Hale, Edward Jones, Papers

Heckstall Papers

Leach, J. P., Papers

London, George E., Collection

Myers, A. C., Papers

*Private Laws of the State of North Carolina, Passed by the General Assembly at
    Its Adjourned Session of 1863.* Raleigh, N.C.: W. W. Holden, 1863.

*Public Laws of the State of North Carolina, Passed by the General Assembly, at
    Its Adjourned Session of 1862–'63.* Raleigh, N.C.: W. W. Holden, 1863.

*Public Laws of the State of North Carolina, Passed by the General Assembly at the
    Adjourned Session of 1863.* Raleigh, N.C.: W. W. Holden, 1863.

*Public Laws of the State of North Carolina, Passed by the General Assembly at Its
    Adjourned Session of 1864.* Raleigh, N.C.: W. W. Holden, 1864.

*Public Laws of the State of North Carolina, Passed by the General Assembly, at Its
    Adjourned Session of 1865.* Raleigh, N.C.: Cannon & Holden, 1865.

*Public Laws of the State of North Carolina, Passed by the General Assembly at Its
    Called Session of 1863.* Raleigh, N.C.: W. W. Holden, 1863.

*Public Laws of the State of North Carolina, Passed by the General Assembly at Its
    Regular Session of 1864—'65.* Raleigh, N.C.: Cannon & Holden, 1865.

*Public Laws of the State of North Carolina, Passed by the General Assembly at Its
    Second Extra Session, 1861.* Raleigh, N.C.: John Spelman, 1861.

*Public Laws of the State of North Carolina, Passed by the General Assembly at Its
    Session of 1862–'63: Together with the Comptroller's Statement of Public
    Revenue and Expenditure.* Raleigh, N.C.: W. W. Holden, 1863.

*Public Laws of the State of North Carolina, Passed by the General Assembly at the
    Sessions of 1861–'62–'63–'64, and One in 1859.* Raleigh, N.C.: Wm. E. Pill,
    1866.

Settle Jr., Thomas, Letters

Starr, Joseph B., Papers

Whitaker, Stephen, Papers

San Marino, Calif.

  The Huntington Library (HL)

    C.S.A. Report of the Joint Select Committee appointed to Investigate the
        Condition and Treatment of Prisoners of War. House of
        Representatives, March 3, 1865.

    Bowley, Freeman S. "Seven Months in Confederate Military Prisons." *A
        Paper Prepared and Read before California Commandery of the Military
        Order of the Loyal Legion of the United States, May 2, 1890.* War Paper
        No. 6. Commandery of the State of California. Military Order of the
        Loyal Legion of the United States.

    Browne, Junius Henri, Letters, Nicholson Collection

Carr, Austin A. *Three Years Cruise of Austin A. Carr in Co. F 2nd N.Y.S.M. or 82nd N.Y. Vol. Second Division, Second Corps, Army of the Potomac.*

Drake, J. Madison. *Narrative of the Capture, Imprisonment and Escape of J. Madison Drake, Captain Ninth New Jersey Volunteers* (1866).

Goodnoh, E. C. *The Famous Tunnel Escape from Libby Prison.*

Hamilton, A. G. *Story of the Famous Tunnel Escape from Libby Prison. As Told by Major A. G. Hamilton, One of the Projectors* (1893).

Hasson, B. F. *Escape from the Confederacy: Overpowering the Guards—Midnight Leap from A Moving Train—Through Swamps and Forest—Blood Hounds—Thrilling Events.*

Henderson, Harvey, Civil War Diary, 1861–65

Kinsman, Oliver D. "A Loyal Man in Florida, 1858–1861." War Paper 81. Military Order of the Loyal Legion of the United States. Commandery of the District of Columbia. Read at the Stated Meeting of May 4, 1910.

The Libby Prison Minstrels! December 24, 1863, Program

McKercher, Duncan, Papers

Mead, Warren Hewitt. *Southern Military Prisons and Escapes. Prepared and Read By Request before the Minnesota Loyal Legion, at Minneapolis, Nov. 11, 1890.*

Narrative of Privations and Sufferings of United States Officers & Soldiers While Prisoners of War in the Hands of the Rebel Authorities. Being the Report of a Commission of Inquiry, Appointed by the United States Sanitary Commission. Boston: Office of "Littrell's Living Age," 1864.

Official Correspondence Between the Agents of Exchange, Together with Mr. Ould's Report. Richmond: Sentinel Job Office, 1864.

Radcliff, J. Napolean. *Journal of the War of the Rebellion.* 5 Vols.

Robbins, Nathaniel A. "Life in Rebel Prisons." War Paper 64. Military Order of the Loyal Legion of the United States. Commandery of the District of Columbia. Read at the Stated Meeting of May 2, 1906.

Sargent, George A., Diary

Stars and Stripes in Rebeldom. A Series of Papers Written by Federal Prisoners (Privates) in Richmond, Tuscaloosa, New Orleans, and Salisbury, N.C. Boston: T. O. H. Burnham, 1862.

U.S. House of Representatives. 38th Cong., 1st Sess., Report No. 67. Joint Commission on the Conduct and Expenditures of the War. Report Returned Prisoners. May 9, 1864.

U.S. House of Representatives, 38th Cong., 2nd Sess., Ex. Doc. No. 32. Exchange of Prisoners. Letter from the Secretary of War. January 23, 1865.

U.S. House of Representatives, 38th Cong., 2nd Sess., Ex. Doc. No. 20. Exchange of Prisoners Of War. Message from the President of the United States. January 9, 1865.

Wilkins, J. E., Civil War Diary, 1862–64

Washington, D.C.

Library of Congress, Rare Books and Manuscripts Division (LC)

"An Account of Captain Conley's Escape from Prison"
Billings, Luther Guiteau, Memoir
Carter, Samuel P., Biographical Sketch
Crossly, Sylvanus, Diary
Dickerson, Edward E., Papers
Hawley, Joseph R., Papers
Spaulding, Oliver L., Diary, Spaulding Family Papers
National Archives (NA)
Record Group (RG) 45, Records of the Naval Records Collection of the
    Office of Naval Records and Library
    Letters Received Relating to Union Naval POWs. Reports from Officers
        and Seamen of the U.S. Navy Who Were Prisoners of War in the
        South
    Log of W. L. F. Golway
    Miscellaneous, Relative to Prisoners of War
RG 109, Confederate Records
    Account Book, Military Prison at Columbia, S.C., 1864–65
    Letters Sent by the Agent for Exchange of Prisoners, Richmond, Va.,
        Nov. 1862–March 1865
    Letters, Orders, and Circulars Issued and Received, Military Prison
        Hospital, Salisbury, N.C., 1864–65
    Papers of General P. G. T. Beauregard, 1864–65
    Papers of Maj. Gen. Sam Jones, 1864–65
    Papers of General Lafayette McLaws, 1861–65
    Papers of Maj. Gen. W. H. C. Whiting, 1861–65
    Schedule of Papers in the Archive Office Relating to Exchange and
        Treatment of Prisoners
RG 249, Records of the Commissary General of Prisoners
    Correspondence and Reports (1863–64) Relating to Federal Citizens,
        Clerks and Sutlers Confined in Castle Thunder Prison,
        Richmond, Va.
    Extract from War Department Special Order No. 43
    List Dated Columbia, S.C., 1864
    List of Federal Prisoners of War Who Escaped from Confederate
        Prisons
    Lists of Escaped Prisoners, Deserters, and Refugees
    List of Escaped Prisoners Forwarded to Camp Parole, Md.
    List of Paroled and Escaped Federal Prisoners Sent from Fort
        Columbus
    List of Paroled Prisoners of War in the Prison Camp Near Columbia
    Memorandum of Escaped Prisoners from the Hands of the Rebels
    Memorandum Slips Containing Individual Histories of Federal
        Prisoners of War
    Register of Federal Prisoners of War Who Escaped from Confederate
        Authorities

Register of Federal Prisoners Whose Cases Were Investigated by
Confederate Authorities

Receipts for Money Sent to Federal Prisoners of War in Charleston

Roll of Escaped Prisoner Bailey Ellis

Rolls and Reports of Federal Prisoners of War Who Escaped from
Confederate Prisons

Rolls of Federal Officers Confined as Prisoners at Camp Asylum

RG 393, Records of United States Army Continental Commands, 1821–1920

Endorsements Sent by the Provost Marshal General, District of East
Tennessee

Letters Sent, April 1864–March 1866, District of East Tennessee

Letters Sent by the Assistant Commissary of Musters, October
1864–March 1865, District of East Tennessee

Letters Sent and Received, Military District of the Etowah

Register of Letters Received by Provost Marshal, District of East
Tennessee, July 1864–February 1865

Register of Letters Sent by the Provost Marshal, District of East
Tennessee, July 1864–August 1865

Record Book of the Provost Marshal General (RBPMG), Hilton Head,
South Carolina

Records of Provost Marshal General, District of East Tennessee,
1863–65, Prisoners and Oaths of Allegiance

Press Copies of Letters Sent by Provost Marshal, District of East
Tennessee, November 1864–April 1865

Press Copies of Telegrams Sent by Provost Marshal, District of East
Tennessee

Rolls and Reports of Federal Prisoners of War Who Escaped from
Confederate Prisons

Special Orders Issued April 1864–March 1866, District of East Tennessee

Special Orders Issued by Provost Marshal General, District of East
Tennessee

Statement Forwarded by Capt. Appleton, Provost Marshal Morris Island
of U.S. Soldiers Who came into our lines on the 5th Nov 1864 at Long
Island, SC. Having escaped from the Southern Confederacy

Statements of Escaped Union Prisoners, Refugees, and Rebel Deserters
Union Prisoners of War—Escaped from Confederate Authorities

Newspapers

Aberdeen Daily News
Albuquerque Morning Journal
Asheville News Weekly
Carolina Watchman (Salisbury)
Charleston Daily Courier
Daily Confederate (Raleigh)

Daily Conservative (Raleigh)
Daily Evening Bulletin (San Francisco)
Daily Picayune (New Orleans)
Daily South Carolinian
Daily Southern Guardian
Daily Watchman (Salisbury)
Edgefield Advertiser
Henderson Times
Leavenworth Bulletin
New York Times
Palmetto Herald
Salt Lake Telegram
Southern Field and Fireside
Times-Picayune (New Orleans)
Weekly Conservative
Weekly Progress (Raleigh)

Published Primary Sources

Abbott, A. O. *Prison Life in the South: At Richmond, Macon, Savannah, Charleston, Columbia, Charlotte, Raleigh, Goldsborough, and Andersonville, during the Years 1864 and 1865.* New York: Harper & Brothers, 1865.

Abbott, Horace R. "My Escape from Belle Isle." *A Paper Prepared and Read before Michigan Commandery of the Military Order of the Loyal Legion of the United States, December 5, 1889, by Companion Lieut. Horace R. Abbott.* Detroit, Mich.: Winn & Hammond Printers and Binders, 1889.

Allen, Theodore F. "The 'Underground Railroad' and the 'Grapevine Telegraph.' An Escaping Prisoner's Experience." In *Sketches of War History, 1861–1865. Papers Prepared for the Commandery of the State of Ohio, Military Order of the Loyal Legion of the United States,* edited by T. F. Allen, E. S. McKee, and J. G. Taylor, 147–67. Vol. 6. Cincinnati: Monfort & Company, 1908.

Anderson, George L., ed. *A Petition regarding the Conditions in the C.S.M. Prison at Columbia, S.C. Addressed to the Confederate Authorities. By Col. John Fraser.* Lawrence: University of Kansas Libraries, 1962.

Basile, Leon, ed. *The Civil War Diary of Amos E. Stearns, a Prisoner at Andersonville.* East Brunswick, N.J.: Associated University Presses, 1981.

Beaudry, Louis N. *The Libby Chronicle. Devoted to Facts and Fun. A True Copy of the Libby Chronicle as Written by the Prisoners of Libby in 1863.* Albany, N.Y.: Louis N. Beaudry, 1889.

Benson, Andrew M. "Prison Life and Escape." *First Maine Bugle* 3 (April 1893): 3–11.

Bixby, O. H. *Incidents in Dixie; Being Ten Months' Experience of a Union Soldier in the Military Prisons of Richmond, N. Orleans and Salisbury.* Baltimore: James Young, 1864.

Bliss, George N. *Prison Life of Lieut. James M. Fales.* Providence: N. Bangs Williams, 1882.

Booth, Benjamin F., and Steve Meyer. *Dark Days of the Rebellion: Life in Southern Military Prisons.* Garrison, Iowa: Meyer Publishing, 1995.

Browne, Junius Henri. *Four Years in Secessia: Adventures within and beyond the Union Lines.* Hartford: O. D. Case, 1865.

———. *The Great Metropolis; A Mirror of New York. A Complete History of Metropolitan Life and Society, with Sketches of Prominent Places, Persons and Things in the City, as They Actually Exist.* Hartford: American Publishing Company, 1869.

Byers, S. H. M. "A Historic War Song. How and Where I Wrote 'Sherman's March to the Sea.' Read at a Banquet of the Loyal Legion, in Des Moines, Iowa, November 21, 1893." In *War Sketches and Incidents as Related by the Companions of the Iowa Commandery, Military Order of the Loyal Legion of the United States*, 393–99. Vol. 1. Des Moines: Kenyon Press, 1898.

———. *What I Saw in Dixie; or Sixteen Months in Rebel Prisons.* Dansville, N.Y.: Robbins & Poore, 1868.

Cavada, F. F. *Libby Life: Experiences of a Prisoner of War in Richmond, VA., 1863–64.* Philadelphia: J. B. Lippincott, 1865.

Cochran, M. A. "Reminiscences of Life in Rebel Prisons." In *Sketches of War History, 1861–1865. Papers Prepared for the Ohio Commandery of the Military Order of the Loyal Legion of the United States. 1890–1896*, edited by W. H. Chamberlin, 46–66. Vol. 4. Cincinnati: Robert Clarke, 1896.

Dowling, Morgan E. *Southern Prisons; or, Josie, the Heroine of Florence.* Detroit: William Graham, 1870.

Drake, J. Madison. *Fast and Loose in Dixie.* New York: The Authors' Publishing Company, 1880.

Dufur, S. M. *Over the Dead Line, or Tracked by Blood Hounds.* Burlington, Vt.: Free Press Association, 1902.

Eldredge, Daniel. *The Third New Hampshire and All about It.* Boston: E. B. Stillings, 1893.

Ellis, Daniel. *Thrilling Adventures of Daniel Ellis, the Great Union Guide of East Tennessee for a Period of Nearly Four Years during the Great Southern Rebellion. Written by Himself.* New York: Harper & Brothers, 1867.

Emerson, W. Eric, and Karen Stokes, eds. *A Confederate Englishman: The Civil War Letters of Henry Wemyss Feilden.* Columbia: University of South Carolina Press, 2013.

Everts, Hermann. *A Complete and Comprehensive History of the Ninth Regiment New Jersey Vols. Infantry from Its First Organization to Its Final Muster Out.* Newark, N.J.: A. Stephen Holbrook, 1865.

Fales, James M. *Prison Life of Lieut. James M. Fales.* Providence: N. B. Williams, 1882.

Ferguson, Joseph. *Life-Struggles in Rebel Prisons; A Record of the Sufferings, Escapes, Adventures and Starvation of the Union Prisoners.* Philadelphia: James M. Ferguson, 1865.

Geer, J. J. *Beyond the Lines: Or a Yankee Prisoner Loose in Dixie.* Philadelphia: J. W. Daughaday, 1863.

Glazier, Willard Worcester. *The Capture, the Prison Pen, and the Escape*. Albany: S. R. Gray, 1865.

———. *The Capture, the Prison Pen, and the Escape*. New York: R. H. Ferguson, 1870.

Hadley, John V. "A Day with Escaping Prisoners." *War Papers Read before the Indiana Commandery Military Order of the Loyal Legion of the United States.* Indianapolis: Published by the Commandery, 1898.

———. *Seven Months a Prisoner*. New York: Charles Scribner's Sons, 1898.

———. *Seven Months a Prisoner; or Thirty-Six Days in the Woods.* Indianapolis: J. M. & F. J. Meikel, 1868.

Hagood, Johnson. *Memoirs of the War of Secession*. Columbia, S.C.: The State Company, 1910.

Harrold, John. *Libby, Andersonville, Florence. The Capture, Imprisonment, Escape and Rescue of John Harrold, a Union Soldier in the War of the Rebellion.* Philadelphia: Wm. B. Selheimer, 1870.

Hazelett, A. H. "Prison Life, East and West." In *War Sketches and Incidents as Related by the Companions of the Iowa Commandery, Military Order of the Loyal Legion of the United States*, 373–388. Vol. 2. Des Moines: Kenyon Press, 1898.

Hobart, Harrison C. "Libby Prison—The Escape." In *War Papers Read before the Commandery of the State of Wisconsin, Military Order of the Loyal Legion of the United States*, 394–408. Vol. 1. Milwaukee: Burdick, Armitage & Allen, 1891.

Howard, Oliver Otis. *Autobiography of Oliver Otis Howard*. Vol. 2. New York: Baker & Taylor, 1907.

Howe, Thomas H. *Adventures of an Escaped Union Soldier from Andersonville Prison in 1864*. San Francisco: H. S. Crocker, 1886.

Hunt, Charles O. "Our Escape from Camp Sorghum. By Lieutenant Charles O. Hunt. Read December 3, 1890." In *War Papers Read before the Commandery of the State of Maine, Military Order of the Loyal Legion of the United States*. Vol. 1. Portland, Me.: The Thurston Print, 1898.

Johnson, Hannibal A. "The Sword of Honor From Captivity to Freedom." *Personal Narratives of Events in the War of the Rebellion, being Papers Read before the Rhode Island Soldiers and Sailors Historical Society.* Providence: Published by the Society, 1903.

Jones, Alex H. *Knocking at the Door. Alex. H. Jones, Member-Elect to Congress: His Course before the War, during the War, and after the War. Adventures and Escapes.* Washington, D.C.: McGill & Witherow, 1866.

Langworthy, Daniel Avery. *Reminiscences of a Prisoner of War and His Escape.* Minneapolis: Byron Printing Company, 1915.

Little, Henry F. W. *The Seventh New Hampshire Volunteers in the War of the Rebellion*. Concord, N.H.: Ira C. Evans, 1896.

Long, Lessel. *Twelve Months in Andersonville: On the March—in the Battle—in the Rebel Prison Pens, and at Last in God's Country*. Huntington, Ind.: Thad and Mark Butler, 1886.

Lyon, W. F. *In and Out of Andersonville Prison*. Detroit: Geo. Harland, 1905.

MacCauley, Clay. "Through Chancellorsville, Into and Out of Libby Prison." *Personal Narratives of Events in the War of the Rebellion, Being Papers Read before the Rhode Island Soldiers and Sailors Historical Society*. 6th series, no. 7. Providence: Published by the Society, 1904.

McCormick, Andrew. "Sixteen Months a Prisoner of War." In *Sketches of War History, 1861–1865. Papers Prepared for the Commandery of the State of Ohio, Military Order of the Loyal Legion of the United States*, edited by W. H. Chamberlin, A. M. Van Dyke, and G. A. Thayer, 69–86. Vol. 5. Cincinnati: Monfort, 1908.

McCreery, Wm. B. "My Experience as a Prisoner of War, and Escape from Libby Prison." *A Paper Read before the Commandery of the State of Michigan, Military Order of the Loyal Legion of the U.S. by Companion Wm. B. McCreery, Late Colonel 21st Regt. Mich. Vol. Infantry, at Detroit, Mich., February 6, 1889*. Detroit: Winn & Hammond, 1893.

McNary, O. R. "What I Saw and Did Inside and Outside of Rebel Prisons." *War Talks in Kansas: A Series of Papers Read before the Kansas Commandery of the Military Order of the Loyal Legion of the United States*. Kansas City, Mo.: Press of the Franklin House Publishing Company, 1906.

Mowris, J. A. *A History of the One Hundred and Seventeenth Regiment, N.Y. Volunteers, (Fourth Oneida) from the Date of Its Organization, August, 1862 till That of Its Muster out, June 1865*. Hartford: Case, Lockwood, 1866.

Murray, Paul, and Stephen Russell Bartlett Jr. "The Letters of Stephen Caulker Bartlett aboard the U.S.S. 'Lenapee,' January to August 1865," *North Carolina Historical Review* 33, no. 1 (January 1956): 66–92.

Murray, William W. "From Macon, Georgia, to the Gulf. An Escaping Prisoner's Experience." In *Sketches of War History, 1861–1865. Papers Read before the Ohio Commandery of the Military Order of the Loyal Legion of the United States*, edited by W. H. Chamberlin, A. M. Van Dyke, and G. A. Thayer, 88–117. Vol. 5. Cincinnati: R. Clark, 1896.

Newlin, W. H. *An Account of the Escape of Six Federal Soldiers from Prison at Danville, VA: Their Travels by Night through the Enemy's Country to the Union Picket at Gauley Bridge, West Virginia, in the Winter of 1863–64*. [1870] Cincinnati: Western Methodist Book Concern Print, 1881.

Nichols, George Ward. *The Story of the Great March from the Diary of a Staff Officer*. New York: Harper and Brothers, 1865.

Nott, Charles C. *Sketches in Prison Camps: A Continuation of Sketches of the War*. New York: Anson D. F. Randolph, 1865.

Parker, Marcellus M. "My Experience as Prisoner of War." *First Maine Bugle* 3 (October 1893): 3–7.

Parker, W. H. *How I Escaped: A Novel*. Ed. by Archibald Clavering Gunter. New York: The Home Publishing Company, 1889.

Price, Isaiah. *History of the Ninety-Seventh Pennsylvania Volunteer Infantry during the War of the Rebellion, 1861–1865*. Philadelphia: Published by the Author, 1875.

Prison Life in Texas. An Account of the Capture, and Imprisonment of a Portion of the 46th Regt. Indiana Veteran Volunteers, in Texas. Logansport, Ind.: Journal Office, 1865.

Proceedings of the Ohio Association of Union Ex-Prisoners of War, at the Reunion Held at Dayton, O., July 29, 30 and 31, 1884, with Register of Members. Columbus, Ohio: Ohio State Journal Printing Establishment, 1884.

Putnam, George Haven. "An Experience in Virginia Prisons during the Last Winter of the War." *Personal Recollections of the War of the Rebellion. Addresses Delivered before the Commandery of the State of New York, Military Order of the Loyal Legion of the United States.* 4th series. New York: Knickerbocker Press, 1912.

Racine, Philip N., ed. *Piedmont Farmer: The Journals of David Golightly Harris, 1855–1870.* Knoxville: University of Tennessee Press, 1990.

——. *"Unspoiled Heart": The Journal of Charles Mattocks of the 17th Maine.* Knoxville: University of Tennessee Press, 1994.

Ragan, R. A. *Escape from East Tennessee to the Federal Lines: The History, Given as Nearly as Possible by Captain R.A. Ragan of His Individual Experience during the War of the Rebellion from 1861 to 1864.* Washington, D.C.: James H. Dony, 1910.

Ransom, John L. *Andersonville Diary, Escape, and List of the Dead, with Name, Co., Regiment, Date of Death and No. of Grave in Cemetary.* Auburn, N.Y.: Published by the Author, 1881.

Read, John. "Texas Prisons and a Comparison of Northern and Southern Prison Camps." *Personal Recollections of the War of the Rebellion. Addresses Delivered before the Commandery of the State of New York, Military Order of the Loyal Legion of the United States.* 4th series. New York: Knickerbocker Press, 1912.

Reports and Resolutions Passed at the Called Session of September, 1863. Columbia, S.C.: Charles P. Pelham, 1863.

Richards, Channing. "Dealing with Slavery." In *Sketches of War History, 1861–1865. Papers Prepared for the Commandery of the State of Ohio, Military Order of the Loyal Legion of the United States,* edited by W. H. Chamberlin, 315–26. Vol. 4. Cincinnati: Monfort, 1908.

Richardson, Abby Sage. *Garnered Sheaves from the Writings of Albert D. Richardson, Collected and Arranged by His Wife; to Which Is Added a Biographical Sketch of the Author.* Hartford: Columbian Book Company, 1871.

Richardson, Albert D. *The Secret Service, the Field, the Dungeon, and the Escape.* Hartford: American Publishing Company, 1865.

Robertson, James I., Jr. "An Indiana Soldier in Love and War: The Civil War Letters of John V. Hadley." *Indiana Magazine of History* 59 (September 1963): 189–288.

Roe, Alfred S. "Richmond, Annapolis, and Home." *Personal Narratives of Events in the War of the Rebellion, Being Papers Read before the Rhode Island Soldiers and Sailors Historical Society.* 4th series, no. 17. Providence: Published by the Society, 1892.

Russell, Milton. "Reminiscences of Prison Life and Escape." In *War Sketches and Incidents as Related by Companions of the Iowa Commandery Military Order of the Loyal Legion of The United States*, 25–59. Vol. 1. Des Moines: Press of P. C. Kenyon, 1893.

Sabre, G. E. *Nineteen Months a Prisoner of War. Narrative of Lieutenant G.E. Sabre, Second Rhode Island Cavalry, of His Experience in the War Prisons and Stockades of Morton, Mobile, Atlanta, Libby, Belle Island, Andersonville, Macon, Charleston, and Columbia, and His Escape to Union Lines.* New York: American News Company, 1865.

Savage, James W. "The Loyal Element of North Carolina during the War." In *Civil War Sketches and Incidents: Papers Read by Companions of the Commandery of the State of Nebraska, Military Order of the Loyal Legion of the United States*, 1–4. Vol. 1. Omaha: Published by the Commandery, 1902.

Scott, Samuel W., and Samuel P. Angel. *History of the Thirteenth Regiment Tennessee Volunteer Cavalry, U.S.A.* Philadelphia: P. W. Ziegler, 1903.

Sherman, William Tecumseh. *Memoirs of General W. T. Sherman.* New York: Library of America, 1990.

Shurtleff, G. W. "A Year with the Rebels." In *Sketches of War History, 1861–1865. Papers Prepared for the Commandery of the State of Ohio, Military Order of the Loyal Legion of the United States*, edited by W. H. Chamberlin, 388–408. Vol. 4. Cincinnati: Monfort, 1908.

Smith, Charles M. "From Andersonville to Freedom." *Personal Narratives of Events in the War of the Rebellion, being Papers Read before the Rhode Island Soldiers and Sailors Historical Society.* 5th ser., no. 3. Providence: Published by the Society, 1894.

The Statutes at Large of South Carolina. Vol. XIII, Containing the Acts from December, 1861, to December, 1866. Columbia, S.C.: Republican Printing, 1875.

Stevens, Leverett C. "A Forlorn Hope." *Personal Narrative of Events in the War of the Rebellion, Being Papers Read before the Rhode Island Soldiers and Sailors Historical Society*, 6th series, no. 1. Providence: Published by the Society, 1903.

Swift, F. W. *My Experiences as a Prisoner of War. A Paper Prepared and Read before Michigan Commandery of the Military Order of the Loyal Legion of the United States, December 1st, 1866.* Detroit: Wm. S. Ostler, 1888.

Thompson, B. F. *History of the 112th Regiment of Illinois Volunteer Infantry in the Great War of the Rebellion 1862–1865.* Toulan, Ill.: Stark County New Office, 1885.

Trautman, Frederic, ed. and trans. *Twenty Months in Captivity: Memoirs of a Union Officer in Confed. Prisons, By Bernhard Domschcke.* Rutherford, N.J.: Fairleigh Dickinson University Press, 1987.

Travis, B. F. *Story of the Twenty-fifth Michigan.* Kalamazoo: Kalamazoo Publishing, 1897.

Trowbridge, Luther S. *A Brief History of the Tenth Michigan Cavalry.* Detroit: Friesema Bros. Printing Co., 1905.

Urban, John W. *Battlefield and Prison Pen, or Through the War, and Thrice a Prisoner.* Philadelphia: Hubbard Brothers, 1882.

U.S. Sanitary Commission, No. 87. *Preliminary Report of the Operations of the U.S. Sanitary Commission in North Carolina, March, 1865, and upon the Physical Condition of Exchanged Prisoners Lately Received at Wilmington, N.C.* New York: Sanford, Harroun, 1865.

U.S. War Department. *The War of the Rebellion: A Compilation of the Official Records of the Union and Confederate Armies.* Washington, D.C.: Government Printing Office, 1880–1901.

Walkley, Stephen. *History of the Seventh Connecticut Volunteer Infantry, Hawley's Brigade, Terry's Division, Tenth Army Corps, 1861–1865.* Southington, Conn.: n.p., 1905.

Weiser, George A. *Nine Months in Rebel Prisons.* Philadelphia: J. N. Reeve, 1890.

Williams, Sidney S. "From Spotsylvania to Wilmington, N.C. by Way of Andersonville and Florence." *Personal Narratives of Events in the War of the Rebellion, Being Papers Read before the Rhode Island Soldiers and Sailors Historical Society.* 5th series, no. 10. Providence: Published by the Society, 1899.

Wilson, Thos. L. *Sufferings Endured for a Free Government; or, A History of the Cruelties and Atrocities of the Rebellion.* Philadelphia: Smith & Peters, 1864.

Secondary Sources

Absher, W. O. *Land Entry Book Wilkes County, North Carolina, 1778–1781.* N.p.: Genealogical Society of the "Original" Wilkes County, 1971.

Abstract of Wills Buncombe County, NC, 1792 to 1904. Asheville, N.C.: Old Buncombe County Genealogical Society, 2001.

Alexander, Virginia, Colleen Morse Elliott, and Betty Willie. *Pendleton District and Anderson County, S.C. Wills, Estates, Inventories, Tax Returns and Census Records.* Easley, S.C.: Southern Historical Press, 1980.

Ash, Stephen V. *When the Yankees Came: Conflict and Chaos in the Occupied South, 1861–1865.* Chapel Hill: University of North Carolina Press, 1995.

Bailey, Anne J. *War and Ruin: William T. Sherman and the Savannah Campaign.* Wilmington, Del.: Scholarly Resources, 2003.

Bailey, Chester P. *Tioga Mountaineers: Company B, 101st Regiment Pennsylvania Volunteers Infantry, 1861–1865.* Mansfield, Pa.: Bailey Printing Co., 1982.

Bailey, Louise Howe. *Remembering Henderson County: A Legacy of Lore.* Charleston: The History Press, 2005.

Barrett, John G. *The Civil War in North Carolina.* Chapel Hill: University of North Carolina Press, 1963.

———. *Sherman's March through the Carolinas.* Chapel Hill: University of North Carolina Press, 1956.

Beilein, Joseph, Jr., and Matthew C. Hulbert. *The Civil War Guerrilla: Unfolding the Black Flag in History, Memory, and Myth.* Lexington: University Press of Kentucky, 2015.

Bennett, William D., ed. *Buncombe Births 1858–1888: Journal of Dr. James Americus Reagan.* Raleigh, N.C.: privately printed, 1989.

Bensel, Richard F. *Yankee Leviathan: The Origins of Central State Authority in America*. Cambridge: Cambridge University Press, 1990.

Beringer, Richard E., Herman Hattaway, Archer Jones, and William N. Still Jr. *Why the South Lost the Civil War*. Athens: University of Georgia Press, 1986.

Berlin, Ira, et al. *The Destruction of Slavery*. Ser. 1, vol. 1 of *Freedom: A Documentary History of Emancipation, 1861–1867*. Cambridge: Cambridge University Press, 1985.

Berry, Stephen. *Weirding the War: Stories from the Civil War's Ragged Edges*. Athens: University of Georgia Press, 2011.

Blair, William. *Virginia's Private War: Feeding Body and Soul in the Confederacy, 1861–1865*. New York: Oxford University Press, 1998.

———. *With Malice toward Some: Treason and Loyalty in the Civil War Era*. Chapel Hill: University of North Carolina Press, 2014.

Bradley, Mark. *This Astounding Close: The Road to Bennett Place*. Chapel Hill: University of North Carolina Press, 2000.

Bradley, Stephen E., Jr. *North Carolina Confederate Militia and Home Guard Records*. 3 Vols. Virginia Beach, Va.: Published by author, 1995.

———. *North Carolina Confederate Militia Officers: Roster as Contained in the Adjutant General's Officers Roster*. Wilmington, N.C.: Broadfoot, 1992.

Brady, Lisa M. *War upon the Land: Military Strategy and the Transformation of Southern Landscapes during the American Civil War*. Athens: University of Georgia Press, 2012.

Brasher, Glenn David. *The Peninsula Campaign and the Necessity of Emancipation: African Americans and the Fight for Freedom*. Chapel Hill: University of North Carolina Press, 2012.

Bridges, Steve A., transcribed. *Henderson County, North Carolina Marriage Records, 1851 to 1872*. N.p.: Published by author, 1984.

Brown, Matthew M., and Michael W. Coffey. *Thomas's Legion*. Vol. 16 of *North Carolina Troops, 1861–1865: A Roster*. Raleigh, N.C.: Office of Archives and History, 2008.

Browning, Judkin. *Shifting Loyalties: The Union Occupation of Eastern North Carolina*. Chapel Hill: University of North Carolina Press, 2011.

Bumgarner, Matthew. *Kirk's Raiders: A Notorious Band of Scoundrels and Thieves*. Hickory, N.C.: Tarheel Press, 2000.

Burton, E. Milby. *The Siege of Charleston, 1861–1865*. Columbia: University of South Carolina Press, 1970.

Burton, Orville Vernon. *The Age of Lincoln*. New York: Hill and Wang, 2007.

Bynum, Victoria E. *The Long Shadow of the Civil War: Southern Dissent and Its Legacies*. Chapel Hill: University of North Carolina Press, 2010.

———. *Unruly Women: The Politics of Social and Sexual Control in the Old South*. Chapel Hill: University of North Carolina Press, 1992.

Camp, Stephanie M. H. *Closer to Freedom: Enslaved Women and Everyday Resistance in the Plantation South*. Chapel Hill: University of North Carolina Press, 2004.

Campbell, Jacqueline Glass. *When Sherman Marched North from the Sea: Resistance on the Confederate Home Front.* Chapel Hill: University of North Carolina Press, 2003.

Campbell, John. "The Seminoles, the 'Bloodhound War,' and Abolitionism, 1796–1865." *Journal of Southern History* 72, no. 2 (May 2006): 259–302.

Carlson, Peter. *Junius and Albert's Adventures in the Confederacy: A Civil War Odyssey.* New York: PublicAffairs, 2013.

Casstevens, Frances H. *"Out of the Mouth of Hell": Civil War Prisons and Escapes.* Jefferson, N.C.: McFarland, 2005.

Castel, Albert. *Decision in the West: The Atlanta Campaign of 1864.* Lawrence: University Press of Kansas, 1992.

Cauthen, Charles Edward. *South Carolina Goes to War, 1860–1865.* Chapel Hill: University of North Carolina Press, 1950.

Cawyer, Shirley Brittain, and Blanche W. Culbreth. *Henderson County, North Carolina Marriages, 1851–1898.* Forest City, N.C.: Genealogical Society of Old Tryon County, 1982.

Christianson, John Benjamin. "'Valley Forge Was a Paradise Compared to It': A Community Study of Columbia, South Carolina's Civil War Prisoner of War Camps." M.A. thesis, University of South Carolina, 2004.

Clarke, Frances M. *War Stories: Suffering and Sacrifice in the Civil War North.* Chicago: University of Chicago Press, 2011.

Cloyd, Benjamin G. *Haunted by Atrocity: Civil War Prisons in American Memory.* Baton Rouge: Louisiana State University Press, 2010.

Cook, Gerald Wilson. *The Last Tarheel Militia, 1861–1865: The History of the North Carolina Militia and Home Guard in the Civil War, and Index to over 1,100 Militia Officers.* Winston-Salem, N.C.: Gerald Wilson Cook, 1987.

Cooper, George. *Lost Love: A True Story of Passion, Murder, and Justice in Old New York.* New York: Vintage Books, 1995.

Cowart, Joe A. *Cowart's 1850 Census Henderson Co., NC with Analysis and Index.* Hendersonville, N.C.: J. A. Cowart, 2003.

Crow, Vernon H. *Storm in the Mountains: Thomas' Confederate Legion of Cherokee Indians and Mountaineers.* Cherokee, N.C.: Press of the Museum of the Cherokee Indian, 1982.

Current, Richard Nelson. *Lincoln's Loyalists: Union Soldiers from the Confederacy.* Boston: Northeastern University Press, 1992.

Danielson, Joseph W. *War's Desolating Scourge: The Union's Occupation of North Alabama.* Lawrence: University Press of Kansas, 2012.

Davis, Nora M. *Military and Naval Operations in South Carolina, 1860–1865: A Chronological List.* Columbia, S.C.: South Carolina Archives Department, 1959.

Davis, William C. *Look Away! A History of the Confederate States of America.* New York: Free Press, 2002.

Denney, Robert E. *Civil War Prisons and Escapes: A Day-by-Day Chronicle.* New York: Sterling Publishers, 1993.

Digges, George A., Jr. *Buncombe County North Carolina Grantor Deed Index.* 3 vols. Asheville, N.C.: Miller Press, 1926.

Dorsey, Lois T. *United States Census 1850 Henderson County, North Carolina.* Hendersonville, N.C.: Genealogy, Ltd., 1983.

Downs, Gregory P. *After Appomattox: Military Occupation and the Ends of War.* Cambridge, Mass.: Harvard University Press, 2015.

———. *Declarations of Dependence: The Long Reconstruction of Popular Politics in the South, 1861–1908.* Chapel Hill: University of North Carolina Press, 2011.

Doyle, Patrick J. "Understanding the Desertion of South Carolinian Soldiers during the Final Years of the Confederacy." *Historical Journal* 56, no. 3 (September 2013): 657–79.

Drago, Edmund L. *Confederate Phoenix: Rebel Children and Their Families in South Carolina.* New York: Fordham University Press, 2008.

Edgar, Walter. *South Carolina: A History.* Columbia: University of South Carolina Press, 1998.

Eicher, John H., and David Eicher. *Civil War High Commands.* Stanford, Calif.: Stanford University Press, 2001.

1860 Census Wilkes County, North Carolina. North Wilkesboro, N.C.: Wilkes Genealogical Society, n.d.

Escott, Paul D. *After Secession: Jefferson Davis and the Failure of Confederate Nationalism.* Baton Rouge: Louisiana State University Press, 1978.

Fabian, Ann. *The Unvarnished Truth: Personal Narratives in Nineteenth-Century America.* Berkeley: University of California Press, 2000.

Fahs, Alice. *The Imagined Civil War: Popular Literature of the North and South, 1861–1865.* Chapel Hill: University of North Carolina Press, 2001.

Faust, Drew Gilpin. *The Creation of Confederate Nationalism: Ideology and Identity in the Civil War South.* Baton Rouge: Louisiana State University Press, 1988.

Fellman, Michael. *The Inside War: The Guerrilla Conflict in Missouri during the American Civil War.* New York: Oxford University Press, 1989.

Fisher, Noel C. *War at Every Door: Partisan Politics and Guerilla Violence in East Tennessee, 1860–1869.* Chapel Hill: University of North Carolina Press, 1997.

Fonvielle, Chris E., Jr. *The Wilmington Campaign: Last Rays of Departing Hope.* Campbell, Calif.: Savas, 1997.

Fountain, Daniel L. *Slavery, Civil War, and Salvation: African American Slaves and Christianity, 1830–1870.* Baton Rouge: Louisiana State University Press, 2010.

Frank, Lisa Tendrich. *The Civilian War: Confederate Women and Union Soldiers during Sherman's March.* Baton Rouge: Louisiana State University Press, 2015.

Freehling, William W. *The South vs. the South: How Anti-Confederate Southerners Shaped the Course of the Civil War.* New York: Oxford University Press, 2001.

Fritz, Stephen G. *Endkampf: Soldiers, Civilians, and the Death of the Third Reich.* Lexington: University Press of Kentucky, 2004.

Gallagher, Gary W. *The Confederate War.* Cambridge, Mass.: Harvard University Press, 1997.

———. "Disaffection, Persistence, and Nation: Some Directions in Recent Scholarship on the Confederacy," *Civil War History* 55, no. 3 (September 2009): 329–53.

———. *The Union War*. Cambridge, Mass.: Harvard University Press, 2011.

———, ed. *The Wilderness Campaign*. Chapel Hill: University of North Carolina Press, 1997.

Gannon, Barbara A. *The Won Cause: Black and White Comradeship in the Grand Army of the Republic*. Chapel Hill: University of North Carolina Press, 2011.

Glatthaar, Joseph. *The March to the Sea and Beyond: Sherman's Troops in the Savannah and Carolinas Campaigns*. New York: New York University Press, 1985.

Greene, Gary Franklin, and the Black History Research Committee of Henderson County. *A Brief History of the Black Presence in Henderson County*. Asheville, N.C.: Biltmore Press, 1996.

Grimsley, Mark. *The Hard Hand of War: Union Military Policy toward Southern Civilians, 1861–1865*. Cambridge: Cambridge University Press, 1995.

Grimsley, Mark, and Brooks D. Simpson, eds. *The Collapse of the Confederacy*. Lincoln: University of Nebraska Press, 2001.

Groce, W. Todd. *Mountain Rebels: East Tennessee Confederates and the Civil War, 1860–1870*. Knoxville: University of Tennessee Press, 1999.

Hadden, Sally E. *Slave Patrols: Law and Violence in Virginia and the Carolinas*. Cambridge, Mass.: Harvard University Press, 2001.

Hess, Earl J. *The Battle of Ezra Church and the Struggle for Atlanta*. Chapel Hill: University of North Carolina Press, 2015.

———. *The Civil War in the West: Victory and Defeat from the Appalachians to the Mississippi*. Chapel Hill: University of North Carolina Press, 2012.

Hesseltine, William Best. *Civil War Prisons: A Study in War Psychology*. New York: Frederick Ungar, 1964.

Holberton, William B. *Homeward Bound: The Demobilization of the Union and Confederate Armies, 1865–1866*. Mechanicsburg, Pa.: Stackpole Books, 2001.

Holcomb, Brent H. *Marriages of Wilkes County, North Carolina, 1778–1868*. Baltimore: Genealogical Publishing, 1983.

Huff, Archie Vernon, Jr. *Greenville: The History of the City and County in the South Carolina Piedmont*. Columbia: University of South Carolina Press, 1995.

Hunt, Robert. *The Good Men Who Won the War: Army of the Cumberland Veterans and Emancipation Memory*. Tuscaloosa: University of Alabama Press, 2010.

Inscoe, John C. *Mountain Masters, Slavery, and the Sectional Crisis in Western North Carolina*. Knoxville: University of Tennessee Press, 1989.

———. *Race, War, and Remembrance in the Appalachian South*. Lexington: University Press of Kentucky, 2008.

Inscoe, John C., and Robert C. Kenzer, eds. *Enemies of the Country: New Perspectives on Unionists in the Civil War South*. Athens: University of Georgia Press, 2001.

Inscoe, John C., and Gordon B. McKinney, eds. *The Heart of Confederate Appalachia: Western North Carolina in the Civil War*. Chapel Hill: University of North Carolina Press, 2000.

Jabour, Anya. *Topsy-Turvy: How the Civil War Turned the World Upside Down for Southern Children.* Chicago: Ivan R. Dee, 2010.

Janney, Caroline E. *Remembering the Civil War: Reunion and the Limits of Reconciliation.* Chapel Hill: University of North Carolina Press, 2013.

Jordan, Brian Matthew. *Marching Home: Union Veterans and Their Unending Civil War.* New York: Liveright, 2014.

Joyner, Charles. *Down by the Riverside: A South Carolina Slave Community.* 2nd ed. Urbana: University of Illinois Press, 2009.

Kaye, Anthony E. *Joining Places: Slave Neighborhoods in the Old South.* Chapel Hill: University of North Carolina Press, 2007.

Killian, Ron V. *A History of the North Carolina Third Mounted Infantry Volunteers, USA. March, 1864 . . . August 1865.* Bowie, Md.: Heritage Books, 2000.

King-Owen, Scott. "Conditional Confederates: Absenteeism among Western North Carolina Soldiers, 1861–1865." *Civil War History* 57, no. 4 (December 2011): 349–79.

Kinsella, Helen M. *The Image before the Weapon: A Critical History of the Distinction between Combatant and Civilian.* Ithaca, N.Y.: Cornell University Press, 2011.

Lanehart, Sonja L., ed. *Sociocultural and Historical Contexts of African American English.* Philadelphia: John Benjamins, 2001.

Lawrence, F. Lee, and Robert W. Glover. *Camp Ford C.S.A.: The Story of Union Prisoners in Texas.* Austin: Texas Civil War Centennial Advisory Committee, 1964.

Lawson, Melinda. "Imagining Slavery: Representations of the Peculiar Institution on the Northern Stage, 1776–1860." *Journal of the Civil War Era* 1, no. 1 (March 2011): 28–42.

Leader, Jonathan M. *Walking the Deadline: The Florence Stockade Revisited.* Florence, S.C.: Florence Historical Society, 1997.

Lowery, Malinda Maynor. *Lumbee Indians in the Jim Crow South: Race, Identity, and the Making of a Nation.* Chapel Hill: University of North Carolina Press, 2010.

Lucas, Marion Brunson. *Sherman and the Burning of Columbia.* College Station: Texas A&M University Press, 1976.

Mackey, Robert R. *The Uncivil War: Irregular Warfare in the Upper South, 1861–1865.* Norman: University of Oklahoma Press, 2004.

Manning, Chandra. *What This Cruel War Was Over: Soldiers, Slavery, and the Civil War.* New York: Alfred A. Knopf, 2007.

Marrs, Aaron W. "Desertion and Loyalty in the South Carolina Infantry." *Civil War History* 50, no. 1 (March 2004): 47–65.

Marten, James. *The Children's Civil War.* Chapel Hill: University of North Carolina Press, 1998.

———. *Sing Not War: The Lives of Union and Confederate Veterans in Gilded Age America.* Chapel Hill: University of North Carolina Press, 2011.

Martinez, Jaime Amanda. *Confederate Slave Impressment in the Upper South.* Chapel Hill: University of North Carolina Press, 2013.

Marvel, William. *Andersonville: The Last Depot*. Chapel Hill: University of North Carolina Press, 1994.

McConnell, Stuart. *Glorious Contentment: The Grand Army of the Republic, 1865–1900*. Chapel Hill: University of North Carolina Press, 1992.

McCuen, Anne K. *Abstracts of Some Greenville County, South Carolina, Records Concerning Black People Free and Slave, 1791–1865*. Vol. 1. Spartanburg, S.C.: Reprint Company, 1991.

McCurry, Stephanie. *Confederate Reckoning: Power and Politics in the Civil War South*. Cambridge, Mass.: Harvard University Press, 2010.

McKenzie, Robert Tracy. *Lincolnites and Rebels: A Divided Town in the American Civil War*. New York: Oxford University Press, 2006.

McMurry, Richard M. *Atlanta 1864: Last Chance for the Confederacy*. Lincoln: University of Nebraska Press, 2000.

———. *Two Great Rebel Armies: An Essay in Confederate Military History*. Chapel Hill: University of North Carolina Press, 1989.

McPherson, James M., and James K. Hogue. *Ordeal by Fire: The Civil War and Reconstruction*. 4th ed. New York: McGraw-Hill, 2010.

McWhiney, Grady. *Battle in the Wilderness: Grant Meets Lee*. Abilene, Tex.: McWhiney Foundation Press, 1998.

Meier, Kathryn Shively. *Nature's Civil War: Common Soldiers and the Environment in 1862 Virginia*. Chapel Hill: University of North Carolina Press, 2013.

Miller, Paul D. *Armed State Building: Confronting State Failure, 1898–2012*. Ithaca, N.Y.: Cornell University Press, 2013.

Mills, Gary B. *Southern Loyalists in the Civil War: The Southern Claims Commission*. Baltimore: Genealogical Publishing, 1994.

Minnick, Lisa Cohen. *Dialect and Dichotomy: Literary Representations of African American Speech*. Tuscaloosa: University of Alabama Press, 2004.

Mitchell, Reid. *Civil War Soldiers*. New York: Viking, 1988.

———. *The Vacant Chair: The Northern Soldier Leaves Home*. New York: Oxford University Press, 1993.

Mohr, Clarence L. *On the Threshold of Freedom: Masters and Slaves in Civil War Georgia*. Athens: University of Georgia Press, 1986.

Montgomery, Michael B., and Guy Bailey, eds. *Language Variety in the South*. Tuscaloosa: University of Alabama Press, 1986.

Moore, John Hammond. *Columbia and Richland County: A South Carolina Community, 1740–1990*. Columbia: University of South Carolina Press, 1993.

Moore, Mark A. *Moore's Historical Guide to the Wilmington Campaign and the Battles for Fort Fisher*. Mason City, Iowa: Savas, 1999.

Mountcastle, Clay. *Punitive War: Confederate Guerrillas and Union Reprisals*. Lawrence: University Press of Kansas, 2009.

Myers, Barton A. *Executing Daniel Bright: Race, Loyalty, and Guerrilla Violence in a Coastal Carolina Community, 1861–1865*. Baton Rouge: Louisiana State University Press, 2009.

———. *Rebels against the Confederacy: North Carolina's Unionists*. New York: Cambridge University Press, 2014.

Neely, Mark E., Jr. *The Civil War and the Limits of Destruction*. Cambridge, Mass.: Harvard University Press, 2007.

Neff, John R. *Honoring the Civil War Dead: Commemoration and the Problem of Reconciliation*. Lawrence: University Press of Kansas, 2005.

Noe, Kenneth W., and Shannon H. Wilson, eds. *The Civil War in Appalachia: Collected Essays*. Knoxville: University of Tennessee Press, 1997.

Owsley, Frank L. *State Rights in the Confederacy*. Chicago: University of Chicago Press, 1925.

Phillips, Jason. *Diehard Rebels: The Confederate Culture of Invincibility*. Athens: University of Georgia Press, 2007.

Pickenpaugh, Roger. *Captives in Blue: The Civil War Prisons of the Confederacy*. Tuscaloosa: University of Alabama Press, 2013.

Poole, W. Scott. *South Carolina's Civil War: A Narrative History*. Macon, Ga.: Mercer University Press, 2005.

Proctor, Tammy M. *Civilians in a World at War, 1914–1918*. New York: New York University Press, 2010.

Quigley, Paul. *Shifting Grounds: Nationalism and the American South, 1848–1865*. New York: Oxford University Press, 2012.

Raboteau, Albert J. *Slave Religion: The "Invisible Institution" in the Antebellum South*. New York: Oxford University Press, 1978.

Racine, Philip N. *Living a Big War in a Small Place: Spartanburg, South Carolina, during the Confederacy*. Columbia: University of South Carolina Press, 2013.

Ray, Lenoir. *Postmarks: A History of Henderson County, North Carolina, 1787–1968*. Chicago: Adams Press, 1970.

Rhea, Gordon C. *The Battle of the Wilderness, May 5–6, 1864*. Baton Rouge: Louisiana State University Press, 1994.

Robinson, Armstead L. *Bitter Fruits of Bondage: The Demise of Slavery and the Collapse of the Confederacy, 1861–1865*. Charlottesville: University of Virginia Press, 2005.

Royster, Charles. *The Destructive War: William Tecumseh Sherman, Stonewall Jackson, and the Americans*. New York: Alfred A. Knopf, 1991.

Rubin, Anne Sarah. *A Shattered Nation: The Rise & Fall of the Confederacy, 1861–1868*. Chapel Hill: University of North Carolina Press, 2005.

Ruscin, Terry. *Hendersonville and Flat Rock: An Intimate Tour*. Charleston, S.C.: History Press, 2007.

Sanders, Charles W., Jr. *While in the Hands of the Enemy: Military Prisons of the Civil War*. Baton Rouge: Louisiana State University Press, 2005.

Sarris, Jonathan Dean. *A Separate Civil War: Communities in Conflict in the Mountain South*. Charlottesville: University of Virginia Press, 2006.

Schwalm, Leslie A. *A Hard Fight for We: Women's Transition from Slavery to Freedom in South Carolina*. Urbana: University of Illinois Press, 1997.

Sheehan-Dean, Aaron. *A Companion to the U.S. Civil War*. 2 vols. New York: Wiley-Blackwell, 2014.

———. *Why Confederates Fought: Family and Nation in Civil War Virginia*. Chapel Hill: University of North Carolina Press, 2007.

Slim, Hugo. *Killing Civilians: Method, Madness, and Morality in War.* New York: Columbia University Press, 2008.

Sondley, F. A. *A History of Buncombe County, North Carolina.* Spartanburg, S.C.: Reprint Company, 1977.

Speer, Lonnie R. *War of Vengeance: Acts of Retaliation against Civil War POWs.* Mechanicsburg, Pa.: Stackpole Books, 2002.

Springer, Paul J. *America's Captives: Treatment of POWs from the Revolutionary War to the War on Terror.* Lawrence: University Press of Kansas, 2010.

Springer, Paul J., and Glenn Robins. *Transforming Civil War Prisons: Lincoln, Lieber, and the Politics of Captivity.* New York: Routledge, 2015.

Staley, Linda M., and John O. Hawkins, compilers. *The 1860 Census of Caldwell County, North Carolina.* Lenoir, N.C.: Caldwell County Genealogical Society, 1983.

Sternhell, Yael A. *Routes of War: The World of Movement in the Confederate South.* Cambridge, Mass.: Harvard University Press, 2012.

Stoker, Donald. *The Grand Design: Strategy and the U.S. Civil War.* New York: Oxford University Press, 2010.

Stone, H. David, Jr. *Vital Rails: The Charleston & Savannah Railroad and the Civil War in Coastal South Carolina.* Columbia: University of South Carolina Press, 2008.

Storie, Melanie. *The Dreaded Thirteenth Tennessee Union Cavalry: Marauding Mountain Men.* Charleston: The History Press, 2013.

Stumpp, Lillian Ledbetter. *Marriages of Transylvania County, North Carolina, 1861 through 1899.* N.p.: Published by author, 1985.

Sutherland, Daniel E., ed. *Guerrillas, Unionists, and Violence on the Confederate Home Front.* Fayetteville: University of Arkansas Press, 1999.

———. *A Savage Conflict: The Decisive Role of Guerrillas in the American Civil War.* Chapel Hill: University of North Carolina Press, 2009.

Taylor, Amy Murrell. *The Divided Family in Civil War America.* Chapel Hill: University of North Carolina Press, 2005.

Thomas, Emory M. *The Confederate Nation, 1861–1865.* New York: Harper & Row, 1979.

Topkins, Robert M. *Marriage and Death Notices from Extant Asheville, N.C. Newspapers, 1840–1870: An Index.* Raleigh: North Carolina Genealogical Society, 1977.

Turner, Grace, and Miles Philbeck. *Caldwell County North Carolina Will Abstracts, 1841–1910.* N.p.: Published by author, 1983.

———. *Henderson County North Carolina Will Abstracts, 1838–1910 and Transylvania County North Carolina Will Abstracts, 1861–1910.* N.p.: Published by authors, 1991.

———. *Wilkes County North Carolina Will Abstracts, 1777–1910.* N.p.: Published by authors, 1988.

Vandiver, Frank E. *Rebel Brass: The Confederate Command System.* Baton Rouge: Louisiana State University Press, 1956.

Van Engeland, Anicée. *Civilian or Combatant? A Challenge for the 21st Century.*
New York: Oxford University Press, 2011.

*Walls that Talk: A Transcript of the Names, Initials and Sentiments Written and
Graven on the Walls, Doors and Windows of the Libby Prison at Richmond by the
Prisoners of 1861–1865.* Richmond: R. E. Lee Camp, no. 1, c.v. 1884.

Weiner, Marli F. *Mistresses and Slaves: Plantation Women in South Carolina,
1830–1880.* Urbana: University of Illinois Press, 1998.

Whites, LeeAnn. "Forty Shirts and a Wagonload of Wheat: Women, the
Domestic Supply Line, and the Civil War on the Western Border." *Journal of
the Civil War Era* 1, no. 1 (March 2011): 56–78.

Whites, LeeAnn, and Alecia P. Long, eds. *Occupied Women: Gender, Military
Occupation and the American Civil War.* Baton Rouge: Louisiana State
University Press, 2009.

Whitescarver, Keith. "Political Economy, Schooling, and Literacy in the South:
A Comparison of Plantation and Yeoman Communities in North Carolina,
1840–1880." Ed.D. thesis, Harvard University, 1995.

Witt, John Fabian. *Lincoln's Code: The Laws of War in American History.*
New York: Simon & Schuster, 2012.

Wolfram, Walt, and Erik R. Thomas. *The Development of African American
English.* Oxford: Blackwell, 2002.

Woodworth, Steven E. *Jefferson Davis and His Generals: The Failure of Confederate
Command in the West.* Lawrence: University Press of Kansas, 1990.

Wooley, James E. *Buncombe County, North Carolina Index to Deeds, 1783–1850.*
Easley, S.C.: Southern Historical Press, 1983.

Index

Note: Page numbers in *italics* indicate illustrations and maps.

Guard for Home Defense units: arrest of women, 80; and collapse of Confederate borders, 108; and collapse of Confederate military, 129; and collapse of local defenses, 70–73; and courts martial, 174 (n. 8); and desertions, 69; and the Holinsworth sisters, 77; and protection from escaped prisoners, 187 (n. 14); and surveillance of Estes family, 66–67; and Unionism in Transylvania County, 83–85. *See also* State militias

Guardian angels, 67, 81, 86, 88

Guerrillas and guerrilla warfare: and aid of mountain women, 79–80, 88, 177 (n. 24); and the Appalachian Mountains, 6; and collapse of Confederate borders, 91–92, 98, 107–9; and collapse of Confederate military, 130; and combatant status, 177 (n. 25); and escape narratives, 144; North and South Carolina compared, 175 (n. 15); Rebel guerrillas, 100–101; and "survival lying," 174 (n. 11); terms for, 178 (n. 27)

Guides, 2, 31, 54, 93

Gullah creole language, 166 (n. 13)

Gunboats, 22

Gunter, Joe, 93, 151

Hadley, John V.: and aid of mountain women, 106, 180 (n. 43); arrival at Union lines, 111; and collapse of Confederate borders, 89, 107–8; encounters during escape, 55; escape from Camp Sorghum, 17–18; and escape narratives, 140–43, 147–48, 176 (n. 21); and the Holinsworth sisters, 77–78; postwar life, 151; prior escape attempts, 184 (n. 31); and routes of escaped prisoners, 24–26, 41, 67, 72–73, 157; and scope of fugitive narratives, 4;

and slave guides, 28; travels home, 132

Hagood, Johnson, 124

Hamilton, Robert, *85,* 87, 150, 181 (n. 13)

Hanby, Benjamin Russell, 145

Hardee, William J., 13–14, 44, 59, 62, 116

Harper's Weekly, 140

Harris, David Golightly, 32–33, 138–39

Harris, Elizabeth Golightly, 32–33, 38–39, 138–39

Harrold, John, 149

Hartley, James, 98, 181–82 (n. 14)

Hasson, Benjamin, 150

Hastings, G. S., 179 (n. 35)

Hatch, John P., 59

Havil, Rebecca, 83–84

Hawley, Joseph R., 128

Health of prisoners and fugitives: foot problems, 30, 84, 91, 109–13, 135; hunger and malnutrition, 6–7, 24, 28, 105–6, 133, 139, 151; illnesses and disease, 20, 133; and prisoner of war policies, 6–7, 121

Highland Rangers, 94

Hilton Head, South Carolina, *156;* arrival of escapees at, 132, 148, 154; and extent of prison escapes, 2; and Federal offensives, 59, 62; and routes of escaped prisoners, 10, 15–16, 18–19, 22–23, 27, 30–31, 53, 165 (n. 5)

Hoke, Robert F., 69, 123–24, 126

Holinsworth, Alice, 77, 87, 106, 151

Holinsworth, Delitha, 77, 106, 151

Holinsworth, Elizabeth, 77, 106, 151

Holinsworth, Josiah, 77–78, 151

Holinsworth, Martha, 77–79, 106, 151

Holst, Charles F. A., 191–92 (n. 4)

Holston River, 100

Horry District, 51, 53

Horse thieves, 101

Howard, O. O., 121

Magrath, Andrew G., 39, 62–63
Manufacturing, 44–45
Marion District, 53
Martin, Henry, 49, 76
Martin, James G., 73–74, 96
Martinez, Jaime Amanda, 168 (n. 39)
Mass escapes, 4
Mattocks, Charles Porter, 15; and aid
    of mountain women, 82–84, 85, 86;
    and aid of slaves, 24, 30, 82; and
    collapse of Confederate borders, 89;
    encounters during escape, 54;
    escape from Camp Sorghum, 14–16;
    and fate of deserters, 183 (n. 27);
    postwar life, 151; recaptured, 104–7;
    and routes of escaped prisoners, 18,
    41, 67, 81, 90–91, 93, 117; and scope
    of fugitive narratives, 4
McCurry, Stephanie, 169 (n. 43), 178
    (n. 26)
McKercher, Duncan, 114
McKinney, Gordon B., 173 (n. 5)
McLaws, Lafayette, 7–8
Means, Robert, 14
Meany, Daniel, 120, 187 (n. 14)
Medal of Honor Legion, 147, 151
Memminger, Christopher G., 77–78
Miasma theory, 102–3
Military Division of the West, 95–96,
    116
Militias: and collapse of state borders,
    91–92, 101–2, 129; and defense
    against Federal advances, 59–62;
    and deserters, 45; fugitives'
    encounters with, 54–55, 59, 183
    (n. 28); and guarding of prisoners,
    8; and manpower shortages, 44, 50,
    51–53, 63, 172 (n. 31); organized by
    slaves, 40; reorganization of, 63; and
    secret societies, 70; and slave
    patrols, 34. See also Guard for Home
    Defense units
Minstrelsy, 21, 164 (n. 1), 165 (n. 12),
    193 (n. 14), 194 (n. 24)
Morgan, James, 27

Morganton, North Carolina, 75–76,
    97, 105, 157, 159, 187 (n. 14)
Mountain passes, 94
Mount Pisgah, 106
Murphy, Francis, 56
Mutinies, 8–9, 110

"The Nameless Heroine," 144–47
*Narrative of the Capture, Imprisonment
    and Escape of J. Madison Drake,
    Captain Ninth New Jersey Volunteers*
    (Drake), 141
Native Americans, 93–94
Newark Advertiser, 140–41
Newberry, South Carolina, 41
New Jersey National Guard, 147
New York Tribune, 88, 143, 144
Ninth New Jersey, 11, 135
Nolichucky River, 99, 144
North Carolina Guard for Home
    Defense, 66–67, 101
North Carolina Railroad, 121
Northeast Cape Fear River, 127, 136, 142
Nullification crisis, 45

Occupation forces, 139
Order of the Heroes of America,
    69–70
Overland campaign, 186 (n. 6)
Oxford, Isaac, 1

Pace, John C., 175 (n. 14)
Pace, Ransom W., 175 (n. 14)
Paint Rock, North Carolina, 107–8
Palmer, John B., 96, 108
Paramilitary groups, 32. See also
    Guerrillas and guerrilla warfare;
    Militias
Pardons, 148
Paroles, 6, 14, 127, 144
Partisans, 100–101. See also Guerrillas
    and guerrilla warfare
Paston, J. L., 27
Payments to soldiers, 35–36, 132,
    134–35